University Campus

Barnsley

Telephone: 01226 216 885

Catalogue: **https://webopac.barnsley.ac.uk/**

Class No: ...... 781.66 ABB ....

This book is to be returned on or before the last date stamped below. Thank you!

Garage Rock and Its Roots

Musical Rebels and the Drive for Individuality

ERIC JAMES ABBEY

McFarland & Company, Inc., Publishers
Jefferson, North Carolina, and London

LIBRARY OF CONGRESS CATALOGUING-IN-PUBLICATION DATA

Abbey, Eric James, 1976–
    Garage rock and its roots : musical rebels and the drive for
individuality / Eric James Abbey.
        p.   cm.
    Includes bibliographical references and index.

    ISBN-13: 978-0-7864-2564-8
    (softcover : 50# alkaline paper) ∞

    1. Garage rock music—History and criticism.   2. Garage rock
music—Social aspects.   I. Title
ML3534.A23   2006
781.66—dc22   2006014347

British Library cataloguing data are available

Cover image ©2006 PhotoSpin

Manufactured in the United States of America

McFarland & Company, Inc., Publishers
    Box 611, Jefferson, North Carolina 28640
    www.mcfarlandpub.com

For Ann

Acknowledgments

This book would not have been possible without the following people who have lent me their support and to whom I am entirely grateful. First and foremost, my wife, for her dedicated and meticulous revisions and support through all of the breakdowns. My entire family for giving me the strength to finish this text. Dr. Thomas Kitts for inspiring me to do my best work and for reading and offering suggestions throughout. Dr. Annette Saddik who guided me from the very beginning and helped to create a paper that would turn into this book. Charlie Kondek for his consistent reading and comments. Dr. Russ Larson and the Eastern Michigan University English Department for granting me the time to write. Brendan O'Malley who saw the potential in a conference paper for this book. Jeff White at jwhitephoto.com for his pictures of the city of Detroit. The Popular and American Culture Associations for continuing the academic study of culture in America and the world. Keuffer's bar in New Orleans, Ship of Fools and DTUT in New York, and the WAB in Detroit for lending spirit to the writing process. The final thanks goes to the entire music scene in Detroit, for their support throughout my career as a musician and writer, especially to those who granted interviews and rehashed old stories of the past. Thank you all.

Table of Contents

Introduction

With the advent of contemporary Garage Rock, the music scene was forced to recognize specific concerns relating to nostalgia and its use in our constructed individualism. Beginning in the city of Detroit, Michigan, and its suburbs, contemporary Garage Rock found its home equally among ruined streets and wealthy neighborhoods. From the start, this underground movement experienced rapid growth due to its insistence on staying away from mainstream culture and its break with traditional popular modes of musical representation.

This book is intended as the beginning of a conversation on the extreme importance that nostalgic representations hold over the current musicians and participants in the Garage Rock scene. Throughout the text is the premise that contemporary Garage Rock relies on these representations to break into its constructed individualism. This premise is the basis for a closer look into what is occurring within mainstream and underground music. Contemporary Garage Rock allows us to become immersed in our own reflections on how we construct ourselves within mainstream capitalist America and provides a structure that attempts to thwart capitalist notions of control over self.

This attempt was often apparent in earlier underground musical movements, but contemporary Garage Rock has allowed the greatest progress toward a constructed individualism. By drawing on nostalgia for specific time periods, this musical movement has developed a way to become immersed in mainstream society. This immersion offers an alternative viewpoint and opportunity to claim a subjectivity that is different from previous capitalist constructions of self.

Like any emerging underground movement, Garage Rock at first met with uncertain response in the mainstream marketplace. Many early

Garage Rockers found this uncertainty liberating and regarded their non-mainstream style as the "real" way to perform music. They relished the challenge of mixing nostalgia and the reconstruction of the past with the harshness and cynicism of postmodern America. Contemporary Garage Rock began in an attempt to stand within musical society and still have the option of constructed individualism.

By taking on performance traits and attitudes of the past and reestablishing them within a contemporary context, the first successful Garage groups challenged the surrounding musical underground. This was not the all-out abrasiveness of Hardcore or the confrontational feel of Punk. This was simply music for music's sake and an attempt to reclaim "real" Rock and Roll. The underground forces were stressful for the participants but also allowed for the creation of a new musical scene. Contemporary Garage Rock demonstrates a desire to return to a time when rebellion was simple and more effective through the music played and the attitude assumed in performance.

The following text sets out to demonstrate that contemporary Garage Rock is based on nostalgic representations within our culture. These representations stem from the British Invasion, Hard Mod and original 1960s Garage Rock culture, but also take their cues from Hollywood films and television shows that demonstrate a culture of rebellion within accepted societal norms. Many participants within the current scene state that these influences are subconscious, while others claim outright that the representations serve as the impetus and drive for the creation of the music and performance principles. While some current groups have grown in popularity, other performers have negative feelings about mainstream acceptance and seek to remain within the underground subset.

Specific periods of representation allow the audience to construct contemporary Garage Rock within a particular time frame of nostalgic rebellion. The periods represented are those that have consistently been viewed as rebellious in nature, periods during which society was shocked into a certain realization. The postmodern world has left many people without a way to effectively rebel, and many are drawn into contemporary Garage Rock as a way to reclaim certain rebellious aspects of society. Even though these forms of rebellion are often cited as outdated and somewhat ineffective, it is the desire to claim individualism within contemporary times that is extremely important to the Garage Rock scene.

Within the context of this scene, it is important that groups remain in opposition to mainstream classification. While certain groups have left the confines of the underground for mainstream success, others still cling heavily to the underground notions that were prevalent during the uprising of the movement. This duality of contemporary Garage Rock allows for groups to create gaps in classification—undefined spaces in which they perform while continually challenging elements of mainstream musical culture, providing a strengthening aspect that colors the music and the surrounding scene.

The spaces carved out by the success of many bands are immense. Many people are now competing to fill these spaces, but the spaces keep the scene and the music at the fore of contemporary thought. Bands performing within and around mainstream and underground connotations allow contemporary Garage Rock to remain a vital part of contemporary music culture.

A difficulty with terminology throughout the contemporary Garage Rock scene is apparent in the number of bands that desire classification outside the Garage label. This text discusses the inherent danger of over-classification within the label and stresses the importance of bands simultaneously remaining within each subset to retain credibility and marketing power. Most groups that subscribe to the label of Garage Rock are, in effect, limiting their marketing power to the area of a trend while discounting the beginnings of the scene.

Many of the newer groups that are simply using the label for success are in fact failing to reach the specific market of underground fans they need. There are many instances of bands that have sprung up just to catch onto the Garage trend. As a result, they have been limited in their success. Even when some of these groups achieve limited success, they are still viewed as contradictory to the original intent of the scene and said to have "sold out" musically through the use of the label.

The dissolution of any underground musical scene usually begins with mainstream infiltration. With contemporary Garage Rock, this negative effect is diluted because many groups have achieved mainstream success while remaining within underground realms. The reason this has been possible is discussed fully within the text. An interesting feature of Garage Rock is its ability to simultaneously purport underground ideals within a mainstream culture.

The differences between Punk, Hardcore and Garage Rock are numerous, but the largest difference lies in Garage Rock's acceptance of mainstream success. There is no selling out within contemporary Garage

Rock if you are an original band. As long as the underground remains in sight and the band members continue to propagate the same feelings and drives as they did in the beginning, they are not removed from the underground. This difference between Garage Rock and other underground movements is extremely important and has led to contemporary Garage Rock's place within musical culture.

Garage Rock and Its Roots begins with a brief but thorough look at the rise of the contemporary scene within Detroit and the surrounding suburbs. This growth is discussed from the perspective of those present at the beginning of the scene, and these early participants are focused on as important aspects of its original development. The performers and participants who allowed this growth did so in an effort to reassert a place in underground music within Detroit out of a frustration with the surrounding music and scenes. The growth of this "new" movement was modeled on the growth of many previous musical movements in Detroit, and the thought processes that were part of the music's development were based on principles from earlier scenes. Contemporary Garage Rock did not begin with one band or with one person's idea for a new sound but was instead created through the efforts of the many performers and participants who hoped to bring something different to musical culture.

A defining feature of Garage Rock discussed here is its effort to reclaim the naiveté of the original rock groups. This goal is shared by many of the original bands and continues to be a characteristic of contemporary Garage. At the beginning of the scene there was a limited amount of live music in Detroit and many people had all but given up hope when a small group of musicians came together just to play live shows again. These shows were not put on to upstage anybody or to remove other bands from the scene. The musicians simply wanted to play live music, and this is what led to the development of the scene.

The book's second chapter takes a close look at the Sights, a group that has continually represented the Garage Rock scene throughout the years. The chapter briefly describes the history of the Sights and links their rise within the underground to the nostalgic traits they portray. The chapter also demonstrates how the Sights constructed and defined themselves from the very beginning.

The Sights are one band discussed in depth, but many other groups are represented in this book, and all the bands demonstrate the importance of the scene's different sounds and attitudes. From bands with a hardcore edge to bands that play dance music, contemporary Garage

Rock is inclusive of all. The focus on the Sights is due to the band's extreme reliance on past influences in musical construction and performance and the way it has remained a part of the scene since its inception but refuses to be linked to the originators.

The culture of contemporary Garage Rock draws heavily on nostalgic representations of the British Invasion and Hard Mod cultures of the 1960s and 1970s, as discussed in Chapter 3. Members of the scene reflect this period in their aspects of dress, sonic performance and attitude in an effort to assert their own constructed individualism within capitalist America. Bands that directly and indirectly base their appearance and sound on these eras of music are a focus of this book.

A reflection on the 1960s and 1970s—two important periods in music and culture—is extremely relevant in a discussion of rebellion. Within these periods one finds most of the first examples of rebellion through music, examples that led many people to develop a definition of rebellion based on musical performers. This book fully discusses the British Invasion as one of the first and most important periods to be nostalgically represented within the Garage scene, with the Hard Mod movement a close second. Together they represent a continued drive toward cultural rebellion.

Another important facet of contemporary Garage Rock is the way it draws on the original sound and focus of 1960s Garage Rock. This era is referenced continuously throughout contemporary Garage music and, although mostly subconsciously, is represented within the style, appearance and attitude of the performers and participants. The original scene was instrumental in attempting the first break into a constructed individualism of musical thought with the arrival of the British Invasion. These musicians attempted to realign the music that they heard into a purely American sound, and many faltered in their approach. This text discusses the reason for their failure as well as the success of the groups that achieved some notoriety throughout. Contemporary Garage Rock relies heavily on the 1960s Garage Rock approach to music and cannot be understood without an appreciation for the original sound and concept.

Many members of the current scene do not realize that groups such as the Count 5 and others have influenced them. This does not mean that they are limited in their approach to the music, but it does mean that they have often ignored the true roots of the music. As discussed in Chapter 4, the original Garage groups of the 1960s play an extremely large role in the thought process of many contemporary bands. With their simplistic, naïve style, these original groups paved the way for the do-it-yourself attitude that has been carried through to contemporary Garage.

Dress has always been an important part of musical movements, and Garage Rock is no exception. Chapter 5 focuses on dress in order to demonstrate the importance of attire based on nostalgic representations of the past. Members of the contemporary Garage Rock scene use items of dress that represent Hard Mod, British Invasion and even 1950s culture in their attempt to construct their individualism. The dress that is more or less required of Garage participants and performers aligns itself with these movements and shows how contemporary Garage Rock reasserts an aspect of rebellion that has already taken place within our American society. In its attempt to assert a difference, dress inherently places demands on the participant and performers within the surrounding culture.

Actually, in comparison with preceding musical movements that relied heavily on inclusion as a way to reinstate family and solidarity, contemporary Garage Rock is very limited in demands it places on participants. Nevertheless, the scene does force its participants to make certain choices, and these choices are often reflected in dress. Here is where the Garage scene is similar to preceding movements but far less harsh.

Whether the original participants of the underground scene continue or withdraw their support for a given group depends largely on how the media constructs that group. Hence media construction plays a large role in determining whether a band remains viable within the underground. In their image, their videos, their advertisements and even their CD production, bands must retain elements of the underground and not give in to mainstream constructions of success. The mainstream media must be relegated to the background within the band's display. In this way, a band that achieves mainstream success can continue within both spheres of music. This is the goal of many bands that achieve a great deal of success. By remaining true to underground goal structures, these bands demonstrate the importance of image and media to the surrounding scene.

The groups that successfully manipulate the mainstream for their own benefit construct themselves as members of the underground who have simply happened upon success. This leads many participants to view success in a completely different way from previous underground musical movements and benefits contemporary Garage Rock by limiting the epithet of "sell out" to a specific few groups that have been fully constructed through mainstream capitalist desires. The underground continuously shapes the way bands display themselves through the media and production qualities. For this, the underground places a specific set of demands on the performers and continues the relationship between all members of the contemporary Garage Rock movement.

Nostalgic images are continually on display in bands' advertisements, videos, and CD cover art. These images strengthen the contemporary scene's reliance on the past and demonstrate the requirements associated with playing Garage Rock in the postmodern world. In their logos and other advertising, groups use images from old movies, album covers or television programs. With this comes the desire to reflect a time period that is different from postmodern surroundings. This structure of nostalgic representation is a key point for bands that achieve mainstream success while maintaining underground intentions, and allows groups to keep a foot in each world.

The traits of contemporary Garage Rock merge into a coherent goal—a drive that has developed and is shared between performers and participants. This goal is what allows for the defining of a movement based on the principles of the participants. The goal of contemporary Garage Rock is to inspire a difference in the way that we construct ourselves as individuals within a capitalist society. With the use of nostalgic representations, contemporary Garage Rock blazes a path into a constructed individualism that goes against the norm and focuses on the importance of self-assertion through uses of the past. Many people have claimed that this occurrence within music is just a fad or a passing fancy, but what this musical movement presents is extremely important and rather effective in its attempt to establish a new type of constructed individualism.

In order to fully discuss this break into individualism, Part II of this text links the contemporary Garage movement to other forms of expression. Many postmodern artists and musicians are attempting this break, and what is essential to Garage Rock is the way that the mainstream has incorporated it. Unlike other forms of postmodern art that have consistently been marginalized, contemporary Garage Rock has been allowed to retain its credibility even as it finds mainstream acceptance. This has been accomplished through its use of nostalgic representations of rebellion.

In postmodern times, nostalgia has been largely viewed with disdain and pushed to the background of contemporary thought. This is disparaging to the thoughts and attitudes that contemporary Garage Rock members are putting forward. Nostalgia has always been and continues to be used in a way that allows members to construct their presence within society in a unique and specific way. The importance of nostalgic representation to Garage Rock cannot be overstated, as it is the basis of individualism constructed throughout the scene. Many theorists scorn nostalgia with blatant disregard for its power within our postmodern society. Contemporary Garage Rock strikes a chord in many with its use of nostalgia in an attempt to reclaim, for a new time period, what has been lost.

Nostalgic thought is often identified with a longing for a better time. This text allows for this identification but also suggests that the longing is due to a perception that something is missing in our current era. By attempting to reclaim specific aspects of the past for personal use, subjects are realigning the present based on a constructed past. It is a given that this past is faulty, but the importance lies in the reason behind the attempt at nostalgia. In our postmodern world we do long for home and we construct this home, through our cultural referents. Contemporary Garage Rock positions this constructed home in the eras discussed throughout this text and allows for us to realign our attempt at individuality.

This book focuses on the strength of the break into constructed individualism in order to show why nostalgic forces are rising to a position of importance in postmodern American thought. The desire to find a constructed individualism has always been relevant to thought processes, but today in America we are continually viewing nostalgic representations as ways to reassert our presence within a fully developed thought process. Postmodernism puts forth the notion that everything has already been accomplished; the strength of Garage Rock is how it presents an affront to this thought process by using nostalgic representations of self and music. This text begins the discussion of how this is accomplished and what contemporary Garage Rock has done in order to affirm its importance within our society. By reasserting specific traits of the 1950s, 1960s and even the 1970s, contemporary Garage Rock reaffirms the rebellion of the past and reinstates it for today. Without this type of rebellion, we would be limited in our view of the present and left without much alternative thought within mainstream music.

Garage Rock and Its Roots focuses on the importance of contemporary Garage Rock in our attempt to construct ourselves. The text is to be used as a starting point for a discussion of musical genres and their ability to confirm or reconfirm specific notions of self through performance and association within the scene. Contemporary Garage Rock allows for this discussion to take place within postmodern capitalist society and strengthens our desire to nostalgically represent the past in our efforts to construct ourselves. Many different musical genres have drawn on nostalgic images in the past, but Garage Rock's choice of time period sets it apart. With Garage Rock we see a largely prosperous time in America being used to represent individuality and rebellion within postmodern times.

Why choose to construct ourselves around images of the past? With the advent of postmodern time and the beginning of cultural despair in many areas of American thought, we are challenged to look to the past for affirmation. Our constructed individuality is based on a hegemony that revolves around capitalist principles, and contemporary Garage Rock offers an alternative far removed from these demands. Reasserting the past, with rebellion as the focal point, allows participants to confirm their identity separate from the standards of society but within certain frameworks of acceptance.

This book stresses the important sociological influences that one musical movement can push forward with the appropriate amount of support from surrounding factions. The support that Garage Rock musicians have found, after a brief struggle, is strong and consistent, from the burgeoning labels that gave them an outlet for their music to the fan base that remains with the groups even after mainstream crossover. Why has Garage Rock been allowed to maintain this cultural status? This and other questions are answered in a discussion of the many important implications of a musical scene remaining viable through mainstream exposure.

The continued support is evident even when bands become larger than many thought possible. Jack White of the White Stripes played in the 2002 feature film *Cold Mountain* and was not condemned by anyone in the underground. Could that ever have occurred with a Punk icon? The importance of this example is easy to see but difficult to explain. Contemporary Garage Rock has remained successful due to the continued support of all surrounding fans and participants. The issue of selling out is not even discussed with the original groups; they have simply been successful.

Many musical movements have emerged and dissolved in accordance with mainstream capitalist desires. With contemporary Garage

Rock the mainstream seems to have a limited effect. The success of Garage Rock seems to be rooted in its message for society and not simply in mass appeal or trendiness. What the future holds for Garage Rock remains to be seen, but the elements of cultural rebellion through nostalgic representation have allowed this genre of music to remain an influential underground and mainstream musical movement.

The differences between Garage Rock and preceding musical movements and their rates of success are discussed throughout the text. What is extremely interesting is the way contemporary Garage Rock has developed, allowing mainstream success to be viewed without negativity and instead with a feeling of cultural gain and recognition for the city of Detroit and other bands' members. This openness to success strengthens the scene and the participants' ability to view the bands and their leaders as examples of the success of rebellion through nostalgia.

Garage Rock and Its Roots covers the development of a musical culture, its mainstream success and its continued underground acceptance. The book is intended as the beginning of a discussion of the elements that have made this musical development relevant to many fans and music representatives. In developing the idea that contemporary Garage Rock began by drawing on earlier musical movements, this text focuses on the strength Garage Rock gained through performance within multiple musical scenes. The book's discussion of the progress of Garage Rock also includes a focus on the preceding musical movements that continue to influence many musicians within the scene. The discussion emphasizes the importance of these movements, which influence everything from the conceptualization of a band to its surrounding scene.

The text is presented here in two sections that encourage the reader to focus first on the scene itself and then on the critical implications of contemporary Garage Rock. The first section takes the audience through the creation of the scene and explains the importance of relationships to the past. The second section demonstrates the relationships to society on which contemporary Garage Rock is structured. The book as a whole shows how both relationships—to the past and to society—are relevant in the continuation of contemporary Garage Rock.

With the structure laid out in this way, *Garage Rock and Its Roots* determines that the continuation of contemporary Garage Rock is based on how the underground situates itself within postmodern society. Throughout the text an effort is made to distinguish the bands that have gone against or been removed from the underground from the bands that remain an important part of its survival. With mainstream record labels and others encouraging rapid success, the way that a band shapes itself determines its dependence on or removal from the underground. The two sections differentiate the culture and society of contemporary Garage Rock in a way that asserts the musical scene's specific importance to the postmodern late capitalist world.

It is important that contemporary Garage Rock remain viable within both the mainstream and underground musical communities. By continuously challenging the hegemonic control of self through nostalgic representations of rebellion, contemporary Garage Rock has developed a place in cultural history where other musical movements failed. Through cultural referents and signifiers based on the past, the music and performance of these new groups effectively allow subjects to witness a new way to construct their individualism within our postmodern capitalist times. *Garage Rock and Its Roots* discusses this relevant development and places contemporary Garage Rock within a significant cultural sphere.

PART I
Foundations

1

Made in Detroit[1]:
How an Underground
Movement Restructured the Past

As the 1990s came to a close, the popular music industry left many individuals searching for an underground musical development that they could call their own. The construction of an underground scene within music is generally based on the alignment of a multitude of factors; among them, band members in agreement on musical style, a common goal of musical practices, club owners' belief in popularity and fan participation. When this occurs, a strong undercurrent of family and solidarity appears. In the past, a coming together of these factors has taken years to come to fruition. This is also true of the contemporary Garage Rock scene.

The first of these traits is a common goal within the music of the surrounding culture. In Detroit, Michigan, and elsewhere, the desire was to escape from the capitalist confines of traditional popular music. This began in the late 1980s with the Punk and Hardcore scenes, was transferred through the Swing and Rock-a-Billy cultures, and landed in the current Garage Rock movement. Bands standing against contemporary notions of late capitalism is the foundation of Garage Rock. Growth is based on the shared desire to go against fixed notions of capitalist control. The contemporary Garage Rock scene developed through the assertions shared by a large community of differing musical groups.

In Detroit, the musical scenes were largely split and could not come to any form of agreement. It took the creation of a new form of music, based on the past, to revive the live music scene and to bring together the members of multiple movements and underground assertions. Contemporary Garage Rock did not begin in an effort to bring together the world or to put forward a political agenda. It began with the desire of musicians to get together and play live music. This led to the beginning and continuation of one of the most successful music scenes to come out of Detroit in recent times.

The Garage Rock underground scene appeals to a large and diverse group of people. Because the music can be classified in a variety of ways, and the scene welcomed differing musical styles, the scene drew members from almost every type of underground affiliation. Present throughout the music scene is the relationship to a formal past group identity that either resides in the type of music played or the fashions worn by the musicians. Through its relationship to many different musical movements, contemporary Garage Rock became one of the largest, fastest growing underground, and eventually mainstream, scenes in Detroit.

The general appeal of contemporary Garage Rock lies in its use of preceding movements and the incorporation of ideals that were displayed previously. This incorporation created a desire within the underground in Detroit and led to the construction of Garage Rock. By forming bands that included members that previously played with Hardcore and Punk bands, the underground gained members from both scenes and rapidly expanded. The welcoming aspect was not witnessed often and became the determining factor in the success of this new underground.

Members of the current manifestation of Garage can often be seen in clothing that represents past scene affiliations. Dress and apparel common in Punk and Hardcore scenes is occasionally witnessed, along with Rock-a-Billy, Mod and Swing fashions. Identity with the past is not limited to dress and appearance but demonstrates the importance of contemporary Garage Rock's reliance on the preceding underground movements in Detroit.

Detroit has always had a strong musical history. While this discussion will be concerned only with the late 90s music scene, a strong musical presence has been a part of Detroit from the beginnings of Jazz in the 20s. As the 90s began, the underground music of Detroit was strongly based on Hardcore music,[2] prevalent throughout the city and surrounding suburbs. The bands involved were influential in exposing members of the contemporary Garage Rock scene to the notions that music can be as raw and powerful as you can make it and should be presented from an outwardly apolitical standpoint. It is an essential element of Detroit

Hardcore music to be as strong in output as possible without defending a specific political side.

The non-political aspect of Hardcore music was not always shared, even within the Hardcore scene, but the emphasis on strong musical power over anything else was. Hardcore and its many variations is an entirely separate discussion itself, but the specific use of power chords and distortion to display raw emotion is the key element that contemporary Garage Rock chose to embrace for its determination into the underground.

It is also extremely important that many of the members of the original Garage groups began their musical career or participation within the Hardcore scene. Some of the groups that made up the Detroit Hardcore scene that influenced the current Garage movement were bands such as Cold as Life, Pist-n-Broke, and Feisty Cadavers. These groups played an extremely important role in exposing members of the current Garage scene to a type of music that did not answer questions but was played only for emotional release. Members of this underground, Ko Shih and others, would later play large roles in contemporary Garage Rock, and most still claim at least an outsider status within this underground, continuing to perform in Hardcore venues and with Hardcore bands. The emotion expressed is the key, and many people still relate to this conception in music.

This stance can be currently witnessed throughout the Garage Rock scene. The reliance on power over musical technique is a consciously made decision within many groups. This aggressiveness continues throughout today's Garage Rock scene, with many of the bands using chord progressions and musical forms similar to those of the previous Hardcore groups. Many listeners to current Garage Rock music can easily relate to the simple chord patterns and the emphasis on power and emotion over explicit musical technique.

This is not to say that Garage musicians are less talented than previous musical bands, but it is a differentiation from the more formulaic and processed music that mainstream labels are producing. The emphasis on emotion over technique is extremely important in the feeling of reclaiming the past and nostalgically representing bands and music from a different era. By playing chord progressions and using the most basic of musical construction, Garage bands allow the listener to remain focused on the lyrical stance and power within the group.

The reliance on emotion over technique becomes specifically important in the construction of a Garage Rock band. Many of the current bands began with the most basic forms of musical construction. Generally there is no strict musical formula in the creation of the current music, although according to *Time Out New York*'s Jay Ruttenberg, the White Stripes claim to focus their music and all aspects of their style around the number three.[3] This lack of formula and concentration on raw emotion can be seen in a variety of musical forms; however, this current phenomenon can be directly linked to exposure within the previous Hardcore scene. Bands including the Dirtbombs, the Detroit Cobras, the Von Bondies and the Come Ons specifically rely on a distinct focus on power and emotion over strict musical technique through their use of lyrical phrasing and powerful stage presence.

The Detroit Cobras and the Come Ons began and continue to play as cover bands using their stage presence and power to differentiate themselves from the surrounding cover bands of Detroit. Specifically, the Detroit Cobras play songs that are obscure with an extreme intensity onstage intensified by the use of guitar sounds and drum patterns. They express the cover of the song in a way that allows them to assert themselves through the song and not simply cover the original. Many groups begin in this way but play the original in the same way that it was originally composed. The Detroit Cobras and the Come Ons both separate themselves by playing covers with a harsh intensity that was prevalent in previous underground movements.

With this focus comes the determination to express a relationship with past forms of music in Detroit and other American cities. Many of the current Garage bands express a strong desire to play a type of music that is the reclamation of the spirit of real Rock and Roll.[4] This conscious attempt to capture the feeling of Rock was apparent within the Hardcore underground and the type of music played. Although Hardcore music was known to be extremely aggressive in its output, apparent throughout was the desire to go back to a raw form of music. It was this desire that developed into contemporary Garage music.

The modern development of Garage music is driven by this attempt to return to a type of music that was "real" and influential in the development of American Rock music. Many of the current musical groups playing Garage music seek this return to a time of glorified music without constraint. This construction is reliant on the feelings that were displayed in the Hardcore scene of the early 90s in Detroit. This feeling continued as the Hardcore scene moved on and the underground focus shifted to the development of a new movement that was, in all aspects, a short-lived trend in Detroit and the rest of America. This movement was called Swing, which later transformed into Rock-a-Billy.

This new development in Detroit arrived with the desire to completely return to a past period of American music. This was based on the premise that music of the late 1920s and early 30s was essential to the development of American music. Big Band Swing, Hot Jazz and Be-Bop were merged with a type of punk ethos that attempted to again reclaim the aspect of music that was more technical and demanding, but still carried with it a desire to go against the popular music fads. This growing determination to rediscover a "true" American music further led to bands looking back to American Roots music.

One of the groups playing Swing at this time in Detroit was the Atomic Fireballs. This group emphasized a reliance on the stage performance and sound of the early 20s Swing bands. It had one of the most active front men in Detroit in Jon Bunkley and led the Detroit Swing underground into the mainstream, eventually playing on national television for the Miss America pageant. This group also based its sound on original Swing music with a mixture of Punk that centered them in the underground and allowed them to influence surrounding groups in Detroit.

With the onset of the Swing underground culture, offshoots of musicians were playing a type of music that was rooted in the classic forms of Country and Folk music. Rock-a-Billy became an underground scene in itself through the many bands that claimed to go against the Swing fad and play, what they considered, true American music. Bands within this scene, in Detroit, such as the Twistin' Tarantulas and the Dangervile Wildcats, were determined to offset the trend of Swing with a strong relationship to the early constructions of Country music. These bands were focused on earlier musicians, including Hank Williams and Carl Perkins, and were consciously asserting a relationship with this past form of music.

The members of the Rock-a-Billy movement, audience and musicians, used historical cultural signs of American rebelliousness to express their individuality. By wearing clothes that were considered rebellious in the 1950s, and even going as far as getting tattoos that were similar in style to the era, members of the scene asserted this type of rebelliousness completely relating to the past. The Twistin' Tarantulas based their appearance entirely on 50s iconography, the lead singer and bass player dressing in leather jackets and tank tops with duck-tailed hair and tattoos. Those involved were completely dependent on cultural signs of the past to assert their rebelliousness. What was essentially important within Rock-a-Billy was the relationship with dress and appearance.

The dress and appearance, to many members of this scene, were considered more important than the musical style and ability of the performers. A band that looked the part and played music that was somewhat similar would be considered part of the scene. The dissolution of the scene occurred when the music began to fail in its interpretation of true American Roots music. With this dissolution, many members were left with a desire to find a way to play real Rock and Roll.

In the 1990s the underground participants in Detroit struggled to find the essence of what real Rock and Roll music was and how they could reinterpret it into a contemporary form that would gain influence on the surrounding underground. The search was difficult and led to many failed attempts at band formation. The music they discovered was not classified as anything but Rock music but would later be titled Garage Rock.

The underground music scene struggle in Detroit has always been a difficult one. Many participants are drawn only to specific forms that go against the mainstream of contemporary music. Granted, this can be a broad base of music depending on what is considered mainstream. This desire is driven by what is considered underground by its participants. A scene begins to assert power over music venues and individuals when its participants do not consider the music performed as mainstream. The participants are strict enforcers over what is to be considered the next underground movement with an asserted attempt at individuality. Whether this is Hardcore, Swing, Rock-a-Billy or Garage Rock, the movement must remain within the underground scene. Throughout the development of the Garage scene in Detroit, emphasis on the music remaining part of the underground subculture was essential. Without such emphasis, the differing groups of musicians and fans would not merge and the scene would not get off the ground.

This occurrence is seen throughout underground types of music and scenes, but in Detroit this is strongly supported throughout the gig-going and playing community. The Club owners, booking agents, venue management and fans come to an agreement when reliance away from the mainstream occurs. The Garage scene developed through the assertion of many differing underground scenes and came to fruition through the combination of many different types of musical movements. Through its demand to remain apart from the mainstream, it became one of the largest underground movements of recent time.

Garage Rock carried with it a strong demand to remain outside the acceptable norm. When the Rock-a-Billy movement began to fade, the underground scene of Detroit was left searching for the next musical form; bands began looking for different ways to express their true musical sensibilities. One of the first bands to attempt to recapture the "real" essence of Rock and Roll was the Sights. These teenagers began to play music within the Ska and Punk scene with a strong desire to reclaim Rock music. They took on the appearance of the early version of the Who, circa 1965, and played a harsh type of music that is now considered Garage Rock. At their creation, this term was not used and they were simply classified by the underground as a Punk or Mod band.

What is distinctly relevant with the Sights is their attraction to a variety of members of differing underground scenes. Their fan base contained members from Ska, Punk, Rock-a-Billy and Swing because they displayed an attempt to recapture a sound that was lost to mainstream music. The Sights were just one of many bands that began to appear in an attempt to assert a new type of sound within the underground music scene of Detroit. Their sound and apparent appeal led the many clubs and booking agents to believe that they would easily sell tickets, draw crowds and be the next big thing. When this occurred, a once unsteady direction became focused and a scene began to develop.

This new direction began an attempt within Detroit to bring together the straggling remainders of the various scenes. It was this togetherness that club owners and agents wanted to take advantage of; and when they discovered a sound that was able to do this, they fully supported its growth. Clubs, such as the Lager House, Small's and others, began to open in Detroit and in Hamtramck and focus themselves on this scene. As the clubs began to book more bands that attempted to recapture an older sound, the scene began to develop strong support. Many of these first bands did not have a classification, but this would soon change. The beginning bands of the scene included the Sights, Ko and the Knockouts, and the White Stripes, among others. This first sign of what was later to be termed Garage Rock took on many characteristics of the earlier scenes and related to all of them because of their attributes.

These attributes consisted of the afore-mentioned assertion of power over technique and a strong desire to return to the real essence of Rock and Roll. What was specifically important was that this music was completely unlike the current mainstream popular music. Mainstream music in the late 90s had become saturated in pop with the Backstreet Boys,

Britney Spears and N'Sync leading and competing for the top of the charts. As bands began to form, and some would re-form from existing bands to become Garage bands, the scene began to take on a shape of its own that was far different from previous underground movements. It relied on almost complete nostalgic representation of the previous form of Garage Rock of the 60s and the British Invasion that immediately preceded it. What became apparent was the conscious desire to recapture the feeling and emotions of these bands.

Many of the difficulties in the beginning of a music scene lie in the ability to get booked into existing clubs and bars that will give the fledgling bands credibility with participants in the underground movement. This difficulty was virtually erased at the onset of the Garage Rock scene when the first bands grabbed opening positions at established venues. They played with almost every differing underground type of music. From opening for Ska bands to headlining shows with Punk and Rock-a-Billy bands, these unclassified Garage bands strongly asserted their presence in the underground. Through their ability to appeal to members of almost every scene, these bands quickly gained a successful following that was comparable to previous underground movements. The bars and club owners took notice.

The first clubs to begin to feature exclusively Garage Rock shows were the Garden Bowl and the Magic Stick, both historic venues for new music in Detroit. In these two clubs, located on different floors within the same building, the Garage scene began to take on a shape of its own. The shows at the Garden Bowl, entitled "In Person," were organized by someone who would go on to front her own band with great success. Ko Shih began to offer shows for any band that wanted to play in the bar at the Garden Bowl, and the majority of these bands would later go on to become Garage bands. These shows relied on the aspect of the most limited and stripped down performance possible. In the bar of a bowling alley, bands performed where tables usually sat with no stage and little room for movement. In addition, microphone use was usually limited to the lead vocalist, and the music tended to take on this type of stripped-down performance.

This space, given the weak marketing promotion of these shows, relied on word of mouth, and the performances were generally sparsely attended. What took place at these shows, however, was the development of many bands that would later go on to be heavily prevalent within the

1. *Made in Detroit*

Garage Rock scene. The beginnings and continuation of groups such as the Go, the Von Bondies, the White Stripes, the Dirtbombs and many others relied on these shows. It was these performances that were instrumental in the development of the movement standing on its own. Before these shows began, the bands had been forced to play opening slots with other genres of music. They were still searching for a place and a name to call their own when Ko and the Garden Bowl came along.

Other venues began to have a great influence on the start of the Garage Rock scene in Detroit. Situated above the Garden Bowl is the Magic Stick and its large performance space that allowed many bands to hone their stage presence. This space began as a pool hall and still has the feeling of the underground within Detroit. The space caters to the underground and local bands that are large enough to fill the space without being mainstream. The stage is large and the venue is immense for a local band, but those that play here successfully have a large following in the underground of Detroit. For many of the beginning Garage bands, this club was the goal in performance. Stage antics and attitudes were perfected on the Magic Stick's stage. Along with the Garden Bowl, the Magic Stick is part of the Majestic Theater Complex and allows for the larger bands of the scene to play shows that are still within underground constraints and demands.

Another venue essential to the development of the scene was the Gold Dollar. Located in the heart of downtown Detroit, as is the Garden Bowl, the Gold Dollar quickly gained the reputation as the place to play if you were involved in a different sound. The owner and booking agent focused his efforts on bands that remained far outside the mainstream of music. The bands booked ranged from avant-garde Jazz groups to Hardcore Punk bands and consistently challenged the audience's expectations. Almost every group that would later go on to Garage Rock fame played some of their first shows at the Gold Dollar and the Garden Bowl.

These two places were favored at the beginning of the scene due to their extreme underground appearance and attitude. The Garden Bowl shows were played inside one of the oldest bowling alleys in Detroit, and, while it was still in business, the Gold Dollar was located in a very underdeveloped area of the city known as Cass Corridor. These two bars were gritty and reminiscent of punk clubs of the past. These bars allowed bands to play whatever they would like and cared only about the number of people who came through the doors. The stage was often barely lit, and at the Gold Dollar, on the point of collapse. Bands that played these shows were given the opportunity to fine-tune their sound in an atmosphere that was equal to the beginning style of the music. Harsh, gritty and fully removed from any corporate attitude, these clubs gave the musicians and the fans of the beginning scene a feeling of originality and a full underground aesthetic.

Many of the participants in this first appearance of the contemporary Garage scene were influenced by the desire to grasp a type of music that asserted a strong force against the typically capitalist constructions of contemporary popular music. These first bands did everything possible to avoid being classified into one type of music or genre. They adamantly claimed to be simply Rock bands, playing music for their personal enjoyment in an attempt to reclaim the current scene from previous musical underground reactions, which had, in their eyes, destroyed the underground. What becomes interesting is that these first bands were actuating a form of music that was similar to most Punk groups, and many performed onstage in ways that were similar to these Punk performers.

The stage presence of the first groups on this scene varied immensely, but they all shared a similarity to that of the early Hardcore and Punk bands. Many of these bands, the Sights included, smashed equipment onstage, did not care about who they angered, in or out of the scene, and asserted they were above retribution from club owners and booking agents. Many different types of underground movements have taken on this attitude, but these became critical traits of the burgeoning Garage Rock scene.

Although the scene began to build its own reputation, its creation and success were based on the reflection of past scenes that had been popular immediately preceding it. The preceding movements were very influential in the creation of the Garage scene, and without a high reliance on these existing scenes, Garage Rock's proliferation would have been questionable. The key to Garage Rock's beginning was its immersion in and influence on the Hardcore and Punk movements. Garage Rock began in an effort to insert a different type of music into these two scenes, one that could be considered hard enough and still appeal to everyone in the Punk scene. To do this, the bands had to play a style of music that related to both. The music was not classified as belonging to any group of musicians and therefore was allowed into all scenes.

The importance of this infiltration into a multitude of scenes cannot be overstated within the Garage Rock movement. As it carries on in the early twenty-first century, the scene would have nothing if it were not for these original members of differing scenes coming together in an effort to express a different style of music. What brought them together in the first place and why was it so important to these musicians? To answer this, we must begin to look at what Garage Rock was attempting to do and what it was trying to insert into the musical environment.

Immediately preceding Garage Rock's creation in Detroit was a lack of leadership and sense of community in the previous musical movements. People had either grown out of belonging to a scene or had grown up and realized other life priorities. While this was occurring, live music in Detroit was at a standstill. Many bands were unable to play due to infringement by the techno and dance cultures, and many others were not creative or original enough to gain widespread notice. The underground musicians and participants within scenes were excluded as the club and bar owners consistently booked disc jockeys spinning records instead of live bands. The Detroit bands and members of the underground scene were stranded without many places to play. This is when the Garden Bowl shows and the beginning of a whole new underground movement emerged.

Along with the clubs that were irregularly offering Garage shows, many individuals and companies gave the scene its initial support. Of these, three were specifically responsible for the boost of popularity and fame that would come to the Garage Rock scene. These three factions were two independent record labels and a small recording studio run by a single individual. Without the encouragement, time and money from these three elements, the Garage scene would not have received its popularity.

At the very beginning of the scene, a small record label formed in order to promote and distribute the first recordings of contemporary Garage Rock. Italy Records was founded by Dave Buick and went on to release the first records of many of the original bands, most notably the White Stripes. By providing a way to get the music heard, bands were now given a focal point for their sound. Italy began by simply putting out music on 45 rpm records that were, at the time, inexpensive to produce and that reflected the nostalgic factor in Garage Rock. The bands on this label made an important break into the underground scene with the help of Dave Buick and Italy Records.

The first band to be placed in the Italy Records lineup was Rocket 455, a band that would go on to popular success. In 1997 they put out their second EP entitled *Ain't the Right Girl* (IR-001) and became influential as the first band on Italy Records to gain recognition and underground support. Rocket 455 won mainstream success and allowed Italy to gather momentum for future releases. This small independent label created a very large stir within the city of Detroit with this release, which propelled it into the ranks of large-scale production houses. Although they were not classified as Garage Rock and leaned more towards a pop sound, Rocket 455 was extremely important in that they provided stability for Italy Records with a strongly supported release.

The second release from Italy was the Dirtys' *It Ain't Easy* (IR-002), which featured a musician of the Detroit scene that continues to play an extremely important role in music, Mick Collins. (Mick would later go on to play with the Dirtbombs and various other groups.) The Dirtys' recognition and success were more at the local level but began to shape the focus, style and thought process behind Italy Records' releases. The Dirtys were a Hard Rock group that shared more qualities with the Hardcore scene than Garage, but the focus on local, talented musicians was present. The most important releases from Italy were still to come, but the Dirtys and Rocket 455 were important first steps for the label that would go on to shape what the contemporary Garage sound would be.

The most important releases from Italy Records, in the eyes of the popular music press, are the first recordings of the White Stripes. The third release from Italy was by the band that would go on to become the "emissaries" of Garage. *Let's Shake Hands* (IR-003), released in 1997, with a re-pressing in 2002, broke Italy Records and the White Stripes into the underground and allowed Italy to proclaim itself as the label for Garage Rock at the time. The second White Stripes EP, *Lafayette Blues* (IR-006), released in 1998 and re-pressed in 2001, solidified Italy's approach and stance within the scene. These two 7-inch records strengthened the definition of Garage Rock in Detroit by allowing a band with only two members to release music that has become referential in sound format to Garage.

Italy Records went on to put out records by the Hentchmen, the Clone Defects and others that would remain influential to the sound and image of Detroit Garage and Punk. Since then, the label has undergone a change with the new moniker of Young Soul Rebels and continues to produce genuine music that is influential to underground fans everywhere. Dave Buick remains an influential part of the scene, playing in various bands and producing records for Young Soul Rebels. His continuing theory on music is what has made his label a success. He states that the most important aspect of the current scene is "maintaining genuine honesty in the songwriting process."[5] This label became one of the most influential forces in the beginning of contemporary Garage Rock, and Dave continues to remain a strong force in underground Detroit music.

The concept of remaining honest and genuine in songwriting is a common thread throughout the contemporary Garage scene. Most participants classify the Garage sound as something that is basic but heartfelt. This is where Garage shines in the eyes of many of the fans and performers. Without a strong stance on remaining true to the music and as far away from capitalist desires as possible, bands would not be labeled or even welcomed within the contemporary Garage Rock scene. The continuing desire of many groups is to produce music that contains the same feeling of honesty and genuineness that they played at the beginning.

The independent record label known as Sympathy for the Record Industry is based in Long Beach, California. While a small and relatively unknown label at the time, it played an influential role in the development of the burgeoning Garage Rock scene. With its independent status and willingness to push the envelope of what is considered popular music, the owners focused on the new sound coming from Detroit. They originally began signing contracts with small, unknown groups and developed the bands through tour support and promotion-driven album sales.

Sympathy for the Record Industry was the second label to release and support the White Stripes and the first to support their European tour that would establish the band as the recognizable musicians they are today. This label also signed many of the original more recent Garage bands from Detroit, such as the Detroit Cobras, Ko and the Knockouts and the Come Ons. Sympathy was one of the only labels to recognize these early bands as an investment and was determined to reap benefits from their discovery.

With Sympathy for the Record Industry's release of its first "Garage Rock" compilation, entitled *The Sympathetic Sounds of Detroit* (SFTRI 623), it promoted the new sound of the underground movement. This first compilation featured many of the bands that would later develop deals with major labels, and still more that are considered the founders of contemporary Garage Rock, and was also influential in categorizing these bands under one moniker: Garage Rock. This compilation was produced and recorded by Jack White of the White Stripes. Mixing and engineering was by Jim Diamond of Ghetto Recorders and Jack White. Although there is no mention of this record as a Garage Rock compilation, it featured bands and music that would later be classified as such. In order for Sympathy or Italy to be able to sign any artist from Detroit, each had to record tracks that would be available for distribution. This is where the third instrumental faction was essential.

Ghetto Recorders is the recording studio in Detroit that became the heart of the Garage Rock music-making scene. With a commitment to recording with less sophisticated equipment in order to acquire a sound that was reminiscent of the past, the Garage sound was created within the confines of this studio. The proprietor of this studio is Jim Diamond, recently dubbed the Phil Specter of Detroit Garage, but considered by many more akin to Sam Philips at Sun Records. His commitment to recording technologies that have long since been replaced by current electronics established a sound many Garage Bands strive to achieve. He also allowed many early bands to record demos at a relatively low cost, which gained them exposure and accessibility within the industry. From recording the first tracks for the White Stripes to the current recordings of bands like the Come Ons, Ghetto Recorders continues to play an influential role in the Garage scene.

It is this type of dedication to older recording equipment and "lo-fi" sound that is desirable to the Garage scene participants. The use of computer-aided recording equipment and programs that construct rhythm patterns is regarded as a negative aspect within Garage Rock. Forgoing modern technology where everything is in perfect placement and fits a preconceived notion of music, Ghetto Recorders and the Garage bands seek to create a sound that nostalgically represents the past. This recording style also allows the music to go against capitalist notions of higher end machinery and technology creating better sounding music. It is this lack of quality that has become so desirable in today's underground music environment where over-produced mainstream music, like that of Britney Spears and the Backstreet Boys, is viewed with disdain.

With the backing of a record label and a recording studio dedicated to a specific recording strategy, the Garage scene began to gain momentum throughout the underground music community. All of these factions were as influential as the previous underground scenes to the developing Garage Rock movement. The favored recording equipment and record labels were important aspects of the emergence of this movement in

Detroit and elsewhere. Without Ghetto Recorders, Italy Records and Sympathy for the Record Industry, the Garage Rock scene would not have developed as rapidly or acquired the momentum to become so influential within the underground music movement. Dave Buick, Jim Diamond and Sympathy are specifically important due to their commitment to older technologies and newer musical sounds.

At first these older technologies were the result of a limited budget within limited studio space. The beginnings of contemporary Garage Rock took place in a run-down warehouse that was converted into a recording studio. Built with barely any sound- proofing technologies within this simple space, the recording studio began with a four-track recorder. The first recordings of the new movement were extremely raw and under-produced, many of them capturing the original Garage sound. Among the various individuals who use older technologies as a way of expressing groups and sounds that they were influenced by, Ko Shih states, "I don't think I've ever recorded to anything but tape. Tape is what the records I like were recorded on, so that's what sounds good to me."[6] This characteristic later developed into a sound that would become synonymous with contemporary Garage bands worldwide, with many bands traveling from other parts of the country to Detroit in order to record.

As Garage Rock began to ascend through the ranks of the underground, where to achieve this sound and how to produce albums with this apparent lack of quality became better known. Ghetto Recorders became the heart of the burgeoning scene and continues to draw artists from around the world to its studio. Without Ghetto Recorders, Sympathy for the Record Industry and Italy Records, the Garage Rock underground would not have begun.

At the beginning of the Garage Rock scene there was a band known as the Gories. This group was one of the first bands to play a style that was similar to 1960s Rock. The band consisted of three members that were determined to play music that reflected the late 50s and early 60s era. Even their name pays homage to a band that appeared in the original *Gidget* series. The Gories consisted of two guitar players and a drummer. With no bass player, they went on to large success due to their harsh sound and simplistic musical concept.

The Gories began in 1986, before the current proliferation of Garage Rock. One of the main members currently plays in the group known as the Demolition Doll Rods, and another performs with the Dirtbombs. They were featured on one of the largest Garage Rock compilations that appeared in 1987, before the current movement. The compilation, entitled *It Came from the Garage II* (Wanghead with Lips WH005), was not well received and would have done much better in sales if it had been released during the current underground movement. Many members of the contemporary scene are unfamiliar with this group; however, they played and still play an influential role in the development and continuation of the Detroit Garage Rock sound.

It has often been stated, among performers of the contemporary scene, that the Gories were one of the first groups to influence them in the determination of what style of music to play. The Gories were extremely focused on playing remakes of Blues numbers and Classic Rock in a way that made the songs more powerful and harsh. Cover songs of John Lee Hooker and Willie Dixon were recorded and used as a stepping point for the group in their determination of sound. What is extremely important in relation to the Gories was, at the time they were performing, there was not a group around that sounded similar to them. They performed in the Hardcore and Punk scenes of Detroit and put out a Blues oriented sound. This was extremely effective for many listeners and gave the original Garage scene a basis for sound and performance attitude.

The proliferation of Garage Rock was due in large part to the many different individuals who participated in the many musical groups at its onset. Another of the main groups influential at this beginning was the Go. The Go was an important band because almost every member of existing Garage bands has played with them at one time or another. Many members received exposure to this type of sound and approach to music from the Go and went on to play with the many groups that began the Detroit Garage underground. Along with the Go, many members of this beginning scene floated from one group to another to help each other in their development.

The Go released their first album, *Whatcha Doin?*, in 1999, on the SubPop label in Seattle. They continued to rise in success through the incorporation of Blues and Soul with a harder Rock edge. They have often been compared to the Kinks and other British groups, and dominated the beginning of the contemporary Garage scene. It is often said that their claim to fame is the fact that they were the first band that Jack White played with, but this is somewhat overstated because of the talent of the surrounding musicians in the group. The Go is filled with great song-writers, especially John Krautner, and have a talented vocalist in Bobby Harlow. The importance of the Go lies within the aspect of performance and how they allowed many of the original bands access to a sound and attitude that would define contemporary Garage Rock.

Members of many of the original groups rotated between bands in order to give participants the chance to come into their own and develop, with the best example being Ko and the Knockouts. This band was formed when the owner of Sympathy approached Ko Shih with an offer for her to front her own band and record a track for the *Sympathetic Sounds of Detroit* album. In the beginning, Ko had no songs written and lacked a band, but Long Gone John, owner of Sympathy, wanted her voice recorded and urged her to form a band for the project. Her band consisted of members from existing groups, including the Sights and the Wildbunch, and quickly developed a sound that showcased Ko's vocal patterns and lyrics. It was this blending and support of musicians and participants that gave the Garage scene its strong beginning and continued development.

The fans and individuals who began to search for a new alternative to the existing underground movements also had an impact on Garage Rock's beginnings. This search gave Garage Rock its strong start and allowed the musicians and fans to become their own underground movement. The drawing on nostalgic representations was deemed important to the Garage Rock sound and scene. These nostalgic representations allowed the participants to become standardized in their beliefs about capitalist notions of control.

Through the continuing search for a new form of music, bands that were already playing a style similar to Garage Rock were rediscovered. These included bands, such as the Hentchmen, and Fortune and Maltese, having started with a strong emphasis on organ-centered music, which allowed the participants to link them immediately to the sound of the new underground that was forming. Both of these groups were influential in the rediscovery of the sound that would influence the current Garage Rock underground. These groups focused on establishing a new sound in the current underground, leaning towards the sounds of the late 1950s and early 60s organ-centered groups.

The Hentchmen began in a small suburban town of Detroit and were, at first, written off as untalented. As they continued traveling through the underground, they began to play shows within a myriad of scenes, from Ska to Punk. This allowed them greater access to a fan base that would go on to support them throughout their career. This also allowed them to maintain an influence within different scenes, and for this reason they were rediscovered as the new underground began to form. The Hentchmen were not originally labeled a Garage band but they have gained recognition through the incorporation of this label. They have also allowed for the continuation of a sound that they enforced from the beginning. The Hentchmen were one of the first groups to express characteristics that would later be associated with contemporary Garage Rock.

The Hentchmen, led by John Syzmanski, were extremely important to the development of the keyboard sound that influenced many of the beginning Garage bands. Now signed to Times Beach Records, they continue to play organ-based Garage Rock. The use of a keyboard is nothing new, but with the Hentchmen, many people felt the nostalgia for the 60s keyboard groups for the first time. This nostalgic sound formation was pivotal to the continued success of the Hentchmen and set them up as one of the first purveyors of this sonic formation.

Fortune and Maltese, who led the organ-based sound into the majority of undergrounds, also shared these characteristics. This group was comprised of musicians who were strongly influenced by 60s rock and British Invasion music and garnered a following through their incorporation of both. They were one of the first bands to be linked with a Garage sound and would go on to influence the majority of bands that play on this scene today. Inclusion of this group in contemporary Garage Rock has been based in the underground, but they allowed for the first sounds to be discovered by the participants who would later go on to Garage Rock fame.

The current participants gained their first understanding of what it meant to play music based on music from this time period from these two groups. They were influential in the determination of the beginning culture and influenced a countless number of bands. By being based in the underground and playing with many different styles of music, the Hentchmen and Fortune and Maltese were the first groups to spread the type of music to which contemporary Garage Rock would cling. For these two groups, organ-based, fuzz-tone Rock was the focus, and they championed a new sound within the Detroit underground long before the current phenomenon of contemporary Garage Rock, giving new participants a starting point in nostalgic representation.

As the Garage underground began, individuals, bars and clubs alike linked it to past musical developments in the underground. Garage Rock owes its immense success to its reliance on previous musical movements. From the Sights to the White Stripes, the bands' popularity was benefited by the support of the existing movements. These movements allowed the burgeoning Garage bands to play at various clubs and develop their own sound. While many people considered the beginning sounds of the movement amateur and crude, they were exposed to these sounds due to the generosity of existing bands within the scene providing opening slots and gigs.

It was at these performances that the first Garage bands developed into something powerful. After the initial reaction of fans, the Garage bands were left with their music and a few die-hard loyalists—one of which was Ko Shih. With her insistence and control of a space, the Garden Bowl, shows began and added another dimension to the Garage bands and their sound. Another loyalist was Neil Yee at the Gold Dollar and the proliferation of music that went against the mainstream ideal. With this development and a place to play, the bands that would become extremely popular within the scene began to gain recognition and a positive reputation. This led club owners and booking agents to recognize a beginning scene and leap to book these bands for their clubs.

With the venues and underground scene established, the Garage movement was allowed to expand its fan base and realize its potential. Now the bands had a venue at which to play, and had access and exposure within the Detroit community. This exposure paved the way for Garage Rock bands to be noticed and to have major label record deals offered. With this popularity also came the insistence on past cultural signs as a breaking away from the mainstream of society.

These past cultural signs began with a reliance on the immediately preceding musical developments and continued, within the music and the scene, as nostalgic representations of the British Invasion and the original Garage Rock of the 1960s. The specific representations will be discussed later, but what becomes important is the reliance on nostalgia and the way it was and is used to determine the establishment of an underground movement and culture of music that continues to infiltrate the mainstream music community. Without this reliance on the immediately preceding musical movements, Garage Rock would not have had the impact and driving force that it held and continues to hold over the underground music scene in Detroit.

2

Setting Your Sights on the Underground

To define the contemporary Garage movement, one must consider an example of the scene as representative in the development of nostalgia and music. In this case, the focus will be on the band the Sights. This group demonstrates the ability of a group of musicians to rise from the underground and break into the mainstream while remaining champions of underground thought. Many people view the Sights as a group that has always been slightly behind the mainstream of popular trends, and because of this they have consistently remained popular in the underground. What is extremely important about the Sights is that they have incorporated many of the defining notions of contemporary Garage Rock, and they were there from the beginning of this new movement within Detroit. Through the influence of preceding musical groups, in and out of Detroit, the Sights focused their music on the attitudes and issues that related to all of the surrounding musical scenes. The performance aspects and sonic representation that the Sights offer is reflective of the contemporary scene and continues today, even with mainstream success. The Sights are a definitive representation of the contemporary movement and demonstrate the importance of preceding musical influences and nostalgic representation in musical construction and performance.

By discussing one specific group from the beginning scene, the development of and reliance upon nostalgic thought can be understood. This is not to say that other groups are not deserving of recognition. It is only suggesting that the Sights most closely represent the ties to nostalgia and the representation of the past in their creation of music, performance attitudes and appearance. The discussion focuses on this group of musicians and their relation to the past, and who continue to revolve around nostalgic representations.

The beginning of the Sights stemmed from lead singer Eddie Baranek's random discovery of the Jam. After a simple listen to Paul Weller, Eddie and three other friends created a group called the Same. The importance of this beginning was that Eddie and his friends were only 17 years old at the time. As seniors in high school, they were not allowed into any bars, and when they did gain access within the underground they were always viewed as the kids to take under your wing. By performing with members of the then underground scene of Ska, the group began to take shape. The importance at the beginning was that this group was relating to music of the Jam, the Small Faces, the Move, and others of the Hard Mod and 60s Garage Rock scene.

This music was not extremely popular in the late 90s and allowed the group to play a type of music that was considered original at the time. The late 90s were largely based on the sounds of British Pop and other formats of music that members of many people, the Sights included, felt limited expressive and creative avenues. Through listening to bands that were extremely influential to the development of music but generally left out of the popular American press, the Sights began to develop a strong musical focus and the band began to grow by playing covers of these often-obscure groups.

The Sights demonstrated their affinity for Hard Mod from the very beginning by dressing in the sharpest of suits and playing a type of music that was aligned with the bands mentioned. The Move was an extremely popular group within the Hard Mod sound, and this group of young kids took their inspiration directly from them. The sound was harsh and basic at first, and allowed the group to develop into a fully functioning nostalgic act based on these influences. They showed up at events dressed in full suits and made their way into the scene through their use of fashion and style, along with musical construction. Where the Hardcore and Punk scenes influenced other beginning groups, the Sights relied on more obscure influences that allowed them to put a different sound into the underground Detroit music scene.

By appearing at events in full suits, the Sights' members looked similar to one another, and they were at first linked to the Ska underground. They would have been limited in playing shows if they had not developed a strong following by playing a type of music that was derived from the Mod sounds of England and not the Ska sound that was dominant in the underground of Detroit at the time. Although they were considered distinct from the underground scene, the Sights began to develop a strong presence that was based on the attitudes and performance aspects of the original Mod groups.

The Move were a large part of the Mod sound of Birmingham and later London, England. They began as a combination drawn from the local groups that had the most success, and continued with the help of legendary manager Tony Secunda. What is extremely important about the Move and their influence on the Sights is their stage presence and the sonic quality of their recordings. The Move championed what was known as the Brum Beat sound and challenged the surrounding fan base with their onstage antics. Rob Craiger states in his history of the Move, "Audiences, drawn to both the musicianship and violence, now saw lead singer Carl Wayne smashing television sets with an axe, showering the packed crowd with glass."[1] This led to an immense following in the surrounding cities and great success on the charts. What these kinds of displays also led to was the band being recognized more for its antics and less for its music.

A large part of what led to the Move's downfall was the harshness of personalities within the band, especially the lead singer and his antics on stage. Although many fans and even the group's manager were thrilled by the display, the other band members did not want to be known only for the actions of one person. This is a common story for many of the original bands, especially ones from the Mod scene that were successful more for the fans that followed them than for what type of music they played. The Move was important in both respects, but it was the performance aspect that subsequent bands like the Sights took directly from the group.

The Move–Sights comparison is not limited to the antics on stage, but the similarities between the two lead singers are remarkably striking. Sights lead Eddie Baranek is known for his often-raucous stage antics, although he has not yet broken a television onstage. The tonality of both singers and the way that they express themselves onstage are both reminiscent of pure emotional release, and this is where both groups gained their following. Baranek has often stated that his main influence in stage performance comes from Tim Vulgar in Detroit. Tim has been a member of various Hardcore and Punk bands, most notably the Clone Defects, and has an almost animal-like stage presence that allows the music expressed to continuously affect the audience. Herein lies the effectiveness and point of all three lead singers and groups: to influence the audience by providing a sonic and visceral experience.

Tim Vulgar's stage presence is generally viewed as extremely harsh and not conducive to drawing many fans, but to the members of the underground and to many in the press, his performance represents the total Detroit experience. Tim has often been mentioned as influential to many musicians in the scene and continues to inspire through the use of his body and voice in any way possible to affect the crowd.

Although the Move were extremely boisterous on and off stage, they played a type of music that was filled with rave-ups and five-part harmonies at the beginning. Their sound was extremely influenced by Motown and Soul and then shifted to the West Coast San Francisco Psychedelic vibe. The group would go on to form the seminal group ELO (Electric Light Orchestra) based on these latter influences. The point of reference for the Sights, however, is on the beginning recordings of the group and how they were using Motown and Soul records and playing with a harsher feel. This sound can be heard on the Sights' first two records and continues to demonstrate how the Sights rely on nostalgic sounds and performance styles for their construction.

The nostalgic sounds recreated by the Sights challenged the first set of contemporary Garage bands in that the music was slightly different and not simply straight Rock and Roll. What this did for the Sights was to allow them to remain a part of the underground, but also to develop a large following based on their use of such a specific past. Many people were drawn to the Sights in an effort to reclaim, or even relearn, a past that they had never shared. When audiences viewed the Sights with such a nostalgic outlook, they grew in great numbers. The construction of music and the formation of attitude within the group led to a focus on sound and appearance that influenced many of the surrounding members of the scene.

It is extremely interesting to consider how the Move were using the nostalgic sounds of Motown, even as the sound was occurring, to create their music, and how the Sights again recreated this type of music with nostalgia for the same time period. The Sights continually display aspects of Motown throughout their recordings and performance. Although they do not use five-part harmony, they base their musical construction on chord voicing that is directly related to the Motown sound. The importance of this link cannot be emphasized enough in the Sights' mass appeal.

By challenging audiences to go back in time through their music, the Sights broke into the underground through nostalgic methods of performance and songwriting.

The aspect of chord voicing displayed in the Sights' music is often considered simplistic. This is not always the case, but the simplicity is what allows the group to display the emotion and strength within the song. The use of chord progressions that are based in simple Motown and Soul progressions allows the band to move through changes rapidly without hesitation and to focus on the performance aspects of the group. This style of writing also forces the listener to hear the group as a representation of nostalgic thought and sound.

Another influential group for the Sights was the Small Faces. This group was a large part of the Hard Mod sound and scene, with their name derived from a top Mod being called "a face." This group was also known for its raucous stage antics and its larger than life attitude. The main difference between the Small Faces and other groups was that they lived the true life of the Hard Mods through their music and actions. Their first show as a group is one of legend in many musicians' and fans' eyes.

The Small Faces were a group that truly lived the life of the Mod. Whenever they received money or any funding from anyone, it was spent on clothing. Their record label even gave them, in exchange for royalties of course, an open account at every store on Carnaby Street. This group was destined for success because they related to the surrounding scene even before they became popular. Here was the real incarnation of the Mod band—Mods playing music for other Mods.

The first show the Small Faces played was at a middle-class bar, and the owner threw them off the stage. After being ousted from their first show, they decided to walk to a pub and drink. They arrived at a small club and within minutes were onstage playing to a full house of Mods. This landed them a monthly gig at the club, the Mojo. This was just the beginning of a group that would go on to influence many of the premier Mod exports to the U.S., including the Who. The Small Faces were revolutionary in their use of the surrounding sounds of American Motown and R & B, with their main influence being Booker T & the MG's.

The Small Faces were extremely influential in their approach to sound and music because of the influences they drew from. Instead of simply following the Motown sound, they infused their music with a harsher R & B sound people could dance to rhythmically. The surrounding scene was extremely taken by this sound and embraced the group as heroes of the Mod underground. Through covering songs by Booker T & the MG's, the Small Faces led the way into the stronger sounds of later Mod bands and championed the look, sound and feel of being a Mod.

Their first full-length album rivals any album put out by the Who, the Jam, or the Rolling Stones. The self-titled album is a classic that showcases the true Mod sound of the day. With Steve Marriot's voice leading and the entire band playing extremely well, the album went to number three on the British charts and set the Small Faces on their way to stardom. Many sounds, such as the quality of the bass and the guitar effects, heard on this album can be witnessed on later Sights albums. The tone of the vocals and the guitar sound are extremely similar, and this album can be viewed as one of the most influential albums on the Sights' look and sound.

The album also gained popularity due to the stage antics of Steve Marriot. He was not as harsh as the lead singer for the Move, but the aspect of throwing yourself into a performance was greatly in evidence. By showcasing the Mod sound and appearance throughout the U.K., the Small Faces were largely responsible for exposing many people to the Mod sound, including the men responsible for the Who and other British exports. The importance here lies in the way that the Small Faces infused their music and performed it onstage with the type of swagger and vigor that was derived from American music but placed in a wholly English context.

The beginnings of both the Small Faces and the Sights are extremely similar as well. By choosing covers of songs to play and then slowly developing original material, both groups gained a large following. The Small Faces originally had only two originals in their set of Motown and Stax covers, while the Sights played a full set of covers. The only difference between the groups, in this respect, is the fact that the Sights chose covers that many people had never heard before, whereas the Small Faces were playing American music for an audience that was familiar with the sound and style.

This difference is important because the Sights broke into the scene through the incorporation of songs that many people thought were their own and not covers. This allowed the band to come together and develop through the playing of someone else's music. By doing so, the group began to develop a writing and performance style based on these covers of, to the scene in Detroit, obscure bands from the 60s.

With these influences, the Sights delved into the Detroit music scene and began to play with anyone and everyone they could. This allowed the group to develop a strong fan base from different, and sometimes competing, underground scenes. The first groups the Sights played with were Ska groups, and then they would turn around and play with bands in the Punk scene. This is what a majority of new bands will do, but the various scenes reacted to the Sights with warmth rather than dismissal. The Sights challenged the underground scene in Detroit with a new sound that was taken directly from the influences that many of the underground movements shared. Ska and Punk followers alike found a link to the music through the use of Mod culture.

The Mod culture and sound resonated through both scenes because of the outlook and stage performance of Eddie Baranek and the rest of the band members. By reconstructing this sound and approach to music, the Sights were given access to many opportunities that newer bands do not normally get. It is also a credit to Eddie's shear tenacity in booking and managing the band that they played the amount of shows they did in the beginning. By doing so, they gained a large following from the outset and continued to influence many groups to come.

From the start, the various scenes took these teenagers under their wings and began to give them more and more shows. The Sights were the beneficiaries of an extremely rare occurrence in Detroit: support from almost every scene. This allowed them to develop strongly and progress through the underground. Many people and groups saw them as important to the continuation of live music in Detroit, and this led to their acceptance and success within Detroit. This is not to say that they did not have any problems at the beginning.

A constant issue with every band is membership; the Sights are no different. Any attempt to get three or more people to agree for a long period of time is extremely difficult, especially when creative personalities are involved. The Sights, especially Eddie Baranek, went through a great number of changes and survived them all to become a breakthrough group with their latest self-titled release on James Iha's Scratchie/New Line label. In examining the history of the Sights, what becomes important is how the band has used the past within their musical production and performance.

As if often the case with newer bands that become successful, the structure of the group is centered on one individual. With the Sights, this is lead singer Eddie Baranek. Without his constant effort in promotion and work ethic the group would not have been as successful as it has. The structure of the Sights has changed multiple times, but the sound and approach has remained intact due to Eddie's insistence on the musical and nostalgic consistency of the band. The importance of remaining with one solid sound is extremely relevant, especially in the beginnings of a group. With a variance of sound, fans begin to fade and lose interest. The Sights avoided this throughout their history, surviving many member and label changes.

Their first album, *Are You Green?* 1999, was produced at Ghetto Recorders and had the production quality of the contemporary Garage bands. The album was recorded through the limited technology and mixing capability of the original 60s groups and sounds as if it is directly from that era. From the guitar to the drum sound, there is a significant effort to play in the style of their influences. The guitar and bass sound extremely reminiscent of the Who, and the drums, although the album features a drummer change, sound as if Keith Moon had been reincarnated. This sound was extremely effective in the development of the Sights' following and their continuation onto bigger things. First released on Spectator, and then re-released on Fall of Rome, *Are You Green?* set the Sights on their way to Garage Rock fame.

The album is often viewed as a starting point for the Sights' sound, but fans and members of the scene heard something that was different and began to hold the group up as a pivotal part of the underground scene in Detroit. With the small success of their first album, the Sights began to increase their use of aggressive stage antics and harsh sounds. This led to many becoming engrossed with their sound and approach to music, and began their ascent into the heights of the underground in Detroit. By infusing their first record with the type of energy and emotion that would classify the group from day one, they displayed to everyone the impact that nostalgia has on the group and the surrounding scene.

What becomes interesting is how the Sights have never championed the label of Garage, yet continue to use the same strategies and sonic qualities as other Detroit bands that play within the genre. The defining aspect of Garage Rock for Eddie Baranek is an innocence and naiveté that newer bands possess.[2] This is a key point in the Sights' outlook on both the music and the scene. Listening to the first album, one can view a group that had not quite found themselves but was enjoying the discovery and journey. This, to many, is Garage Rock in its newest form.

What then became of the group when they discovered the music scene's realities and the management and business side of things? According to Eddie and others, this is where the breakdown of the underground starts.

The breakdown of any underground scene is usually determined in advance through the many bands attempting to catch onto a trend simply to make money and become successful. The Sights and others of the original movement have begun to question many rising bands and the attitudes of the mainstream press in defining Garage Rock. Through the manipulation of many groups, the underground gradually begins to fail, but somehow contemporary Garage Rock has remained and has continued to play a large part in the underground and mainstream of society.

If there is a breakdown within the scene caused by the introduction of business into music, why then haven't the Sights failed? This question can be answered through looking at how the band remains centered on their goal to remain in the underground, even with significant mainstream exposure. The continuation stems from rooting the band in an attitude that is focused away from the mainstream capitalist desires that have affected so many bands of the Garage Rock scene. Through remembering first witnessing a show that allowed access to the music, and by playing shows that are geared toward influencing fans in the same way, the Sights have remained an important band within the scene.

While bringing up the recent past, Eddie Baranek recalls many shows that influenced him musically and pushed him into forming and playing music. "It's cool ... going to the Garden Bowl in 2001 and seeing Tim Vulgar sing. The Done Wrongs were playing a show and Tim Vulgar grabbed the mike, Jack [White] played guitar, and Pat Keeler of the Greenhorns grabbed the drums ... and that's what I could call the scene."[3] This hesitancy to group himself into the beginning of the scene allows him and the Sights to stay within the underground. There is still a notion in the band that they are a young group and everyone around them is helping them develop, when in reality the Sights have developed into a group that has increasing popularity and continues to profess the same nostalgic traits as the contemporary Garage groups that have helped them reach their current status.

This naiveté still prevalent within the group allows the Sights to maintain their underground status and champion the bands that continue to remain on the outside of the scene. By claiming to not be a part of any beginning scene or movement, the Sights allow themselves to consistently remain as a band that belongs to multiple scenes. This is extremely important in the outlook of the Sights and continues to allow them access to many different shows and venues throughout the world. By championing the underground of Detroit and remaining nostalgic in their approach, they continue as a band that has achieved success but remains an active part of the underground.

While sharing the same beginnings as the surrounding Garage groups, the Sights often were pushed into the background of the popular groups. They were viewed within the scene as the young ones, and that has allowed them to continue as a band within the underground and remain apart from the more popular groups that have been said to have sold out. This allows the group to become more focused on musical production and not simply on attaining fame and fortune. With all of the fame and recognition that has come their way, Eddie still lives with his mother. This attitude towards music and the mainstream press has allowed them to become representative of contemporary Garage Rock and its insertion through nostalgia into society.

It is extremely important to realize that the Sights still view themselves as a newer band that is just playing for the fun of it. Throughout photo shoots, press releases, even the construction of their latest video, they have remained a band that is still enjoying the ride. While many bands view success as the final destination, the Sights continue to view it as a part of the journey. The main reason for this is the effort that has been put into the band by Eddie and the existing members. By remaining dedicated to nostalgic representations and constructions based on the past, the Sights continually shape the underground and mainstream music of today.

To understand the importance of the Sights, one simply needs to look at the groups that have appeared after formation of the Sights. These groups, although sonically different, share a great deal of performance aspects and musical constructions with the Sights. Groups such as the Hard Lessons and others continue to display raucous stage antics that are similar to the Sights. This is not to say that the Sights created these antics but rather displayed them again through the beginnings of the scene. The way that the lead singer/guitar player reacts on stage is extremely similar in these two groups, and the comparison can be extended to include vocal styling as well. Although Eddie has stated that the style of the Sights is based on multiple influences, his stage presence is one that continues to influence newer bands in Detroit.

The sound of the Sights is also influential to many of the newer bands. The band now consists of a keyboardist, guitarist/singer and a drummer, which is exactly the same format the Hard Lessons and other newer groups have adopted. This does not mean that these newer groups are the same in sound or approach, but it does demonstrate the impact that the Sights have had on the Detroit scene. The Hard Mod sound and approach to music has often been codified and reformed, but never has it been represented so completely in music as by the Sights.

To relate the influences of the Sights is to view the extreme differences within the contemporary Garage scene. The band began under the moniker of the Same, and the logo they chose was a rip-off of the Who, with their letter being combined in the text to reference the Mod leanings of the early band. The Jam and the Rolling Stones also play a large role in their determination of sound and style. Finally, on their newest album, the sound is reminiscent of the Beatles and other British Invasion bands. This is extremely important in the realization that the Sights continue to view themselves in relation to the past. There is no consideration for the newer sounds of the mainstream music world.

The newer sounds of the mainstream music world are often viewed as limiting in emotion and feel. Many bands regard the recording strategies of overdubbing vocals and sounds as inauthentic, but the Sights also refuse to manipulate their tracks with newer technologies. Their recent sound also represents a more refined style of music that is not related to the original Rock and Roll that many groups in the contemporary Garage world are striving for. The Sights chose their nostalgic era and have been rewarded for it. The sound of the mainstream has become watered down and filled with fake Pop music, and the Sights and others are successfully attempting a change.

The group even constructs their music in a way that is reminiscent of the past. While many groups write music in an attempt to copy a newer sound, the Sights use the past to gain ideas and chord progressions that have influenced them musically. In fact, Eddie has stated that Mod, British Invasion and the original Garage sound are all places in which to access ideas. He claims that these are all musical realms that are superior to the Rock music of today. There is nothing in the music of the Sights that relates to the music of the Rock and Roll of today.

The group has always relied on influences that were beyond the majority of Pop record fans. Eddie Baranek takes great pride in his record collection and often ventures into record shows simply to find something from the Small Faces or other bands that have continued to dominate his love of rare sounds from the past. While many musicians strive to remain current with the surrounding scene, Eddie Baranek and the Sights consistently delve into the past. This does not mean that they are ignorant of their surroundings, only that they choose to find their influence nostalgically.

While this may be limiting in the aspect of mainstream success, the Sights continue to remain fixated on the past for their inspiration and ideas. This generates a multitude of comparisons to other groups within the Garage scene, but the Sights were one of the first to construct themselves in this manner. With this construction comes their unwillingness to submit to mainstream musical demands. The group has received countless accolades in the press and has now released a record on a semi-independent label. Eddie Baranek admits that he is wary of what happens to bands when they sign with a major label. In a *Metro Times* interview with Brian Smith, Eddie states, "We didn't really want to be on a major label because we see what happens to the bands."[4] This statement is key to the Sights' success. Eddie Baranek has suffered for his success and remained focused on a do-it-yourself ethos that has let the Sights remain a part of the underground even with label success.

The crossover from the underground to the mainstream is extremely difficult to accomplish without alienating fans and supporters. The Sights have achieved this crossover and been allowed to remain a part of the underground due to their insistence on the music and by not giving in to corporate record label demands. They also continuously challenge the notions of the Detroit scene that are perpetuated in the press. The conception that all of the Detroit scene hangs out and relates to one another continuously is inaccurate, though the press, especially in Europe, continue to make this claim. Members of the bands within the scene do not all hang out at one another's houses. Many do not relate to one another except when playing shows together. Some members even disassociate themselves from the scene in order to claim a further underground stance within the scene. By allowing different fans and members of the surrounding scene to view the Sights in a way that challenges the mainstream notions of music, the Sights continue to be a part of the underground in Detroit and elsewhere.

The importance here lies in the way that the Sights retain their underground status. By claiming a type of outsider status, in contrast to mainstream popular groups like the Hives and others, they align themselves with groups that remain undiscovered. The Sights' status within Detroit also allows them to maneuver without any conflict. While other groups name-call, steal girlfriends and even get into fistfights, the Sights avoid these negative occurrences. They also continuously demonstrate an allegiance to groups that have come before them and remain emphatic in their support of up and coming bands that relate to them musically.

There is also a perception in the press that only certain groups play at certain venues in Detroit. The thought has become that you must play a certain venue to remain an effective and successful member of the scene. Whether it is Punk and Hardcore bands playing at Alvin's, or Garage Rock groups playing at the Lager House, this perception is rooted in the surrounding members of the musical community. This aspect is one that must be changed, and the Sights attempt to play with as many different sounding groups as possible to continue to challenge the notions of their mainstream removal from the underground. By doing so, they remain active within the scene. The Sights were the beneficiaries of multiple styles at the beginning, and by allowing different bands to play on the same bill they give back to the underground of Detroit.

The most important methodology that the band uses to remain a part of the underground is their insistence on playing music that is representative of the group's beginnings. The sound on their first record is almost exactly the same as their newest release. The songs may be more polished and formed, but the sonic quality is extremely similar. This is due to the band's insistence on using Jim Diamond's Ghetto Recorders for recording, production and post-production. By doing so, their sound retains the qualities of what has come to be known as Garage today.

Another important aspect of sound is the thought process put forward in recording by the group. The key viewpoint of the recording process is the aspect of recording a *song*, not simply laying down tracks. According to Baranek, "I don't cut tracks, I never have cut any track. I record songs."[5] This may seem like a simple assertion, but it becomes extremely important in the way that songs are recorded and placed onto tape. By only recording full songs and not simply laying down guitar tracks and overdubbing, the Sights adhere to the original methodology of recording. It would be extremely simple for the group to lay tracks and overdub, like countless other mainstream bands do, but they choose to record in one full take, like their influences did. The band plays the song together and records each track simultaneously. This leads to a consistency in the music.

Another key aspect of the sonic quality of the Sights is their writing style. They continue to use a method used by many of the original groups of the 60s and British Invasion. By using one member, usually Eddie, to form and create the structure of the song, i.e. writing lyrics, and then bringing it to the group to be enhanced with a bass line or drum pattern, the Sights again reinstate a past method of writing. This methodology may sound simplistic, but it remains integral to the Sights' sonic output. Other rock groups of the day usually hire songwriters and producers to form the song and then simply play the song the way they are told. In other cases the group writes the song collaboratively, which lends to the song feeling less complete. Eddie Baranek admits that he borrows from multiple influences to write and construct songs, and by doing so, the band expands to include these influences. Instead of paying outside writers and producers to construct songs and then playing them, the Sights adamantly insist on writing their own music.

Throughout the contemporary Garage world are many instances of groups that are prepackaged and formed by record executives, even down to the writing of music by others. This is what the Sights have come to stand against. In a world where groups are constructed by the mainstream labels in an attempt to make money, the Sights champion the notion that anyone can make music for the love of it and can be successful. Their story allows for people in Detroit and elsewhere to hear a band that withstood the pressures of mainstream success and continues to offer an alternative to the thought processes put forward by mainstream music. By continuing to champion the underground in their music, the Sights remain an integral part of the contemporary Garage movement.

Are they a part of a movement to make a difference? According to Eddie Baranek they are, and if people do not realize that, they are fooling themselves.[6] The construction of a representative is nothing new, but the fact that Eddie Baranek and the Sights have remained at the forefront of the Garage underground from the very beginning is pivotal to their success and continued inclusion within the underground. The Sights thrive on making music that they enjoy and have grown up with, and their continued apparent naiveté within the scene allows them to champion the contemporary Garage movement. They do not readily wear the label of Garage but continue to challenge the press's definition of Garage. By doing so, they remain a part of a movement and express a format of music that is theirs alone.

The Sights began before the consolidation of the Garage scene in

Detroit. Although the Gories and others were playing a similar style of music, the Sights formed before the term began to gain popularity. This allowed them to incorporate the surrounding influences in Detroit and stretch out into the realm of Garage. For many, the beginning of the Garage scene stemmed from the idea that anyone could form a band and play. This is still the feeling within the Sights and allows them to strongly push against the capitalist constructions of music. Through playing with many other styles of music, they were focusing on the way music was based in a community, and they were desperate to become a focus within this community.

The Detroit music scene has always been extremely competitive and often leads to bands and people becoming ostracized. The Sights avoided this at first by incorporating themselves into as many scenes as possible. This led to their status within the music community being challenged, but it also led to their success. From the first shows at the Wired Frog to larger venues like the Magic Bag, the Sights claimed a large following from every underground scene.

Nostalgia has always been a part of the Sights. They always record to tape and consistently use dress to represent themselves outside of the popular capitalist constructions. This becomes extremely important in the way they challenge the capitalist constructions of music. The press cannot stop comparing the Sights to older bands and nostalgic sounds. James Oldham's review of their second release, *Got What We Want,* in *New Musical Express,* focuses the group's nostalgia. "Taking its cue from scuzzed 60s beatpop, it manages to cram echoes of Supergrass, the Who and (soon-to-be-hip-again) 70s rockers Humble Pie into its 11 tracks. It's the coolest and most accomplished rock 'n' roll record to come out of Detroit since 'White Blood Cells.'"[7] The group relies on musical inspiration and construction from sources that were never extremely popular but were successful within the underground of music. They also effectively demonstrate a means to construct individuality through the music played and performance aspects that relate to the past. By doing so they consistently challenge what it means to be a success within capitalist America, especially within music.

Without instituting this force into the contemporary music scene, the Sights would not be as successful throughout the underground. They continue to remain as a part of the underground simply through this challenge to reconstruct identity through the past. The nostalgic use of music and dress relays this message, and countless fans relate to the image and sound of the Sights. By gaining success in the mainstream music world, the band will face their greatest challenge to remaining true to the concepts that put them on the map. The main concept of naiveté and playing music for yourself and for the fun of it must remain in order for the Sights to continue their dominance of the underground in Detroit.

Throughout the Sights' existence has been a desire to play music that is influenced by the past and displays characteristics of musicians that have been viewed as influential to the group. By continuing to create a type of music that relates to the past in this way, the group will continue to dominate the Garage scene. The creation of music through a wealth of past sources has allowed them to remain relevant and to place old sources back into the forefront of underground thought. This must continue in order for the band to survive within the ever-changing underground musical climate. The Sights' nostalgia is easily viewed in their record sleeves and must continue to be displayed within the entirety of their music and presentation.

With their first album, *Are You Green?*, the Sights chose to display themselves through the use of the 60s and 70s Mod culture. The front of the album cover displays a group picture along with the logo of the group at the time, simply their name. The back is a photo of an amplifier in a studio and a piece of paper with the track listing lying haphazardly on the floor. The entire album is framed in a lime green color that strikes the viewer as older and more nostalgic than anything else. The reference to the past is immediately relevant through the display of objects and the use of color on the album. Their next album was strikingly similar in look and feel.

Got What We Want was designed in a very similar way, with a slight modification to the color scheme and pictures shown. Here you have a group that is again using nostalgia in an effort to demonstrate their influences. The color scheme on this album was red and black, and the pictures used represent different aspects of the Sights' stage shows. The referent here is to performance, and the album is filled with songs that discuss performing for the crowd and themselves. This album is generally considered their finest work by many fans, and the sleeve demonstrates a creativity that goes along with the music.

Even their newest release on New Line continues to reflect the nostalgic traits of the band. The cover of *The Sights* is reminiscent of the past with its nod to the 70s in color and design. The album is centered on a beige background that brings the 70s immediately to mind. There is no art on the cover except for the logo, leading to a direct comparison to album covers from the 60s and 70s. The Sights have achieved a nostalgic look that represents an old Chicago album.

The use of nostalgia, even in their largest label release, continues to solidify the Sights place in the underground and allows them to remain a part of the community within Detroit and beyond. They have continuously challenged the contemporary musical world and have influenced the mainstream through their nostalgic traits. By doing so, they continue to influence underground groups within Detroit and around the world with their brand of nostalgic Rock and Roll and their style of Mod dress. The Sights have always attempted to remain a part of the underground and have achieved this by remaining true to the nostalgia of their music. This allows them to stand as a true representation of the contemporary Garage Rock movement. By using nostalgia of the 50s and 60s within music construction and stage presence to determine their attempted individuality, the Sights continue to be representatives of the new movement and will remain as proponents of the underground.

3

Invasion of the British

As the British Invasion began its assimilation into popular music, many people began to view the bands as antithetical to the current mainstream of music. This led to these bands being construed as outcasts and rebels. Bands like the Kinks, the Rolling Stones and others were all banned from playing certain venues within the United States, with the Kinks being banned from the country for a period of approximately 4 years.[1] It wasn't until the Beatles and the Stones began to achieve monetary success in America that the doors began to open to other British bands. The continued success of British Invasion bands within postmodern society has allowed a new generation of people to become influenced by their attempt at a different form of music. This new generation has carried the influence of the British Invasion forward and allowed these bands to remain vital to the musical world. Bands from the British Invasion still continue to influence many forms of underground and mainstream music, but it is with Garage Rock that this influence is directly correlated. In order to fulfill this relationship, many members of the current scene cite the British Invasion as their starting point into the form of music that they now play. From the Who to the Rolling Stones, these bands have created a style of music that has continually dominated the charts, and music that holds great influence over many new underground developments. Contemporary Garage Rock is greatly influenced by these bands, and it looks back to the British Invasion for the structure of their sound, appearance and musical approach. By doing so, they continue to champion a sound and attitude that was influential in changing the musical landscape of the world.

The British Invasion is viewed as a defining time in Rock music. This period saw the talent and music of Britain become immersed in

American society. With the Beatles's explosion into mainstream America, the British Invasion began and its influence is still prevalent in many musical styles today. The critically acclaimed groups of the British Invasion are still viewed as founding fathers of Rock music and are held in great esteem. Many of these bands relied heavily on the success of the Beatles, who broke into America first, but this reliance was often challenged in an attempt to inject a difference into the musical realm. Through this challenge, bands that directed their music away from suburban desires gained a new acceptance into the mainstream of music and were allowed to influence generations of music performers and participants. The Who (1965), the Jam (1978), the Kinks (1964) and the Rolling Stones (1964) are the direct links to the current manifestation of Garage Rock and can be viewed in relation to the forming of this new underground trend in music. (Both the Who and the Jam are included in this discussion because of their influence on the contemporary Garage Rock scene. While not considered a part of the original British Invasion, these groups [along with many others from a later period] play a large role within the development and continuation of contemporary Garage Rock. Besides, these bands are also often incorrectly considered British Invasion bands by many participants within the scene due to their confusion of time and style of playing.)

The Kinks began in a suburb of London and were determined to promote animosity toward governmentally controlled life. This determination was based on the fact that members of the Kinks grew up in working class London and were relocated to the suburbs by a government decision to clean up the lower class slums of the city. Many of the Kinks' songs relate to a feeling of abandonment by present society. Their method of regaining individuality stems from looking to a past form of "Englishness." This aspect of looking to the past and the sense of abandonment from the suburban world is crucial to the contemporary Garage Rock movement. The Kinks are referenced many times in song formats and structures, with some Garage bands even covering their songs as a starting point.

The Kinks have often been considered the preeminent group in regards to nostalgia from England. Their use of Music Hall constructions that defined early British music are legendary and can be consistently heard throughout their music. The Kinks champion the use of nostalgia and relate strongly to the reintegration of the past into a modern time period. Here is the relationship to contemporary Garage Rock and the importance of the Kinks to today's bands. While many members of the scene do not necessarily think of the Kinks as a Garage band, the performers often cite them as one of their first and most important influences.

The expansion of the Kinks into American popular music was severely delayed when they were banned from playing in the U.S. (for a reason that has still not been fully determined). The Kinks' success lagged behind other bands in America due to this ban, but they also developed a mythic quality to which American underground culture would cling. Many members of the current Garage scene are drawn to this period of the Kinks' history, and it is this ban that has allowed the Kinks to become thought of as a group that almost completely resides outside of mainstream popular music.

While being banned led to a mythic quality being bestowed upon the Kinks, many members of the contemporary scene reference the earliest Kinks recordings as the most influential. Many performers view these early recordings as the first form of Rock music that was based purely on emotion. Thanks to the ban, the Kinks took hold of America's consciousness and influenced many of the surrounding scenes through their music and sonic qualities. Their guitar sound is deeply aligned with contemporary Garage Rock.

The Kinks' use of a fuzzed guitar sound came about from Dave Davies and his use of a razor blade, although his brother Ray claims it was their mother's knitting needles. Jon Savage in *The Kinks: The Official Biography* states, "In 1963, Davies took the 8-inch speaker of a 4-watt amplifier and severely cut it with a razor blade, put tape over it and placed it on top of his 30-watt amp to create the sound that is known as the Kinks."[2] This sound was influential to many musicians of the 60s and is still present today. The sound that was achieved through this method is still attempted within contemporary Garage Rock, and it is this fuzz-type of distortion that is relevant in the production of contemporary Garage recordings. The Kinks' use of chord progressions and power chords also played a large part in the development of contemporary Garage Rock.

The Kinks, specifically Dave Davies, was the first band to develop power chords, and they became known for this simplistic style of playing music. These types of chords only require the root notes and are played in such a way that the sound resolution is clipped at the end, which delivers a strong, harsh sound that was influential to every musician that followed. The Kinks' use of this sound allowed them to become a viable part of mainstream music and to assert their individuality and presence within the current musical development known as the British Invasion. The importance of the development of a fuzz tone distortion and the use of power chords cannot be overlooked within the current Garage scene.

Another important development in the sound of the Kinks was their use of simplistic guitar solos that are based on the entirety of the song and not merely a statement by one individual. The guitar solos on many Kinks tracks are short and fairly simplistic but played in a style that fits extremely well within the whole song. The use of one string throughout a guitar solo is something that is rarely utilized by today's mainstream Rock groups, but in contemporary Garage Rock the short and simple solo is again at the forefront. Dave Davies constructed these solos to fit within the song, not to show off his prowess or to stand out as an individual, and this is where the similarities within solo structures come into play.

Just as important as the introduction of power chords, fuzz tone distortion and solo structure, is the comment that the Kinks made on the nature of life in suburbia. The distancing of the band from suburban desires comes across in many of their songs, but in "Sunny Afternoon" they demonstrate their insistence on remaining outside of monetary desires. In *The Kink Kronikles* Ray Davies claims, "The importance of lazing around on a sunny afternoon takes precedence over the taxman's claim on money and the time spent working falls to the aspect of relaxing with nothing on a sunny day."[3] Although this is one of the lighter songs from the Kinks, it allows for the emphasis against the suburban working life to be put forward. The Kinks were influential by displaying animosity toward suburban life throughout many of their songs; they stress the importance of remaining outside of capitalist goals.

This is not the only song that has spoken out against suburban goals and pursuits. Many songs depict people and places that stand against something the Kinks are determined to go against. Take "Dedicated Follower of Fashion" and "A Well Respected Man" as just two instances of the Kinks' irony towards people that claim to be above others in their pursuit of suburban goals. Here, Music Hall is used in an effort to strip both characters of their claims to popularity. These songs are just two of the many that have consistently made comment on suburban social life and the pursuit of capitalist goals within society.

With the rise of the Kinks in England and America, many bands were influenced by their music and the feeling of animosity towards suburban life. Although the Kinks' songs speak mostly of English life, Americans have been, and still are, drawn to their depictions of individuality and feelings of angst regarding modern society. This feeling and this display of removal from suburban life influence the current group of Garage bands.

The depictions of individuality that the Kinks generate generally involve irony, with the main character of the song being used as a warning or threat to the listener. In many cases, this irony has permeated musical history and continues to influence many bands. For contemporary Garage Rock, the depiction of a character in such a way has been an effective and frequent tool for songwriting. While many of today's groups shy away from such direct comparisons and comment, others boldly demonstrate their affinity for the Kinks and other British bands that came after them.

Immersed in contemporary 60s mainstream music, the Who became one the biggest bands to come out of the British Invasion. The Who became fixated on the scene that was known as "Mod," short for "Modern," and inserted a new sound into American and British music. Their use of simple power chords and loud, abrasive drumming allowed them to stand within this movement. Many people were drawn to this raw sound, and the Who began to dominate mainstream charts. This sound would go on to influence a countless number of young musicians who have continually referenced the Who as a starting point for appreciation of Rock music. The Who's cult movie hit, *Quadrophenia* (1979), displayed their use of the underground and gave many people of the contemporary Garage Rock culture their first look into the life of Mod music and culture.

This movie has often been cited as the avenue into contemporary Garage Rock for many performers and participants. Whether it was the soundtrack or the movie itself, people are greatly influenced by the depiction of life and the storyline of *Quadrophenia* and the Who. This extremely important movie was the way that the Who used the Mod scene to gain recognition, but its influence on culture still remains. Contemporary Garage Rock has been greatly influenced by this movie in the fact that most people gained their first glimpse of this type of culture through the viewing of the film.

The Who are still a large part of the current musical society and have remained one of the most influential groups in the world. They have dominated many forms of underground music, from Punk to Rock, and continue to hold major sway over underground developments. The importance of the Who stems from their immersion into the Mod culture of the late 60s, and they are consistently referenced in regards to contemporary Garage Rock. Their influence has played out in many different underground scenes, but their use of the Mod culture and consideration for these tendencies allowed them to play a distinct role in the development of contemporary Garage Rock.

While the Who were not the first Mod band, and many people state that they simply stole the entire scene from the Small Faces, their songwriting and style of performance were entirely Mod and led to their success and their influence on many bands to come. Without the music of the Who, many people would not have gained access to the original Mod bands and would have been limited in their appreciation of the music. Although the Who are often viewed in this way, the music they played is a great factor in the Rock music of today and continues to be held up as extremely important within many Rock circles.

The Who are perceived, by many members of the contemporary Garage Rock scene to be a part of the British Invasion. In actuality they came *after* the British Invasion, and some would argue that they used the British Invasion as a means of success. This misperception has allowed the Who to play a large part in the determination of the sound and style of many bands. While their inclusion in the British Invasion is inaccurate, their music and production of the Mod documentary *Quadrophenia* has given members of the contemporary scene a starting point into what has come to be known as modern day Garage Rock. This starting point is often alluded to by the founders of the contemporary scene and is viewed as a defining moment in the development of style and structure.

While the Who, and their movie, are said to be the starting point for many musicians, other groups play a role as well in the developing of the contemporary scene. One of the later Mod bands that play an extremely important part in contemporary Garage Rock is the Jam. The members joined together with a harder sound than the Who's musical output. Many people consider the Jam to be one of the first popular Punk bands, and they inserted a harsh reality into their music. Their lyrics reflect a strong street sense that influence their sound and approach as well. Lyrics from their hit song, entitled "A Town Called Malice," are representational of their depiction of street life. The emphasis on street life and gaining strength from the struggle of the quiet, harsh reality of urban life is brought to the forefront with this song.[4] This became the focal point of the Jam's music and allowed for a complete anti-establishment viewpoint. They constructed their appearance in standard Mod fashion, consisting of tonic suits, thin neck ties and sharply polished boots, but their lyrics and musical style placed them into the classification of Hard Mod.

The Jam were extremely influential on many members of the contemporary Garage scene. The Sights began in response to hearing the Jam and other Mod bands. The importance of the Jam lies in the harsh sound that was played and the appearance that they carried throughout the scene. While people often criticized the Who for their use of the scene, the Jam were as much a part of the scene as the participants and expressed the concerns and emotions of the fans from the start. The influence that the Jam have on the contemporary scene cannot be understated in their songwriting and onstage performance aspects.

One of the main elements in the classification of Hard Mod was appearance and image. Many members of this original scene in England were determined to dress in a way that was deemed sharp. This aspect linked high fashion within England to a street-tough image. The Hard Mod fashion included the highest priced suits, blue, green or black in color, with labels like Ben Sherman or Merc. With this type of style and fashion, the Hard Mods became focused on attaining the latest and most contemporary clothing from the best manufacturers.

The Carnaby Street shops were the highlight of the Mods' shopping experience, and many often spent all of what little money they had on procuring the newest look. It is interesting to note that a scene based on attaining the highest in fashion was embraced by the working class youth of England. This led to an extreme disparity among the participants, due to the fact that the scene was based on a look, and to be a "face" was the goal of every Mod.

The image of the Hard Mod was constructed around a specific fashion-based look. This look is generally determined through the use of clothing manufacturers such as those described above. These manufacturers were known to produce a style of clothing that allowed for the proliferation of this ideal. This look is generally composed of suits with pants that are tapered at the ankle, allowing for boot or brogue (shoe) to be viewed, a shirt tailored to a close fit of the body and a coat that was cut in a similar way. The colors of these suits varied, but the heavily favored color was black in any form of tonic fabric, a type of material that allowed a sheen to come across. The most heavily favored boot was by Doc Marten, due to their durability and their representation of hard-working individuals. With this look, many people came to view the Hard Mods as fashion icons, but this also allowed them to become immersed in violence and hooliganism without drawing an extensive amount of attention from the authorities.

Their street-tough image led to the Hard Mods being involved in a great number of confrontations and battles in the streets, in clubs and at many public events, including British football (soccer) matches. The image that was constructed by this youth underground led to the development of many different offshoots, but this movement was strongly based in the middle class, members of which were able to afford the latest clothes and records. Charlie Gillett relates that "The core of the Mods was composed of fifteen to eighteen-year-old teenagers from the East End suburbs or the new housing estates in South London who belong to a social milieu made up of a section of the working class which was participating, within certain limits, in the increasing prosperity of the consumer society and which had a secure basis for its livelihood."[5] Music played a large part in the Hard Mod lifestyle, with scooter rallies and concerts being the place to show off the newest styles and marks of the streets. The many local bands that were part of the scene were influential in their contributions to the latest fashions and the determination of what it meant to be a Hard Mod.

The music heard at these events was generally much harsher than the earlier construction of the Mod sound. Bands that played these events were determined to set themselves apart from the middle class groups that could afford the latest clothes. Although the groups were still considered Mod, they were branching off into a street sound, called "Oi!" and "Hardcore," that would come to dominate later music culture and go on to influence the succeeding scene of contemporary Garage Rock.

The local British underground bands[6] that played a part in this youth culture were in some ways obsessed with the aspect of appearance and sound. Their sound was based on the street and contained a harsher outlook on life. The sound of these bands would later carry over into the first representations of Oi! and other forms of Hard Punk music. This led the followers of these groups to consider this outlook as completely rebellious and confrontational, and allowed for them to express desires away from the confining middle class norm. Many of these local groups only played at the scooter rallies and local pubs, but bands such as the Jam felt their influence.

The classification of Hard Mod carries over to the current Garage Rock movement in many ways. This underground movement was focused on remaining apart from the mainstream and inserting a street-tough image into the music that was performed. Many participants in the current Garage scene are drawn to this outlook and have become fixated on the aspect of a street appearance. This focal point carries over to the many bands that have relied on the images that the Hard Mods have put forward, a thought process involving gaining strength from a hard upbringing and a reliance on the street underground for survival and acceptance.

The underground plays an important role in determining status within the contemporary Garage scene. It is often the case that bands will be removed from the underground simply by not sharing the street-tough image displayed first by the Hard Mods and then others. The bands that displayed the feeling of aggression and survival through emotion and performance were the bands that would later influence the Garage Rock scene. While the Jam was critical to this feeling, another band from the British Invasion who plays a large part in the existing Garage Rock scene is the Rolling Stones.

The Rolling Stones hold a significant influence over contemporary Garage Rock with their straight Rock approach and insistence on remaining part of a rebellious culture. Many of their songs relate to a similar feeling of anger against society but are rooted more in the experiences of urban life. The Stones' music impacted the current scene with its loud aggression and lyrical content, and this has become enmeshed within the contemporary underground feeling.

The Stones' aggression and musical power displayed one of the first harsh Rock approaches to music. By championing a sound that focused on power they blew away American audiences and helped to influence many bands of the time and today. The sound of Charlie Watt's drums can be heard on multiple recordings of the new Garage bands, and the laid back style has been extremely beneficial to many groups throughout the world. The Rolling Stones' stage performance also plays an influential role in contemporary Garage Rock.

The stage presence and aggression of a Rolling Stones performance can be witnessed within the current scene at almost every show. Contemporary Garage bands continually rehash Jagger's performance principles, with some bands going so far as to represent, completely and nostalgically, the dress and attitude of these musicians. The Stones' stage presence and musical approach allowed them to gain fans from every walk of underground life, with the biker group known as Hells Angels being their most well known group of fans. This attraction to what some consider a deviant subculture has allowed the Stones to play an influential role in contemporary Garage Rock.

This relationship within society is often characterized in a negative light, but with contemporary Garage Rock, we again witness the benefit of remaining apart from the mainstream elements of society. The Stones were adept at doing so, which allowed their music to relate to anyone that would listen. To continually relate to any part of the underground society is a key goal for every Garage Rock band today.

This ability to relate to groups such as the Hells Angels and other underground movements allowed the Stones to become extremely important to many American sub-cultures, and their fan base arose from these types of underground movements. While they began to gain mainstream recognition and press for their music and stage presence, the Stones also gained a large fan following from these types of groups, something that very few bands from England have ever achieved. Through their music and approach to society, the Stones play an influential role in the current Garage Rock movement, and are central to performance aspects and relationships within the underground population.

The Stones also epitomize how many participants within the contemporary scene react to their inclusion in mainstream music. Many of the bands and fans view the mainstream as antithetical, unless it displays traits of rebellion from within. This aspect of rebellion from within plays out extremely well in the Rolling Stones' presentation and relationship within the music world. Through incorporating such a rebellious stance within society, the Stones became an extremely influential Rock group, not only on contemporary Garage Rock but on forms of Rock music as well.

One of the key participants in the development of the current Garage Rock movement is a big fan of British Invasion music and the recording techniques that were used by these bands. Jim Diamond, proprietor and recording engineer at Ghetto Recorders, is a dedicated devotee of the British Invasion, with a continuation into the new wave sounds of the Zombies in America. To many participants in the original scene, the Zombies cannot be held up as a part of Garage Rock in any way; but to many members of the current scene, the Zombies are directly linked to this sound and outlook towards music, and perceived as a part of Garage Rock. At the onset of the contemporary movement, if someone was not familiar with the Zombies they were not considered a part of the scene, especially in Detroit.

The Zombies were influential to the beginning of contemporary Garage Rock because of their attitude and approach to music. Many people during the beginning scene were drawn to the flair and distinctiveness of this seminal Rock group. Even if the beginning members had no prior knowledge of the Zombies, they soon found out how influential the Zombies were on many of the groups that adopted the British-style sound. The Zombies are often linked with the groups of the British Invasion, and they rode the success of the Beatles to a number one hit in America with "She's Not There." This allowed many people in the contemporary movement to construct a sound that has been thoroughly influenced by the Zombies.

The Zombies play a large part in the new movement of Garage Rock. Their inclusion in what is considered Garage is directly linked to both the type of music played and their outlook. Many people cite the Zombies as a part of the British Invasion due to their use of a newer style of playing and performance. Although they are sometimes considered part of the musical development *after* the British Invasion because of the late release of their hit album, they exert a strong influence over today's Garage Rock scene. For many people in the contemporary scene, the Zombies allowed for the further removal of music from mainstream conceptions and continued a strong stance of non-conformity and musical creativity set up away from mainstream ideals.

Contemporary Garage Rock uses the nostalgic representations of the British Invasion to construct one aspect of their individuality. Bands like the Sights, the Hives, the Vines, Jet and the Indecisives take their appearance and sound from these early Rock bands, deriving their entire concept from rehashing the British Invasion. This allows the current structure of Garage Rock a classical referent to the music of the past. This referent is an essential part of the Garage Rock scene. With the nostalgic representations of the British Invasion, Garage Rock acquires a status outside of the mainstream of society.

The nostalgic use of the British Invasion centers the contemporary scene on a sound that remains fixated within specific styles of writing and performance. By constructing sounds and songs that are based on the musical approach of the British Invasion, many young bands are given the opportunity to succeed and the ability to gain a significant following within the underground music scene. Many groups achieved their success through the use of the British Invasion as a focal point, and many continue to do so.

After a period of time, as the popularity of the Sights began to climb, and with the label of Garage Rock sufficiently in place, the Hives brought their sound to America from Sweden. The Hives have patterned their sound and appearance on later Mod bands, such as the Jam. The Hives formed, or were formed by an outside source (this is still being debated), in reaction to the growing Garage scene and took America by storm with their live shows and harsh sound. Their nostalgic representations are based on the look of the Hard Mods in England through the wearing of black or tonic suits with razor ties and dark glasses. This look allowed them to become accepted within the contemporary Garage underground, and they became, like many of the original Garage bands, one-hit wonders in the mainstream arena. Their live shows are also strongly linked to the performances of the past.

The Hives grew in popularity based on their raucous live shows and their front man's strong reliance on nostalgic performance. It was this attitude that allowed the Hives to make their presence felt in the existing Garage scene. With their sharp black suits and Punk ethos, they emerged seemingly out of nowhere and rose to the top of the charts without any hindrance. The Hives relied heavily on nostalgic representations of the British Mod movement to insert their notion of Garage Rock into the underground and mainstream of American music.

The Hives' relationship to the Hard Mod sounds is significant within the contemporary scene. What has happened to the Hives is extremely interesting in the fact that they have often been removed from the underground by members of the scene because of the band's rapid appearance and climb to success. The Hives acquired the appearance and sound of the Mods and became exemplars to the newer constructions of Garage, but quickly fell out of favor with many participants due to their lack of rebellion from within the mainstream. Even though they offered raucous stage antics and songs that were harsher in tone than the surrounding mainstream groups, they were viewed as a group that represents what happens when the underground becomes mainstream.

Many of the current bands within the Garage Rock scene are assuming a form of dress that nostalgically represents the British Invasion bands. The Hives are only one specific example, but other groups, such as the Vines, use this style of dress in an attempt to set themselves apart from the current mainstream of music. Many groups in the Garage Rock scene use this technique to point out the difference between the musical underground and mainstream music. While this dress code allows for a stance outside of the mainstream, it has become a way to conform to a set notion of what it means to be a Garage band. This notion of conformity is based strongly on borrowing from the British Invasion for its dress and musical sound.

The aspect of dress is extremely important throughout contemporary Garage and will be discussed fully later; however, the aspect of the British Invasion and Mod style of dress plays a specifically important role on many participants' determination of acceptance or removal from the scene. Through dressing in a nostalgic fashion, many people display their alliance with the thought process of the bands that are similarly representing the British Invasion style.

The sound of the contemporary Garage Rock underground is also specifically reliant on the musical sound and structure of the British Invasion. The use of short, choppy lyrics and relatively easy chord structures lends itself to a myriad of comparisons, but it is the sound of the British Invasion that many of the current groups lean toward. This sound, although not easily classifiable, can be heard in many of the original British Invasion bands. From the Beatles to the Jam, a similar sound can be heard. This sound is one that allows for the lyrics and the lead singer to become the prominent focus of the group. To allow for this, music of the British Invasion was structured in a limited way. It is this structure that is found in the music of contemporary Garage Rock.

The lyrical structure of the British Invasion was one that was heavily based in the sound of the 1950s and the early incarnations of DooWop, Soul and Blues that were heard throughout England and were influential to many of the British Invasion bands. This sound is characterized by a musical structure that fully allows the singer to take the lead and determine where the song will progress. The lyrics and style of the singer or singers defined the song and its progression, and keys were often based on the singer's ability and style.

The chord progressions of the British Invasion bands were set up in ways that were rooted in American Blues, Folk and early Rock and Roll, and were played heavily in order to change the focus or feeling of the song. The Beatles used the power of simple chord progressions and non-technical drum patterns to allow the lyrics to come through within the song. Although the Beatles are one of the few bands, even today, who can change time signatures with ease, they still based their songwriting on the power of simple chord progressions.

This simplicity is not in any way a limitation of writing style. Many people believe that these first songs were simplistic in order to relate to the majority of people, and that is why they were so popular. It is also extremely important to realize that the structure of the first songs that broke through to American audiences was based on styles that America was originally producing. The British Invasion bands simply changed the style of playing certain progressions on their way towards changing the way the world heard Rock and Roll.

Many of the original British Invasion bands offered a similar style within their performance and recordings. The focal point was the lyrical patterns and words that were being sung. This allowed for the back line of musicians, drums, bass guitar, rhythm guitar and keys to become easily immersed in the song and maintain a consistent feel. The current state of Garage Rock retains many of these musical functions, and insists on technically simplistic chord progressions and rhythm patterns. A majority of Garage bands base their music on the lyrics and performance of the lead vocalist and insist that the music play a secondary role to the lyrical content.

By placing the importance on the lead singer, the other musicians are forced to play technically accurate. It takes extreme talent to play in a relaxed and limited way, and the reason that many new bands fail is that they believe that this method of playing music is easy. The constructions are simple technically but rely on a style and grace that is not achieved at the early stages of playing an instrument. Leading the formation of sound and focusing on supporting the lead singer is pivotal to the contemporary scene. One of the main proponents of this structure is the White Stripes.

The White Stripes use a variety of styles and chord structures but all are based on simplistic rhythmic patterns. This group consists of only two musicians, and their music is completely based on lyrical content with simple chord progressions. With a love for Loretta Lynn and the music of America's past, the White Stripes have consistently played simplistic music that has its roots in American Blues and Folk. This emphasis on songwriting over technicality in chord progression allows for the White Stripes to focus on style, performance and sound.

The White Stripes were also determined to reflect the recorded sound of the British Invasion and original Garage Rock through the use of older technologies and methods of recording that go against the mainstream, advanced studios. Along with many other groups of the current Garage scene, they have made a name for themselves with a minimalist, roots-oriented approach. By focusing on lyrical content and this recording approach, they nostalgically link themselves to the British Invasion. This link, within contemporary Garage Rock, was also witnessed in the original Garage Rock scene in America.

The Garage Rock scene of the 1960s began with a desire to emulate the rise and popularity of the British Invasion bands. Many of these original Garage bands were determined to put forward an American version of what the British Invasion bands made famous. Through the use of similar chord progressions, appearance and musical outlook, these bands relied heavily on the British Invasion for their inspiration. Much like contemporary Garage bands, with their reliance on the British Invasion, the original Garage bands were drawn to the British Invasion as a way to reclaim Rock and Roll and its roots.

While many of the original Garage bands believed that they could achieve success easily through music, the contemporary bands that share this viewpoint are often removed from the underground scene. Although the British Invasion influenced both, the latter is driven towards capitalist desires, while the original Garage bands of the 60s were mainly focused on producing music based on what was around them at the time. The use of the British Invasion by both the original scene and today's incarnation is paramount in comparing the nostalgia of each. While the original scene was using what was immediately around them, the contemporary scene is relating the past to contemporary times and reinstating the sounds of the British Invasion.

This current goal to reclaim Rock and Roll and to insert a new sound into the mainstream of music demonstrates the similarities of the contemporary and original movements. This first link with the British Invasion is an important realization for many of the newer Garage bands. Although the music is classified as Garage Rock, the British Invasion plays an integral part in the development and sound of the contemporary groups. The original movement was created in an attempt to match the British Invasion's popularity, and the current movement is an effort to reclaim the style and success of the British Invasion.

This desire to nostalgically represent the British Invasion bands is critical to the success of the current Garage Rock underground. Without being allowed access to these bands, the contemporary movement would be limited in its sound and approach to music. By taking on the appearance and sonic representation of the British Invasion, Garage Rock inserts a different aspect into mainstream musical society. This occurs through the use of sound structure and the acquisition of dress as a representation of the past form of popular music. With the rise of the contemporary movement, bands such as the Who, the Zombies, and many others are given new life, with groups performing covers of their songs and being aligned with their approaches to music.

What contemporary Garage Rock has allowed for is the reinsertion of British Invasion groups into the framework of mainstream music. These groups have never fallen far away from the mainstream, but groups such as the Zombies and the Jam shared a limited appeal in the past. With the influence being shifted to the British Invasion groups through the nostalgic representation used in contemporary Garage Rock, these groups are again achieving popularity.

The distinctive sound and approach to music that has been developed by contemporary Garage Rock musicians is also linked to the British Invasion by its emphasis on a release of tensions from the oppression of suburban life. These tensions have often been reflected in music, but it was with the British Invasion that they were first appropriated. Many of these tensions are based on the societal construction of middle-class life. The current wave of Garage Rock is determined to stave off these associations, and the British Invasion was as well. The music created in this environment is consistently viewed as anti-conformist and against the mainstream of America. These tensions were first displayed to America within the music of the British Invasion.

The British Invasion groups were determined to insert a new sound into the then-current musical movement. This determination led to a release of the tensions of suburban life. Within contemporary Garage Rock, this release is witnessed within the present late capitalist world. The music performed becomes a way to construct a focus away from the expectations of middle-class life. Without the British Invasion asserting this notion of anti-conformity, the contemporary Garage Rock scene would not have been as effective in its approach. By assuming nostalgic representations of performance and sound, contemporary Garage Rock accomplishes this release of tensions from suburban life.

The majority of underground musical movements contemplate this release of tensions, but contemporary Garage Rock directly aligns itself with the British Invasion's stance against the suburban middle-class lifestyle. By doing so, the contemporary movement continues a stance that was strongly put forward by the British Invasion. The current bands that are assuming the nostalgic representations of the first British Invasion groups now carry this anti-suburban–middle-class flag.

Without the influence of the British Invasion, the current assertions made by the Garage Rock scene would fail in their effect on underground musical society. The impact of these assertions against suburban middle-class life is an essential part of the Garage Rock movement. These assertions allow for the participants within the scene to bear witness to a break away from the late capitalist notions of conformity. The British Invasion plays an influential role in the sound, appearance and assertions against conformity within the current Garage Rock scene.

With the development of bands such as the Sights, the Hives and the Vines, many members of the modern Garage Rock scene were able to construct a new definition of what Garage Rock means. The British Invasion is directly related to the upsurge of bands and groups within this scene. The mixing of two completely different historical periods of music has, in some cases, failed in its attempt (i.e. Ska and Punk), but Garage Rock successfully combines the sounds, attitudes and recording techniques of the British Invasion and the original Garage Rock of the 1960s. This combining of musical time periods and styles has allowed the contemporary Garage scene to maintain a large underground following, with many different bands being classified as Garage.

The progression of contemporary Garage Rock from the underground to the mainstream is reliant on this aspect of multiple musical influences. These influences are mainly rooted in the past, with many of the bands nostalgically representing what has influenced them. The British Invasion plays a direct impact on these modern day constructions and is strongly aligned with many of the existing groups within the scene. A simple glance at any of the above mentioned bands' websites would allow the viewer a way to understand the nostalgia that these groups take from the British Invasion.[7] The Garage Rock scene is reliant on the past representations of anti-conformity and rebelliousness that the British Invasion displayed to America.

As the British Invasion took over America, the next historical musical development impacted the contemporary Garage scene completely and is what has led to the classification and naming of Garage Rock. This development would go on to influence the contemporary scene from within and in subconscious ways. The original Garage Rock scene of the 60s in America plays a direct role in the formation and nostalgic representations of the current scene and has a direct impact on the sound and attitude of the contemporary movement. Without the Garage Rock of the 60s, modern day Garage music would lack its appeal and would not have been able to successfully gain widespread popularity.

4

The Count Who?

Along with the music of the British Invasion, the original Garage Rock scene of the 60s played a pivotal role in the current manifestation of Garage Rock. This musical movement is barely recognized within the contemporary scene, but gave many of the current bands a basis for their sound and development. While most individuals within the scene have not even heard of many of the original Garage Rock bands, they have still been influenced by these earlier bands' retreat from suburbia and musical emphasis. Many of these original bands were barely recognized at the time they were around, but this lack of recognition does not make this movement insignificant to the contemporary scene. Bands such as the Count Five, the Chocolate Watch Band, Paul Revere and the Raiders, and the Music Machine all played a large role in the development of the contemporary scene. Taking most of their cues from the British Invasion, these bands were determined to make a stand within the music industry. The fact that many of these groups were, at the most, one-hit wonders did not limit their impact on the musical society of the time. This impact is what has carried through to the contemporary scene and can be witnessed through the presentation of the bands and their music.

Despite the lack of recognition by the current scene, the influence that many of the original Garage bands had on future recordings and musical outlooks is extremely important. Many other musical undergrounds have been influenced and have taken their cues from 60s Garage, and this has led to a great undervaluation of these groups. From the very beginning, the groups that followed found themselves weighed down by the fact that they were attempting to re-create a sound and feeling brought overseas by the British Invasion. This aspect has extreme relevance for the contemporary scene and is reflected continuously through the perform-ance and sonic representations of contemporary Garage Rock.

The 1960s Garage Rock scene was considered by many to be a lim-ited underground movement. The many groups that were part of this scene include the Count Five, the Shadows of Knight, the Chocolate Watch Band, Paul Revere and the Raiders, the Music Machine and many others that are relatively unknown. These five groups will be the focus of this discussion, with the remainder still playing a role in the current movement. While the original movement took place throughout the country, these bands were at the forefront of what was known as Garage Rock. Whether this was due to their remaking of a British Invasion song or their original hit, they became a representation of what many people dubbed Garage Rock.

Even from the onset, Garage Rock was difficult to classify, but all of these groups shared common characteristics that allowed them to advo-cate for and display their removal from suburban life. These groups chose to play a type of music that allowed them to access a different sound and a different attitude from what surrounded them. Through the constant reinforcement of a simplistic musical ideal, these bands paved the way for Punk and contemporary Garage Rock and are extremely important in their contribution to the attitude and feeling that is expressed through contemporary Garage.

Bands in this musical movement shared a common goal of reliev-ing the oppression of suburban life. Many of these groups were founded on the mere idea of escaping from the suburbs in which they resided. They began playing music as a means of withdrawal from their current arrangement in life as middle class suburban youth "trapped" in a neigh-borhood that was stifling to their individuality, and this is one of the most significant aspects that has carried through to the contemporary scene. Though the impetus for the formation of these groups is often cited as an attempt to latch onto a trend, they were instrumental in pro-moting an attempted removal from suburban norms. What specifically linked these groups was a sense of belonging to an outside world that did not revolve around the late capitalist notions of suburban conform-ity.

This has occurred throughout youth culture and history. The desire to remain fixated outside of suburban norms and constructions of indi-viduality is not entirely new, but what happened with the British Inva-sion was that many youth had their first exposure to escaping through music. The opportunity for anyone to play music to escape from the boredoms of suburbia became a trend within American society and led to the formation of the 60s Garage scene. This feeling is still present in many of today's music scenes, and many owe their start to the groups of the British Invasion.

Throughout the presentations of the early Garage groups remains the constant notion of not succumbing to capitalist goals of conformity. The groups strived to promote a different path towards individualism, and herein lay the similarity between the original groups and the contemporary ones. The path was not defined for many, and still isn't, but the assertion of a new way of thought and constructed identity focused many youth on musical goals. The use of song structure, chord format and the presence of the lead singer were all extremely important to these groups, and the music displayed a strong feel that still remains prevalent in most current Rock music.

Critics and others often grouped the bands that inhabited this underground scene into two distinct camps. Charlie Gillet suggests that the camps consisted of bands that were playing Garage Rock *before* the British Invasion occurred, and those that were mere imitators. "The differing groups consisted of the first type, mainly from the Pacific Northwest, the Midwest and Texas who began playing rhythm and blues oriented Rock before the British Invasion and continued playing afterwards, and the latter group who were trying to catch onto the fad that was the British Invasion."[1] These two camps paved the way for a multitude of musicians, and their sound can still be heard today. Whether it was Paul Revere and the Raiders or the Count Five, these groups led to the delineation of Garage Rock and influenced underground music.

The groups that were playing a form of rhythm and blues before the British Invasion are often viewed as the precursors to contemporary Garage Rock, but the later also come into play within the discussion of Garage. With the appearance of the British Invasion, many groups were formed in an effort to latch onto a trend, and this is no different from the contemporary scene. The scene today consists of both types of Garage bands, but the groups playing at the onset carry much more credibility than ones that are seen to be jumping onto a music trend.

The original bands and their critics had difficulty with the classification of Garage since many of the groups labeled as Garage did not share common musical influences and sound. Whether or not these groups shared similar sounds, they often times shared a similar outlook on the surrounding musical scene. They were grouped together in an effort to garner attention from the mainstream musical society and displayed a strong yearning for success. This classification allowed for writers and fans to be drawn to a specific band that may or may not have similar characteristics to other groups in the movement, and it is this over-classification that permeates the contemporary Garage scene.

The original over-classification has often been viewed in a negative light, but without the broad labeling of Garage Rock, there would not be as many groups from the original scene that have carried over to today. The extent of the classification allowed many bands to be lumped together into a label that signaled success, propelling them into the mainstream of musical society. While this is consistently thought of within the underground as a negative, the original Garage scene did profit from it.

Along with this over-classification, the 60s movement of Garage Rock became more solidified in its "Garage-ness." Many artists attempted to make the aspect of playing in a garage or suburban practice space seem gritty and more "real." This led to a feeling of elitism in the music and antics of these original bands. Many of these bands felt they were truly getting back to the original Rock and Roll that was played before them. The music style and approach that was often referenced was American Blues and Folk with a harder edge. This edge usually came from the inability of the musicians to play their instruments as well as their predecessors. With this in mind, they aligned themselves with an elite mentality. It is also a common occurrence within the contemporary Garage scene to share this feeling of elitism.

An elitist view of music is common in underground movements. It is the view of being above the pretensions held by proponents of mainstream music. This thought process continues even when the music played is inherently more limited than that of the mainstream. It is this limited specification that focuses the dominant thought of many underground musical scenes and allows for the proliferation of these scenes through and against mainstream constructions of music. Within the contemporary Garage scene, this aspect has been extended to include shunning mainstream recording practices and even traditional band composition. It is these elite notions that many of the current bands carry through their presentation and musical construction.

The elite feeling of the original Garage Scene of the 60s differed greatly from the contemporary underground, but the feeling of superiority to other musicians is no different. Many of the original groups felt that they were superior to other bands because they played a certain form of Blues or Folk, or because of the way they composed and expressed their music. The current manifestation of Garage focuses this feeling in the direction of band composition and recording strategies that remain fixated on nostalgic formations. These elite feelings are nothing new, but continue to be prevalent within contemporary Garage.

The aspect of exerting authority over the construction of the scene through music also links itself to the original 60s Garage Rock. Many contemporary groups assert their individuality and musical form via a sense of rising above the existing music scene. This allows for the band members and the participants of the scene to place themselves above the organized and manipulated notions of mainstream music. Garage Rock of the 60s was determined to suggest that their music was comparable to the British Invasion and deserving of mainstream attention, which allowed them to place themselves above the past underground movements. These past movements consisted of groups playing Surf and Country music with a slightly harder edge. The original groups of the 60s Garage movement consisted mostly of performers that were previously aligned with these genres.

It is easy to see how these assumptions and feelings of superiority come into play, considering that the first bands that featured many of these musicians failed due to a lack of popularity. The original scene offered many bands that had been formed from members who had played in the surrounding scenes with little, if any, outright success. This led to a rejection of the surrounding scenes in an effort to establish the new band as a factor within the "new" underground that was developing. Such circumstances and sentiments are common in underground developments and are shared by contemporary Garage as well.

Many current musicians within the modern Garage movement assume that they are truly expressing the roots of Rock and Roll. Many feel that their style and method of playing music leads to this solidarity. With this assumption, the musicians of the contemporary scene begin to assert this elite feeling over the surrounding underground networks. The current manifestation was aimed against the underground movements of Punk and Hardcore that were prevalent in the Detroit underground. The Garage bands claimed to be above these musical movements due to their insistence on a return to Rock. Many participants in the original Garage scene shared a disdain for imitators and others that were not playing Garage Rock. For them, it was solely about reclaiming real Rock and Roll.

The feeling of removal and withdrawal from the previous undergrounds applies to many underground movements, but with contemporary Garage it was extremely harsh. Club owners and others will not even book a band that is considered Punk or Hardcore simply because of the implications involved with the previous scene. Many of the first contemporary Garage groups were also determined to play only with bands that shared a similar outlook and sound within Detroit.

The original Garage Rock scene was dominated by another aspect: the bands were determined to gain widespread recognition for the British Invasion bands. Many groups believed that the British Invasion provided an opening within music through which they could easily become a part of the scene. Bands such as the Shadows of Knight and others quickly became determined to become a part of this newly popular Rock music. A new following began to form that was split between the two underground groups.

The Shadows of Knight were determined to insert their version of the British Invasion into mainstream music. This led to their claim of adding a Chicago style to the English Blues that played a part in the British Invasion. Although they only charted a limited amount of times, usually with covers, they were influential in their effort to cling onto the British Invasion and gain the attendant popularity. Their biggest hit was a remake of the tune "Gloria," originally by Them, which inserted a more Americanized style of Blues into a British song. It was this attempt to reclaim the original sounds of Blues and the British Invasion that allowed the Shadows of Knight to produce hits. They charted in the mainstream with other songs, but none as popular "Gloria."

The Shadows of Knight were determined to gain success in any way possible and only truly achieved it through the performance of an already-proven song. The Shadows of Knight based their sound on an attempted reclamation of the British Invasion groups, with a new emphasis added. Like the British Invasion bands, they opted for a Blues feel; but the Shadows of Night shifted the music to create a more powerful and determined sound compared to the British Invasion music, and cemented their distinction within Garage Rock.

Throughout the 60s, these bands were determined to assert their dominance over underground music. They also strived for success in the mainstream, with many breaking through only to become one hit wonders. In fact, the term "one hit wonder" is thought to have been conceived during this period of music to reflect certain bands that were not talented enough to gain widespread, continued mainstream success. It was these bands that would go on to influence contemporary Garage Rock. This influence, while often times unknown, can be witnessed throughout the contemporary scene. It was the few bands that broke through to the mainstream that allowed people to witness an American version of what was from Britain.

The emphasis placed on reacting to the British Invasion was extremely important in the original formation of Garage. Many of the first bands were focused on asserting their Americanism in the music that was being played. After all, the British Invasion bands became popular in America because they were playing a form of American music in a different way. The original Garage groups found that they could re-assert the feeling that was being expressed by the British Invasion but with an entirely American approach. This attitude led to the difficulty in classification, as groups were very different in their approach to music; but they all shared a desire to express a form of American music.

These groups, comprised mostly of teenagers, had the desire to break away from their suburban homes and status. It was this desire that led many of them to form bands in the first place. Unlike the later bands of Punk, they had few political desires except to escape from middle-class suburbia. They became determined to assert the fact they could assault their upbringing in any way they deemed appropriate. This led to many groups claiming that they began in a more urban setting than their suburban middle-class homes, when, according to Peter Wicke, "...in reality most rock musicians come from the *petit bourgeois* middle classes and have never experienced the every day life of working-class teenagers."[2] The issue of a lower-co-opting class status is common throughout musical undergrounds, and the original Garage bands were influential in its inclusion in the contemporary Garage Rock movement.

Displaying a removal from suburbia and capitalist constructions of individuality was and still is an extremely important part of Garage Rock. The reason behind the formation of many of the original groups was to distance themselves from their surroundings and place their own version of individuality into the mainstream of music. This aspect of displacement plays out within a multitude of underground music scenes, but the emphasis of the original Garage bands was specifically on removal from the suburbs, and this is what is present in contemporary Garage Rock.

In Detroit, the aspect of coming from the "inner city" resounds throughout many musical scenes. With contemporary Garage Rock, this is viewed as the only legitimate way to succeed. If you happen to be from the suburbs, like most of the bands in the scene, there is an extreme desire to re-make the image of the band as actually being from the city of Detroit. Outside of Michigan, little is known about the extreme differences between the suburbs and the city, but within Michigan this can make or break a band from the outset. To be from the city is extremely important to many participants and performers within the contemporary Garage scene. What is interesting is that many of the original members of the contemporary scene grew up not in Detroit, but in the surrounding suburbs, and have now relocated to the city for various reasons. To justify the claim that you are actually from the city of Detroit, you must include the city's "sound" within your music. Many bands of the contemporary Garage scene accomplish this feat, but are left out of the underground when their actual origins are exposed.

The concept of portraying the city of Detroit through music is inherent to the success of the contemporary Garage bands in the Detroit area. This is accomplished through the feelings of separation from suburbia, with specifically working class ideals and goals, that are placed within the music. Many contemporary groups have clung to these notions as important elements of their musical outlook. Without these concepts being portrayed through their music, many bands and participants in the scene would not believe in the shared relationship that is a large part of many underground scenes.

If a group attempts to display attitudes that are different from the above, they are considered as irrelevant to the contemporary Garage scene. Even when groups consciously attempt to gain mainstream or monetary success, if they remain focused on the city and its working class ideals they will generally remain welcome within the Garage underground. This seeming contradiction is often discussed in terms of the labeling of the music, but it remains similar to the original scene. To express a viewpoint that is taken from the city is as important now as it was for the original scene.

Groups in the contemporary scene must display attributes of the city, such as expressions of hard work and references to locations in the city, within their musical output in order to be considered relevant to the scene. Many groups completely base their sound on what they believe is an expression of the city, whether by referencing events or landmarks or from the constant referral to the city in performance. Many groups, in and out of Garage Rock, attempt to assert this facet in their music. It is with contemporary Garage Rock that this is blatantly displayed within the music and performance.

This aspect continues the line of reasoning that suburbia is a place to escape from, and that to be from the city deserves greater respect within the Garage Rock community. Much like during the original 60s Garage scene, the suburbs are viewed as the place where American capitalism best succeeds. This stance was taken due to the insistence that the suburbs were a place that fostered the traditional views of late capitalism. These traditional views consisted of many different notions that went against the tenor of original Garage Rock, and it is these notions that have carried on through today's underground scene.

The similarities between the original and contemporary Garage scenes stem primarily from escapism. But there are other similarities that often go unnoticed and remain buried within the mindset of the contemporary movement. While they are below the surface, they play a significant role in defining what is to be considered a Garage Rock band. These similarities consist of the use of a garage as a practice space, the use of short choppy rhythm and guitar patterns, the British Invasion having played a strong role in development, and the use of limited recording capabilities.

By remaining below common perception, these shared characteristics have become more important and relevant to the contemporary scene. Through remaining nostalgically linked to the original Garage Rock scene, contemporary groups align themselves in strikingly similar ways. This structures contemporary Garage Rock with an almost backwards-looking stance within music and allows for the reincorporation of the original 60s thought processes. The comparison also mandates that groups adhere to specific principles in order to remain a part of the Garage underground.

The development of the garage as a practice space began after the British Invasion took over America. Many people were inspired by the notion that anyone could play Rock music, and bands began to sprout up throughout the country. Many of these groups began in an effort to emulate the success of the British Invasion and, in doing so, began playing music in their suburban garages. The use of the garage as a practice space came about due to the spatial relationship to the home and the fact that it was easy to set up and rehearse in the garage. It was this development that led to the classification known as Garage Rock.

Many groups simply had no other place to perform, and what became increasingly important was the issue of noise and disturbance to the surrounding community. The original groups used this sound to create a space within the community that belonged to the band. For many, this was the first time that music was heard in such a setting, and the fact that anyone could accomplish this type of sound, with the right amount of practice, allowed for the expansion of Garage Rock throughout America. The thought process was simply to make music that represented where you came from and demonstrated your affinity for certain sounds and groups. Beginning with a simple guitar progression and usually a cover song of another band's music, these bands rose and fell quickly.

While there was no requirement to practice in a garage, this was the easiest place to come together to perform music. Whether or not that music was heard outside of the local town was to be determined, but the issue of performing music within a suburban space began to grow. This limited space would go on to become an integral part of the limited music that was performed, with some groups using drum kits that consisted of only a bass drum and a snare, and others using whatever they could find to make music. It was this desire that the British Invasion provided the American public, the desire and knowledge that anyone had the opportunity to become famous through music.

Even the groups that were playing before the Invasion took place garnered a renewed focus and appreciation from the surrounding fans and media after the arrival of the British bands. This breakthrough in mainstream music allowed many of the existing bands a shot at breaking into the mainstream, whereas most would have been limited to the local underground networks of the community. This is not to say that some bands would not have been successful without the British Invasion, but that it opened the door for many of these original Garage groups.

The focus on becoming famous led to the majority of the original Garage bands failing to achieve the mainstream success that they desired. Many of the original groups were thrown together quickly in this effort to gain widespread recognition. By doing so, their music was mediocre and lacked much of the power and style the British Invasion bands carried with them. Again, this can also be witnessed throughout the contemporary scene, with bands being formed simply for the goal of recognition. While many groups, then and now, were overlooked due to various reasons, the majority of groups claiming to play Garage Rock are and were simply trying to latch onto an existing trend. It was these groups in the 60s, and it is these groups currently, that led to a partial dissolution of the scene.

While many of the groups that began to practice in the garage were limited in their playing capability, they put forward another aspect that is important within the current Garage Rock scene. This aspect is the ability of a band to play music that is considered unpolished or unskilled and yet still be considered great in style and content. While this often occurs in the mainstream pop-centered world, it was the original Garage bands that gave limited quality musical performance a new importance, and it is this importance that has carried through to the contemporary underground movement. While many contemporary groups play music that challenges mainstream ideals, they lack the quality in musical ability to be recognized outside of their own communities. It is these groups that are deeply aligned with the many 60s Garage bands that strived for recognition that never came.

The many groups that remain fixated on the underground of their communities consistently demonstrate their alliance with the original Garage groups through performance and sonic qualities of recording. These groups are usually not as skilled in the construction of music as their counterparts that achieve mainstream success. The main similarity between these underground groups and the groups of the 60s lies in the determination that anyone can play music, and the desire to instill a different type of sound into musical society. Recognition aside, many groups then and now play for the joy of playing music within their community and do not care about breaking into the mainstream.

One of the most influential 60s Garage bands on the contemporary musical movement is the Count Five. With their hit song "Psychotic Reaction," and their insistence on flange and fuzz-tone guitars, they paved the way for Punk Rock and contemporary Garage Rock. Although they are constantly referenced as the original one hit wonder, their music in this one hit played an influential role in defining a musical style and image. This group began in an effort to mix the surrounding musical influences into a solid group. The group consisted of members who were formally involved with surf groups and other styles of Rock and Roll. Mixed in with the British Invasion, the Count Five put out their one and only single and reached number five on the mainstream charts. Their song is a classic that revolves around changing rhythm patterns to elicit a feeling of discord and originality.

It was this unique rhythm change that made the song a hit and that influenced countless groups. This shift in musical style mid-song was one of the first instances of a group placing itself outside of the easily conceived constructions of the mainstream. The Count Five challenged their audience and the mainstream musical press by changing tempo and rhythm pattern midstream. With this occurrence they put their construction of rebellion into the mainstream. Although they were on Double Shot, which was not a major label, they gained popularity and recognition as an influential group through their musical construction.

The Count Five also benefited the contemporary scene in how they were picked up by their record label. After being rejected seven times by other labels, Double Shot finally gave them a chance. Their brief stay near the top made the Count Five accessible to many of the contemporary Garage bands. With the "rave up" quality of their music and the extreme use of the British Invasion groups, the Count Five sound can be heard throughout contemporary Garage and continues to influence countless musicians around the world.

The way that musical construction defines a band also fits the group known as the Chocolate Watch Band. This group featured a wide array of musicians during a short period of time, but their music remained focused on rebellion. Because of this strong focus, one of the original Punk thought processes, the Chocolate Watch Band failed to chart with any of their songs. The Chocolate Watch Band failed to chart because of their musical output, but some say it was because they could not hold a full band together due to creative differences and personality issues. Although they failed to chart, their music would go on to influence the contemporary Garage scene through its insistence on harsh tones and lyrical notions of rebellion against authority.

The Chocolate Watch Band's underground hits include versions of "Come On" and "In the Midnight Hour" that have been classified as the first constructions of Punk by many writers and fans. These versions, along with originals such as "Let's Talk About Girls" and "Expo 2000," displayed a strong leaning toward the aggressive sound that can be readily heard in the music of many contemporary Garage bands, most notably the Von Bondies and the Hard Lessons. While aggressive for the time, their sound became one of the first to be strictly based on going against mainstream constructions of music. This allowed the Chocolate Watch Band to carry a strong message to the contemporary underground movement. It was this harsh aspect to their music that led them to become one of the founding groups of Punk Rock and to go on influencing contemporary Garage.

The Chocolate Watch Band was extremely influential to many contemporary musicians due to their focus on sound and their aggressive approach. What many bands think of as a Punk sound can be directly attributed to this band. The outlook and approach to performance was also influential to today's groups. By performing with a deep sense of irony and sly wit, the Chocolate Watch Band demonstrated their relationship to British bands like the Rolling Stones. The emphasis was on a harsher tone and a loud stage presence that resonated among the youth and continues to exert an influence today.

Throughout the development of the original Garage Rock scene was a desire to represent the British Invasion groups. In style and musical approach, these bands drew on the influence of the British Invasion. Many of these groups were destined to fail because of this, but the few that broke through into the mainstream were influential to the current scene. The destiny of a majority of these bands was greatly shaped by their production of music on a limited scale. Very few groups could construct music that was representational of the British Invasion with limited notions of music and equipment. Although the British Invasion displayed a way to achieve success through music, they did not leave a blueprint for everyone to follow. The groups that did succeed did so because they were talented musicians who latched onto the British Invasion style and success.

Through the use of the British Invasion's influence on American teens, these bands broke into the surrounding mainstream with a reliance on sound and performance aspects that mimicked the British Invasion bands. Many of these groups were said to be copying other bands that already had success, but the best bands to break through into the mainstream were bands that put their own influences on the British Invasion sound. Again, placing an American spin back onto the British sound, Paul

Revere and the Raiders and the Music Machine were two of these groups that broke through, and their influence can be witnessed throughout the Garage Rock scene.

Paul Revere and the Raiders, with their hit "Louie Go Home," went on to significant mainstream success, and it was this aspect that led to their influence on the contemporary scene. They played a style of music that was deeply grounded in the music of the British Invasion, but with an American aspect deeply rooted in the Blues. Their music became popular due to this difference, as it made them stand out from the myriad other Garage bands. Their music concentrated on the relationship between the Blues and Rock and Roll. Much like the Beatles and the Rolling Stones, they were focused on a faster version of Blues, but what made this group important was the fact that they added an element of Americanism to their music.

Paul Revere and the Raiders was the first "Rock" group to be signed by Columbia records, and their career included over 20 charted singles. The group influenced many bands of the time through their appearances on multiple ABC television shows, such as "Where the Action Is" with Dick Clark. They also broke into the mainstream by covering the Kingsmen's "Louie, Louie" and many associate the group with being the first band to break into the mainstream with a different variation of a previously popular song. Paul Revere and the Raiders' influence on the contemporary Garage groups cannot be overstated due to their sound and Americanized take on British Invasion music and the surrounding musical community.

This aspect of Americanism was added through the lyrical content and the method of playing the Blues. While the bands from the British Invasion began with a concern for a certain aspect of American Blues, Paul Revere and the Raiders were concerned with how Blues could be significantly manipulated in an effort to assert a different approach in their music. Instead of following Blues progressions that were inherently the same as the British Invasion groups, they modified the chord changes to impart a sense of rebellion to a classical structure.

Another influential group was the Music Machine. This group was founded upon the intent to put forward another aspect of the original Garage Rock scene: making a break from capitalist notions of control over music. This group was influential in bringing a completely different and new sound into the music world. They used a different style of tuning and very minimalist drumming to portray a deep, dark sound. It was this sound that allowed them to go against the typical, often heard notions of mainstream music.

This sound differed from the current styles and formats that were being played. Through the use of detuning, the Music Machine completely changed the face of Garage Rock and Rock and Roll. Their approach to music was one that continuously influenced other groups, and they are one of the most influential bands on the new Garage sound. By constructing their sound in a way that aligned them with a murky Blues sound, they riveted audiences and challenged the record labels to sign them. Many fans and participants of the current scene are unaware of the Music Machine, but their presence is felt throughout the contemporary Garage world.

The Music Machine was known for their interpretation of music in a manner that was true to the original Blues format but which consisted of variants in style and sonority. They played the guitar and bass with a tuning that allowed for the depth of the music to be brought to the forefront. By tuning the guitar and bass down a half step, they allowed deeper tones to be brought out. This sound, though initially strongly frowned upon and limited only to the group (until their song gained recognition), would eventually change the thought processes of mainstream music fans. Many people cite the Music Machine as one of the most influential groups of this time period due to their constructions of sound and the way they approached their music. This tuning and approach has influenced countless bands throughout the years and continues to play an influential role in contemporary Garage Rock.

With this detuning of the instruments, the Music Machine challenged the existing notion of mainstream music and gained recognition based on this challenge. Their sound was different and new and something that was more aggressive in nature. They moved away from the lighter sounds that were dominating the mainstream charts and consistently offered a darker version of songs that had previously been viewed as light and poppy. They challenged the mainstream notion of happy and upbeat music with the simple detuning of their instruments.

The Music Machine was extremely beneficial to its surrounding scene because of their difference in sound and approach. They all wore the same clothes onstage and dyed their hair in the same manner. By doing so, they gained the reputation of a group that was one entity, and their music relayed this sound. The constant drone of the music is one of the most challenging and interesting things from this period of music and still challenges listeners today. By constructing a sound and feel that envelopes the audience in a dark manner, the Music Machine created the first incarnations of a Punk sound.

This group also played an influential role with its use of minimalist drumming through their aversion to the use of cymbals. Their drum patterns rely heavily on the use of toms and snare drums to give a solid background to the detuned guitars. The drummer consistently focuses on the impact of each hit of the drum, placing the distinction on the simplicity of the music and the harsh, strong feel that dominates the sound. People continue to attempt to recreate this sound on the drums, but fail due to the sound's simplistic but powerful nature. This method of drumming also led to a feel that was reminiscent of the older sounding recordings and song styles, which allowed the Music Machine to heavily influence the surrounding musicians at the time.

By not using cymbals to create a light splash sound or an accent to the beat, the accent then falls on the bass drum and the floor tom. This roots the music in a dense and sonically deep sound. This also allows the lead singer and the rest of the band to construct a sound that springs from the denseness of the bass drum, as opposed to the lightness of the cymbals. The Music Machine became known for this sound and focused their outlook and approach on the darkness and density of the bass drum's reverberations, which causes the entirety of their music to have a completely different feel than the surrounding groups of the time.

The Music Machine's biggest hit came with a reworking of "Hey Joe," a classic Folk song written by Billy Roberts. This song was originally a hit, and with this cover the Music Machine gained greater popularity. Many people cite the Music Machine's version as the impetus for Jimmy Hendrix covering the song. What is significantly important about their reworking is the slow tempo and the introspective approach to the music. With the detuned guitars and drum style, they gave this song a different feel altogether. After this reworking, many bands, garage and otherwise, took on "Hey Joe" with a new approach.

The importance of the new sound of "Hey Joe" cannot be overstated, and the Music Machine gave new life to the Folk song through the use of a sound that was completely different for the time. This version of the classic song has influenced countless musicians and can still be heard in any version of the song played on an electric guitar. Many people fail to realize the influence of simple detuning on a classic Folk tune, but this version demonstrated the important role of the sonic quality of the guitar and the group's use of tuning. The style of this song has remained a precursor to Punk and has resurfaced in countless contemporary Garage bands.

Still, a final influence that the Music Machine had on contemporary groups was in the area of vocal prowess. Sean Bonniwell's voice was a mixture of Mick Jagger's and his own that perfectly suited the tuned down guitars and simple drumming. His influence can be heard today in many of the contemporary Garage groups, including the White Stripes. Bonniwell's voice was instrumental in the Music Machine's break from the mainstream focus in music at the time. Michael Hicks has written extensively on Bonniwell and the Music Machine, and states, "To have such control over a different range of notes and to put forward a style that was mixed and powerful allowed for his voice to be authoritative in essence and ambivalent in every detail."[3] They were successful based on their approach to the music that was surrounding them and due to their going against the grain of mainstream music.

Bonniwell's voice became the center of attention throughout the band's career, and his sound continues to influence countless musicians in many areas of music. The drone and control of vocal patterns became a singular sound of the time and allowed the Music Machine access to a limited amount of success. Bonniwell challenged the sound of the day and also used his voice to signify a new focus in music and society. By relying on the incorporation of his voice with the different tuning and structure of the band, he began an approach to music that would go on to influence countless other Punk and Garage bands.

Bonniwell's voice and the Music Machine's style of playing broke from the mainstream notion of music and can be witnessed throughout the contemporary scene. Many musicians in the contemporary Garage Rock movement are not aware of the Music Machine's influence, but continue to express the same notions and sound of music that this influential group put forward. Without the Music Machine and their insistence on this break from the mainstream, the contemporary Garage scene would not be able to function against the mainstream musical paradigm.

The impact of the original groups of the 60s is not readily recognized within the current musical scene. Although many members of the contemporary scene share musical influences, many are not fully aware of the original Garage Rock scene and its importance to the current musical output.

This lack of knowledge has led to many groups citing influences that are outside of the original Garage Rock scene. Like members of the 60s Garage movement, these current groups cite the music of the British Invasion as a major influence, as opposed to the original Garage Rock movement.

But by citing the British Invasion as a major influence, contemporary Garage bands inadvertently link themselves to Garage Rock of the 60s. The original Garage bands formed and patterned themselves after the British Invasion bands who broke into the mainstream. This break allowed many Americans to view music in a different light, and the first Garage Bands began in an attempt to duplicate this success. Contemporary groups are again attempting to duplicate the success and popularity of the British Invasion groups by sublimating their image and approach to music. This is inherent in many of the constructions of contemporary Garage Rock, but it is an essential link to the similarity between the original and current manifestations.

While the original Garage scene began as a reaction to the British Invasion and its success, contemporary Garage Rock is influenced by both of these founding movements. The constructions that are portrayed by the current scene are taken from direct links to the British Invasion while mixing the musical style and attitude of the original Garage movement. It is this blending of different influences that many bands fail to notice, but both musical scenes play influential roles in the current ideal.

The style of the contemporary Garage scene plays one of the most influential roles in the movement's continuation, and it is this style that has risen from the original Garage rock of the 60s and mixed with the appearance of the British Invasion. Bands have used the musical actions of the 60s Garage Bands in conjunction with the British Invasion to create their contemporary sound and attitude. It is this joining of influences that has allowed the contemporary scene to impact the underground and eventually the mainstream of musical society.

5

You're Going to Wear That?

The aspect of dress within the contemporary Garage scene plays a dramatic part in performance. This performance relies on the ability to represent past forms of style within dress. Performers and participants within the scene directly align themselves with the past by acquiring specific remnants of 50s and 60s nostalgic dress. Many of the performers base their production solely on nostalgic dress, putting forward the notion of rebelliousness that has been portrayed before. Bands such as Black Rebel Motorcycle Club, the Strokes and many others nostalgically adhere to this dress code, and the participants in the scene are drawn to this sense of rebellion and anti-conformity. What becomes important is the aspect of forced conformity to a set notion of nostalgic fashion and iconography. The ability of the performers in the scene to make subconscious demands on the participants is specifically relevant to the success of the music and the scene. Without the bands accepting a joint notion of fashion and apparel, the participants would be disjointed in their outlook as a scene. This creates a tension within all members through the consistent premise of anti-conformity through conformation.

It is this tension that is so remarkable within the myriad underground musical movements. The contemporary Garage Rock scene plays to these notions of conformity through dress. Many members of the current scene are dependant on the use of dress to show their removal from mainstream society. Much like Punk and other underground movements, the contemporary Garage scene displays these notions first within their performers and then within the participants. Although not readily admitted, this aspect allows the members to convey their alliance to the particular scene as well as their rebellion against the mainstream.

The use of dress determines a great deal of how the participants within the scene construct their rebellion and attitudes against society. Through the use of dress, the thoughts and requirements of the scene are displayed and allowed to become a focal point in the community of contemporary Garage. These rules form a structure that is related to consistently through performances on and off stage. Hilda Kuper relates, "The rules for that structure are assimilated over time together with other rules of thought and behavior...."[1] By allowing this assimilation to take place through dress, the Garage Rock scene challenges the surrounding participants to rebel through the incorporation of fashion. The incorporation of fashion is used in this way to strengthen the participants' construction of the scene and their outlook on the surrounding culture of contemporary Garage Rock. Dress becomes a focal point both within and outside the community, but is hardly as steadfast as in earlier music movements.

It is often the case that participants do not admit or even allude to the fact that dress plays an important role in the determination of the scene. By denying or not accepting that the scene is dependant on some type of fashion, the participants perpetuate the notion of a shared removal from society through the use of dress. This also allows for the members of the scene to take a position of control through the structure of dress and appearance as it is placed throughout the scene on stage. The fans then relate to the performers, and a system of control is perpetuated through dress.

Throughout the Garage movement dress is specifically used to create a constructed individuality far removed from the late capitalist notions of conformity that postmodern America displays. This is accomplished through the extreme reliance on past forms of rebellious iconography that was portrayed during the 50s and 60s through televised advertisements and Hollywood productions. It was these first instances of rebellion that the contemporary Garage scene relied on for their depictions away from the mainstream of music and society. These first images from movies like *Rebel Without a Cause*, *The Wild One* and *Quadrophenia* serve as focal points for the underground Garage movement and their style of dress.

There are other nostalgic links throughout the contemporary scene in regards to dress; however, these movies play direct roles in determining relationships between the participants within the scene and movies from the past. The way that these movies are used focuses the performer and participant into a construction of rebellion that was, at the time, fabricated and continues to revolve around difficult issues of rebellion and control. While displaying this rebellion through the use of nostalgic fashion, contemporary Garage Rock strengthens its hold on the surrounding audience by inserting a different viewpoint into society and the postmodern capitalist community.

Within these movies is a constant parade of anti-authority figures, and this is first displayed to the viewing audience through the use of non-conforming dress. James Dean, playing Jim Stark, in *Rebel Without a Cause* (1955) displays this dress during his transformation within the movie. His first appearance as a rebellious character occurs when he puts on his leather jacket. Through this simple assimilation into rebellious dress, the audience is drawn into his performance of anti-conformity and anti-authority. His parents are overwhelmed by this display and serve as a continuous reference point of overprotective parents within our society. Director Nicholas Ray uses many other forms of rebellious iconography, such as a knife, but the audience is drawn into Jim Stark's rebellion from the onset (and some may argue even from before entering the theater due to the movie poster's portrayal of James Dean) via his mode of dress.

The movie poster for *Rebel Without a Cause* includes an iconographic image of Dean is his full rebel outfit of leather jacket, white t-shirt, and jeans. This image would go on to influence many musicians and fans, but it has the greatest impact on the contemporary scene due to the emotion and thought that is discussed and displayed throughout the movie. James Dean characterizes what many in the contemporary scene feel is the best example of a rebel, and the dress has followed this thought process entirely.

Rebel Without a Cause easily constructs what some believe to be the first appearance, to the majority of the public, of a teenage rebel. With his bright white t-shirt, blue jeans and leather jacket, Jim Stark serves as the epitome of rebellion in the 50s. It is this rebellion to which the current Garage scene has clung. What Nicholas Ray's depiction of rebellion stems from is a flight from parental restrictions and psychopathology. The film leads the audience to see the parents as Jim Stark does, as confused subjects in a world of delusion. Nicholas Ray seems to be critiquing the role of parental influence when it becomes masked by its own psychological confusion. Although this may have been the director's intent, the Garage movement clings to the aspect of rebellion against authority figures.

The director's intent is not the concern of the majority of fans and participants within the scene. What is more important is the escape from parental control that is the focus of the movie for many people. This escape can be viewed as an escape from many things within society, but often has been construed as an escape from suburban values and attitudes. The capitalist system of thought has led to the parents' restrictive nature, and Jim Stark cannot handle it, so he must rebel in order to exert his own individualism.

This rebelliousness is witnessed throughout the movie but comes to a head at the climax with Jim and Judy's flight from all forms of authority within the abandoned home. It is this stage of the movie that the members of the Garage scene often cite as influential. What occurs during this part of the movie reflects the desire to be apart from the created normalcy of society. Although Jim's family cannot be considered solely as the mainstream, his aversion to authority leads to a direct confrontation with police. Throughout these scenes, Jim is dressed in his rebellious attire.

This climax is influential in determining the way that Jim's rebellion is focused. There is no desire here to kill or harm anyone in society; it is more a way to escape from the older ways of the past and to cling to a new type of individuality. This is the case in contemporary Garage as well. The desire of this rebellion is not to harm or change the world; it is simply to insert a new thought process into the surrounding society. Jim and Judy's flight is a pivotal scene in this development and lends itself to the aspect of rebellion through simple means.

Rebel Without a Cause serves the contemporary Garage scene in many ways but none as heavily as in the aspect of appearance. There are a countless number of bands that choose to portray themselves as rebellious through their wearing of a leather jacket, ripped jeans and white t-shirts. Although this attire has become common since the release of the movie, it has received a new life through the Garage Rock movement. With this first instance of Hollywood rebellion many members of the Garage scene were allowed access to a depiction of rebellion that went against the mainstream construction of society. *Rebel Without a Cause* had many people co-opting this viewpoint, but it has been rekindled within the contemporary scene.

It is extremely important to realize that this form of dress is a simple statement within society today. Members of the Garage scene are continuously attempting to withdraw from the fashion plates of mainstream musical production. It is almost as if the members of the scene are once again rebelling against the "preppies" of *Rebel Without a Cause*. With a simple removal of high fashion clothing, the members of the scene nostalgically rebel against their counterparts in mainstream music. Jean jackets and ripped jeans became something of a fashion statement with the advent of Punk's incorporation by the masses, but in the contemporary music industry these forms of dress have again been relegated to the underground. It is striking to realize that rebellion can occur through a black t-shirt and ripped jeans.

While Jim Stark defied authority through dress and actions, another occurrence of rebellion can be witnessed in *The Wild One*. Marlon Brando's depiction of rebellion, in the character of Johnny, was the first Hollywood portrayal of a motorcycle gang and the violence surrounding these groups. From the beginning of *The Wild One* (1954), the audience is put on the lookout for displays of violence and anti-conformity. The film begins with a warning to society about violence and then explores the behavior of a motorcycle gang and the townspeople's reactions. Throughout the entire movie Brando displays signs of his rebellion against authority and society. From his gang's leather jackets (with their symbol of a skull above two automobile pistons) to Johnny's brooding sense of justice and removal from society, this aspect of rebellion is continuously asserted. Throughout their stay in Wrightsville, the gang looks to rebel in any way, shape or form. They drag race for beer and generally cause havoc for whomever approaches them. Their rebellious nature is much harsher than that seen in *Rebel Without a Cause*, leading to strong identification from within the contemporary Garage movement.

While the rebellion is harsher throughout this movie, the aspect of a removal from society is more focused on actions that relate to Punk ideals. Contemporary Garage Rock is extremely influenced by these notions, but the majority of fans and participants do not have the same relationship to *The Wild One* as they do to *Rebel Without a Cause*. This is due to the nature of the rebellion in both movies. While Johnny (Brando) asserts his rebellion from the fringes of society as an outlaw, Jim's (Dean) rebellion is from within and is much more threatening to the whole of society. But both movies receive constant nostalgic attention regarding their portrayal of rebellion through dress.

The most obvious sign of *The Wild One*'s influence is in the naming of one of the bands that has broken through to the contemporary mainstream. The band Black Rebel Motorcycle Club derives its name (almost exactly—it drops one letter) from the name of Johnny's gang. Johnny's gang is dubbed the Black Rebels Motorcycle Club and shortened to BRMC. The contemporary band also shortens their name in the same manner. This band constructs its entire image through the use of *The Wild One* and its depictions of rebellion. They are known by their attire and attitude of rebellion against authority. Every member of Black Rebel Motorcycle Club in both the movie and the current band wear black leather jackets and other associations of rebellion.

The contemporary band goes beyond simple fashion statements as rebellion to include stage performance and other aspects of nostalgic rebellion. Black Rebel Motorcycle Club aligns itself with a biker image in order to express their association with the fringes of society. Whether this works or not as an aspect of rebellion is the participant's decision, but the relationship to the past is easily viewed and the entire band was created in reference to the movie.

The music of Black Rebel Motorcycle Club is even slightly harsher than other Garage groups. They choose to uphold the comparison to *The Wild One* by playing music that is more closely related to Punk than 60s Garage, and do so while attired in black leather jackets. This is not just a simple marketing device, but it was extremely important to their mainstream acceptance. Although they have already been somewhat removed from the underground scene, they continue to represent the nostalgic dress that is important to the rebellion mentality of the current Garage movement. Black Rebel Motorcycle Club won brief mainstream popularity while demonstrating the extremity of nostalgic dress within the scene.

While Black Rebel Motorcycle Club asserts its rebellion through the nostalgic borrowing from *The Wild One*, other bands choose to present themselves in more subtle ways. As the scene began, bands were determined to disassociate themselves from previous underground movements. This distancing led to many bands focusing on outward appearance along with the music that was played. These groups, such as the Von Bondies, Ko and the Knockouts and others, expressed themselves through the use of jean jackets, shaggy hair and dirty appearances. This led to a desire within the scene to appear as if fashion and dress did not matter, and that what was at stake and important was the music. It was this type of attitude that allowed the contemporary Garage scene to stand against the majority of mainstream artists who were completely focused on image.

Another essential Hollywood depiction of rebellion used extensively within the Garage underground is *Quadrophenia* (1979). With Phil Daniels as Jimmy, the audience is given an example of what many consider to be the "true" rebel. His loner attitude leads viewers to see him as completely outside of the mainstream of society. While Jimmy constructs himself within the Mod movement, he remains an outsider to his friends and enemies, and insists that his individuality stems from this. Many instances throughout the movie convey the image of Jimmy standing alone against the world, and this concept has been influential within the Garage scene.

The Who's contribution within Contemporary Garage Rock can not be overlooked, and *Quadrophenia* is what many participants cite as their first look into the Mod and underground culture. When asked what was the first movie that led her into the scene, Ko Shih (like many others) stated, "*Quadrophenia*, cuz it got me into all the Mod stuff."[2] Although the movie is considered an exploitation of an underground movement, the depictions stem from a hyper-reality to which many contemporary participants cling. The underground is blatantly exaggerated throughout this movie, which led to a backlash from the original participants of the Mod scene. Although the movie is considered among the best Rock and Roll movies, its manipulation of the underground is often debated. The overextension of fashion and appearance is seen through Jimmy. He appears most often in a Crombie coat riding a scooter in the full throes of Mod stardom. The incorporation of *Quadrophenia* into the Garage scene stems from this fashion statement, and the depiction of Jimmy as a rebel through his moody schizophrenia plays a large role in the determination of fashion within the underground culture.

Many critics and reviewers point to the aspect of internal rebellion and response to internal separation throughout *Quadrophenia,* and place these aspects as a reflection of societal rebellion. Without internal strife and displeasure there would be no cause for rebellion. While this concept is prevalent within the movie, it also allows the audience to witness these splits in psyche and construct their own conceptualization of rebellion. Lenny Kaye, in *Rolling Stone,* suggests, "Torn between identities, Townsend has gifted him with four, all competing for top speed within Jimmy's psyche."[3] While this allows Jimmy to be portrayed with psychological issues, it also constructs Jimmy in a way that has been traditionally defined as rebellious. To go against society one must perform certain roles as a rebel, and one of these roles coincides with appearance and image.

Jimmy Livingston Seagull's appearance is one of pure Mod fashion and diction. He is consistently seen with a full suit and/or Crombie coat. This construction seems to conflict with the images *Rebel Without a Cause* and *The Wild One* have put forward, but their similarities go along with their reliance on rebellion. The wearing of the highest make of suit and riding the best scooter possible was viewed as a rebellious statement within late 60s and early 70s England. The portrayal of the Mod culture in *Quadrophenia* allowed many individuals access to another mode of dress that has become an important statement within contemporary Garage Rock. A full suit and a nice coat do not fit with a pair of ripped jeans and a t-shirt, but both modes of dress are witnessed throughout the Garage scene and are linked through the viewing of *Quadrophenia* to Garage culture.

The contemporary Garage underground grew out of aspects of other undergrounds, and the instances of fashion from these cultures have carried over. Although most have been modified to reflect a tougher street image, the Hard Mod classification and the images displayed in *Quadrophenia* remain important aspects of appearance within the current scene. Jimmy's dress and fight within himself and against society link him to the other Hollywood depictions of rebellion and serve to demonstrate to the current Garage underground avenues toward rebellion in dress and performance.

This rebellion was also focused on the surrounding underground of Detroit, which many people thought was deteriorating due to a lack of reality and simply-played Rock and Roll. By recovering the dress and appearances of the past in an effort to look as if little or no effort was put into appearance, many groups inserted a new thought process into the surrounding scene. This was viewed as something fresh and new, but in reality was nostalgically representing fashions and performance aspects throughout the underground.

The focus began to shift as the scene grew in popularity. An emphasis on appearance and outward signs of expression became dominant within the participants in the scene as well as the performers. It expanded until what was worn to a show depended on whether or not you were accepted as part of the Garage underground. While many musicians and scene members would deny this aspect right away, by witnessing reactions from the crowd toward various aspects of attire one may experience this dichotomy of style. It progressed to where what was worn became more important, in some cases, than what type of music was played.

An extreme example is the reaction at shows to participants that appear in the older style of Swing attire. While there are many people that remain a part of this underground scene, its removal from the show scene is apparent at every performance. The participant that appears in attire based on this movement is not shunned outright but is generally made to feel out of place and awkward within the new scene of Garage. Trying too hard to fit in has always been a downside to any underground, and within Garage this is becoming the case.

The importance of dress within the scene has even come to be known by a specific piece of clothing. This piece has often been said to represent the people who are trying to latch onto the trend of contemporary Garage Rock, and is often viewed with anger because the music has become associated with this type of trend. The piece in question is the white belt, and it is often looked upon with disdain by people who were at the beginning of the scene. What this shows, however, is the strong reliance on outward appearance for belonging within the scene. The white belt can be replaced with a myriad of options for any past or present musical subculture and is simply a signifier of what happens to an underground scene with the onset of mainstream popularity.

What this simple piece of fashion demonstrates is the same thing that the appearance of ripped jeans with safety pins holding them together in shopping mall stores did for the Punk movement. A signifier that is incorporated and shifted from the underground to the mainstream loses its relevance and strength of its original statement. For the contemporary Garage scene, this white belt constitutes a shift from the original focus being on the music played to the current focus on the fashion and appearance that is involved with being a member of the Garage scene.

This instance of import being placed on style over musical technique aligns itself with the original upsurge of Garage Rock in the 60s. Many of the original bands were focused, almost exclusively, on their appearance. It was groups like the Chocolate Watch Band, by wearing all black clothing, which displayed this aspect of style that has led to the current reliance on appearance. Many groups of the contemporary scene have embraced this aspect of appearance over musical representation. By doing so, they have begun to remove the important aspect of the musical culture and are transforming the scene into an area where fashion and outward appearance rides above musical performance.

This relationship to fashion and appearance has led to the downfall of many musical scenes and is equally detrimental to the contemporary Garage scene. While many bands stress the fact that fashion does not matter, others still rely on appearance in order to succeed. Through all of this lies the confusion of the participant, and to know with what they should align themselves becomes increasingly difficult. The downfall of underground and mainstream scenes usually begins when participants are not given a consistent thought process to follow, and the reliance on fashion is antithetical to the contemporary Garage thought process of residing outside of capitalist norms.

The focus on the appearance of performers plays a secondary role to the importance of dress among the participants of the scene. It is these participants that rely heavily on what they wear to embrace their so-called individualism, and they are the strict enforcers of the dress codes within contemporary Garage Rock. While many of these participants determine what they wear based on the performers in the bands, they have aligned themselves against the mainstream of society through their insistence on rebellious attire. Assuming nostalgic dress roles of rebellion allows the participants to establish one method of breaking into a form of counter-culture.

This counter-culture is displayed as a removal from the capitalist constructions of postmodern America. Through the use of rebellious iconography and modes of dress, these participants are attempting to remake themselves outside of the mainstream ideal of culture and music. The representatives of the underground movement have always been aligned in a similar manner, but with Garage Rock a reliance on past forms of dress and representation as an expression of this rebellion is paramount. Many of the current participants allow their dress to be the main, even only, thing that leads to their determination within the scene. While this may seem alarming, it is this code of dress that plays a determinate role in defining the individuals within the scene.

It is this code of dress that becomes the dominant factor in the composition of the contemporary underground. When witnessing underground shows, one can easily determine how this code plays such a defining role. This dress is inherent in the determination of fitting into the scene. Even what one drinks has become important when at shows or events. This concept of dress and appearance has influenced many underground scenes, but within Garage Rock its influence thrives in the many individual participants.

The followers of the Garage Rock scene of music are deeply aligned with the attitude and dress of the performers. They reconfigure these traits into their own expressions of individuality by taking on the performer's style. Audience members wear similar attire and express similar attitudes towards society and capitalist conformity. Most of the time they have a deep refusal of conformity within the scene and believe that their style and dress is their own. This allows for the participant in the scene to construct an individuality that remains outside of capitalist notions of conformity.

Many followers of the Garage Rock scene thrive on such notions of individualism and rebelliousness. They are allowed to remain outside of societal norms and within a subculture that expresses similar desires. This also allows for the performers to have more power and control over the scene and their demands over the participants can become extremely strict and forced. The dress code and style of rebellion become fixed notions of conformity and, according to Walter Benjamin, "Instead of being based on ritual, it begins to be based on another practice—politics...."[4] Both performers and participants are aligned against the mainstream of society and pride themselves in their ability to rebel, but what must be realized is that all participants in the scene use nostalgic representations to gain this sense of a constructed individuality.

It is this sense of politics that the contemporary Garage movement allows to remain through their insistence on a particular style of appearance. These politics are enforced through image and the removal of members from the scene who break the rules. A prime example of this can be easily witnessed through what is considered appropriate to drink at a show. For members of the scene, it is viewed as antithetical to their construction within Garage Rock to drink anything other than Pabst Blue Ribbon, Black Label or any other form of cheap beer. When this is mentioned, it becomes an extreme argumentative point, but the instance of realization comes from the fact that many bars that hold Garage shows in Detroit sell these beers. Sales have doubled, sometimes tripled, since the arrival of the Garage scene. Although what you drink is not as important as what you wear, it is another example of the importance of appearance within the contemporary Garage scene.

This extreme emphasis on appearance links itself with multiple preceding underground movements. However, with the Garage scene, the reliance on nostalgic dress and rebellious attire sets it apart from those precedents. Most of the focus on appearance within the scene revolves around this fact, and it is this nostalgia that plays an important part in the aspect of rebellion against the contrived notion of the mainstream in music and society. Many participants in the scene rely on this form of dress to express their attitudes towards rebellion.

The aspect of expression through dress is extremely important to the Garage underground. Multiple styles of dress can be prevalent, but it is the nostalgic rebellion that is important. The Garage scene is made up of multiple people who dress in a variety of ways, but it is the self-imposed construction of the nostalgic rebel that becomes rehashed over and over again. With this construction, participants are struggling to remain outside of the norm and within the underground culture. They begin to assert notions of rebellion through their dress within the movement. This allows for their mode of dress to take extreme precedence over other aspects of the burgeoning underground.

The assertion that the mode and style of dress is reliant on Hollywood movies and depictions allows for the insertion of the notion that these depictions are faulty. Although many people have brought forward this idea, the reliance on faulty images from Hollywood is extremely important within the current scene. Hollywood interpretations of what was and is considered rebellious have always been, to a certain extent, flawed. The multitude of films that portray rebels that are linked with Garage Rock focus on the appearance and attitude of the rebel in ways that can immediately be viewed as faulty to the reality involved.

Rebel Without a Cause, The Wild One and *Quadrophenia* all seek to portray rebels as being completely removed from the realm of mainstream society. While this is an aspect that many cling to, the only way to rebel is to be within a society and act against it. These productions allow the viewer to witness the filmmakers' interpretation of rebel culture and attitude. It is this interpretation that is most susceptible to Hollywood manipulation and control. With the spinning of the rebel image, audiences are drawn into a depiction that is over-generalized and enhanced in a way to glorify the existence and necessity of rebel culture within our society.

The aspect of glorifying the counterculture is often discussed with these types of Hollywood constructions of the rebel. What is important to realize is that these depictions led to this rebellion being partially accepted within mainstream society. According to Ron Briley, "...this very commercialization of the counterculture led to its being absorbed into the mainstream of American culture and capitalism."[5] Contemporary Garage Rock has, like these rebel images, gained acceptance within society. A Hollywood portrayal of rebels often leads to this type of incorporation, but with the above-mentioned movies comes a re-incorporation within a contemporary scene.

Another aspect of faulty representation can be witnessed through the actual display of rebellion found within Hollywood and the Garage Rock culture. To wear certain clothes and assemble certain character traits for a small period of time (at a concert or event) does not fully signify the individual as a rebel. Through the use of Hollywood depictions, participants within the scene become functioning performers of the role of a rebel. They attempt to portray what has been witnessed within these movies without consideration of the demand of actual rebellion. To fully rebel against societal demands is not even shown in *Rebel Without a Cause*.

The ending of *Rebel Without a Cause* links the movie to a very conservative notion of rebellion. Why then have the participants aligned themselves so strongly with this movie? Jim is brought back into the household and reunited with his reformed parents. They all hug, having found the reasons behind Jim's rebellion. With this, the movie ends and perpetuates the notion that rebelling against society will allow you to gain access within that society. Much like these Hollywood productions that allow rebellion to become part of the mainstream, Garage Rock allows for the incorporation of the rebel within a new form of underground music.

Garage Rock has taken this rebellion and shaped it to meet the demands of the underground culture. The contemporary Garage scene is dependant on these notions of rebellion as witnessed in Hollywood depictions and nostalgic representations. They have allowed themselves to become dominated by what is believed to be rebellion instead of the actuality of rebelling. The movement allows participants to construct themselves within these parameters and, to a certain extent, demands conformity through them. These depictions are faulty but allow for a brief, if inaccurate, glimpse into the nostalgic rebel.

The aspect of faulty depictions is important but not inherently relevant in the discussion of appearance and appropriation. The contemporary scene does not focus on why or how these images are faulty within our society. They become reliant on these Hollywood performances as a starting point for their assimilation into the counterculture. Because these images are faulty does not make them useless within the postmodern context. They become a representation of the effects of the mainstream on notions such as rebellion and are displayed throughout contemporary Garage culture by the dress and attitude that are affected in an effort to distance oneself from the mainstream. The Garage culture insists that these representations play an increasingly viable role within the scene and become determinate on aspects of control.

The concept of control over these permutations sits with the performers of the music and the leaders of the underground movement. Without avid participation by the members of the bands, these concepts of rebellion through dress would not be distributed throughout the culture. Band members align themselves with particular aspects of nostalgic dress, either appropriated from movies or through other nostalgic avenues. It is these appropriations that allow the members of the scene to witness what must be considered as rebellious in nature. For many of the band members this aspect is not conscious; for others it remains a fully functioning aspect of their makeup as a group.

Bands such as Black Rebel Motorcycle Club consciously assimilate these nostalgic images and display them within the scene in an effort to assert their control over what it means to rebel against the mainstream. They are determined to instill the notions that rebellion through dress is just as important as actual rebellion. The focus has shifted into a construction away from mainstream fashion and toward the fashion displayed through performance. By aligning themselves with *The Wild One*, Black Rebel Motorcycle Club portrays the way that they believe leads to a counterculture and rebellion against the mainstream.

The unconscious aspects of this control remain heavily prevalent within most groups. These groups, oftentimes, do not forcefully dress in rebellious attire. They do, however, focus their representation and performance on the nostalgic aspects of rebellion. It is this focus that drives the participants in the scene towards aspects that they find oppositional to mainstream society. Contemporary Garage Rock bands allow their followers to witness these traits of rebellion in order to confirm that they belong to the scene.

The majority of participants within the scene take a strong stance against conforming. This goes right along with the Hollywood reproductions of rebellion and the culture of underground music scenes. When the entirety of the underground is focused in this manner, it takes on the aspect of conforming to rebellion and, even though the participants remain certain of non-conformity, it remains a strong basis for representation within the culture. It is this representation through performance that the majority of the members of the scene take for granted and use to assert their dominance and control over certain parts of the culture and environment at shows and elsewhere.

By witnessing many events that cater to the underground scene of Garage Rock, one can ascertain this conformity to dress. This conformity is usually below the surface in the majority of participants and is clung to in an effort to assert rebellion against the mainstream society. Through the use of Hollywood productions and the performance of appearance, many participants have developed a style that can be readily held up as Garage Rock. Although one style is limiting, there is a strong desire to dress in a reflection of rebellious iconography that has been witnessed through film. For some it is a conscious depiction of rebellion, while for others it remains within the subconscious desires to conform to and be a part of the underground music scene.

Contemporary Garage Rock has allowed for the style and attitude of the 50s to again be brought to the present society. Through nostalgic representations of films, participants link themselves to the faulty display of rebellion that is present throughout. The members of the bands and the participants are linked in this desire to portray a style that is as anti-mainstream and rebellious as possible, but are projecting their own sense of rules and regulations subconsciously within the scene. These rules, and the sense of power that is gained, allow the contemporary Garage scene to conform to anti-conformity and display a conscious desire to remain outside of the mainstream of musical society.

6

What Is Garage Rock?

Underlying this discussion has been the premise of similarity in a form of music dubbed Garage Rock. The difficulty with this classification is that, since the original scene in the 60s, no one has been able to rightly define the parameters that would assign the title of Garage Rock to a band or scene. Originally, this movement arose as a reaction to the British Invasion, and the name sprang from the notion of practicing in a suburban garage; but what is currently being called Garage Rock ranges from Alternative-Country to Hardcore Punk. The differentiations within the scene are strongly referenced in contemporary Garage Rock's attempt to remain focused away from mainstream incorporation. The trend has been to label music in order to garner increased sales figures. Garage Rock's popularity has led to many of the mainstream record labels attaching this moniker to bands that share nothing with what many people consider Garage Rock. This has led to a great deal of difficulty, with many groups shying away from this classification. The over-classification of contemporary Garage Rock has allowed success for many groups, as well as the continuation of an underground movement alongside the mainstream groups.

The continued over-classification of music has always led to confusion among the participants. This results in many people constructing their own definitions of music. From the very beginning of Rock and Roll, the debate has always been about what Rock and Roll even means. It has usually been stated to represent a rebellion of youth culture against the mainstream, but that could include any representation throughout our society. In Lawerence Grossberg's study on youth and Rock, he suggests, "If Rock and Roll music is a response to an environment that is boring, repressive, and crazy, it suggests that these structures coincide within the regimentation of desire in the contemporary world."[1] This regimentation is the cause of the majority of youth fomation throughout history and is part of the determination behind contemporary Garage Rock and its insistence on a return to Rock and Roll.

The demands of the original contemporary participants on the type of music played were not strictly enforced. The surrounding musicians simply played music that was constructed based on their influences and exposure to previous forms of Rock and Roll. The beginnings of the contemporary scene saw a large number of people determined to construct a new scene based on the return to Rock.

What resulted from this desire was the formation of a certain type of community based on original music played in a certain manner. Throughout music has been a consistent viewpoint that a community of thought be represented through the music played. Simon Frith states, "The Rock claim was that if a song or record or performance had, in itself, the necessary signs of authenticity, then it could be interpreted, in turn, as the sign of a real community—the musical judgment guaranteed the sociological judgment rather than vice versa."[2] This goal of an authentic and natural stance within music can easily be viewed throughout the contemporary Garage scene. The musical output of the beginning bands was reflective of the surrounding culture and attempted to put a new sound into the underground that would stand up against the current musical underground that was detrimental to live music.

In order for many groups to begin, they must decide on a style of music to play. For the founders of the current Garage scene, this music was linked directly to the past forms of the British Invasion, Punk and 60s Garage Rock. What began to form was a similarity of style, attitude and stance within the music that was being played, and with the development of record labels and recording studios, the label of Garage Rock was thrust onto the underground and, eventually, mainstream society. At first this label suggested a multitude of things, and it was these suggestions that allowed contemporary Garage Rock to stand on its own.

In the beginning of the 90s, the label Garage Rock held many different connotations. The bands associated with this early label were extremely different in their approach to music, but all shared certain similarities. These similarities consisted of a desire to create music away from the mainstream and a strong will to place real Rock and Roll back into the underground. These similarities stood out even when the sound of the music within the groups was very different. The Sights and the Von Bondies have differences in sound and their approach to music, but both groups are consistently labeled with the Garage moniker.

The label of Garage Rock is often misused, as are most labels in music. The interesting thing about this labeling is the different ways bands have reacted to it. From bands grasping the label in an effort to become successful to bands rejecting the label in an effort to reassert their rebellion against the mainstream, the label of Garage consistently shapes the attitudes and outlook of performers and participants alike. By witnessing reactions to the label of Garage Rock in multiple contexts, such as record reviews and concert listings, these differences appear. Whether it is the band that goes against the mainstream label or the band latching onto a trend, everyone in the scene has an opinion on the label.

The labeling of music has always been a touchy but often debated subject. With underground forms of music, this has especially been the case. It is extremely difficult to classify and label any form of underground music due to the multiple levels of grouping that remain hidden except to the participants. The extent to which underground music is labeled is greatly dependent on the amount of mainstream acceptance and diversification within the underground movement. Contemporary Garage Rock allows for both of these occurrences to become recognized. This has also been the case with almost every form of music that has had mainstream success following underground acceptance. The preceding musical underground of Hardcore was similar in many ways to Garage Rock regarding this over-classification.

Within the music that was labeled Hardcore in the early 90s existed extreme differences in style, and those differences extended even to the definition of Hardcore. Within the time period and continuing on through today we have bands as different as Madball and Minor Threat labeled as Hardcore. This overt use of terminology allowed many bands to jump on the bandwagon and claim to be playing Hardcore in order to garner the attention of record labels and fans. Madball and Minor Threat are two extremely different sounding bands with completely different approaches to politics, but they are labeled in the same way. This demonstrates the difficulty of defining Hardcore. What Hardcore is in reality is another discussion, but the similarities within this musical development and Garage Rock's are striking.

The reasons behind this over-use of labeling are many and allow many observers to retreat from the definitions attached to any label of music. While referring to a form of music will usually force the constructions of labels, many bands and participants simply say they are a Rock band or a Rock fan. This leads to a construction of the groups within a certain context and forces the participant, or listener, to hear the band before making a decision. This becomes extremely important in the expansion of Garage Rock throughout underground society. By limiting the exposure of the label of Garage, many groups were allowed to remain active in the perpetuation of the music and thought process.

Any musical growth is immediately thrown into classification and labeling. This allows record labels and others to begin a process of marketing and promotion within the classification of a musical style. This classification has often led to false claims and faulty representation in order to boost sales figures. The difficulty of classification and over-generalization allows participants to be tricked into purchasing music that in no way relates to previously purchased groups categorized as playing the same music type.

The expansion of a label to include groups that are completely different in sound and approach inspires rebellion and rejection from the original participants in the scene. When marketing takes the focus away from the music being played, the music begins to lose its place and its acceptance within the underground becomes challenged. This is the case with many of the later Garage Rock bands that are simply using the term to gain success. As the label continues to expand and relate to more and more bands, the original bands will resist and rebel in differing ways.

The marketing effects of labeling continue to wield an immense power over the performers and participants within any music scene. By slapping a name onto a style or sound of music, people can group multiple bands under a certain moniker. The false theory of the music industry is that in order for an underground musical development to become popular it must be labeled so that participants can have something to relate to. Herein lies the trouble with contemporary Garage Rock and the way that bands construct themselves in relation to the label.

The hastily labeled groups often view the label as limiting and controlling, and within contemporary Garage Rock this is witnessed continuously. Many bands, when questioned, do not claim the label of Garage Rock for themselves and discuss how this label is limiting and should not be associated with many bands. Both the Sights and the Dirtbombs have been known to claim outsider status regarding this label.

However, these groups have consistently been dubbed Garage Bands throughout the media. The performers that carry this attitude remain adamant about their music representing a certain sound and attitude that is different from what has been labeled Garage Rock.

If many of the founding groups and members of the scene do not claim to be Garage Bands, what does it mean to play Garage Music and Garage Rock? How do the participants within the scene claim and remove bands without a clear definition of the terminology? These questions must be considered alongside the development of the Garage underground and its continuation into the mainstream. Many participants still consider the founding bands of this musical development to be Garage, but the bands resist this label. If this label has any worthwhile connotations, do they revolve around money and sales, or is there a definitive response to the question of what is Garage Rock?

Throughout the entirety of music, these types of questions arise, and the way they are answered usually determines the continuation or downfall of a scene. As far back as Jazz, the argument of what is considered Jazz arose over and over again. Even today, people will argue what should or should not be labeled Jazz or Classical or any other moniker that can be thought of. The insistence on these types of labels usually leads to the listeners becoming confused and frustrated. It is this frustration that can either force the listeners to decide for themselves or ignore the genre and the label completely. These questions also demand that the listener know what is being discussed and be familiar with the music that is considered part of the label.

The Garage Rock of the 60s also faced this general desire for classification. Many of the original groups sound very different from one another, with bands from the later 60s beginning to sound Punk. Within the original 60s scene was a desire to use the term Garage Rock to cast a band in a negative light, as in not being skilled enough to get out of the garage. This began to change when groups such as the Music Machine and Paul Revere and the Raiders reached the mainstream charts, and the label of Garage Rock began to wield marketing power within America.

The marketing power of the term Garage is extremely interesting due to the way the term can be used negatively or positively depending on the reviewer and marketing team. The challenge is in the usage of the term and the meaning behind it. While many bands and mainstream record labels are continuously reworking the term to include other styles of music, the label begins to lose some of its power, and the argument over what the term actually means and signifies continues.

With the success of the Music Machine and other 60s underground groups began the fiery debate over what is considered Garage Rock. Bands considered too weak to break into the mainstream were being linked to bands that had achieved great monetary success. The term Garage Rock came to mean completely different things to critics and fans. For many, the main reason that 60s Garage Rock did not claim a greater popularity was this direct split in classification. What it meant to be a Garage band in the 60s was split in many ways by the mainstream labeling of the music, and it is this debate and the multitude of splits within the scene that have carried over to the contemporary Garage Rock movement.

The marketing of a term has consistently been reflected in the mainstream musical press. This labeling has often led to over-generalizations and conceptions of the term that do not relate in any way to the original meaning. The corporate record labels must find ways to group bands into a style of music that will allow its marketing efforts to be focused and to thrive. When this occurs, many bands fall under a label they originally resided outside of. This may be easily viewed within any type of underground music that has gained mainstream acceptance. When this grouping happens, the remainder of the underground scene is often split in its attitude toward bands that have fallen into the category.

When the labeling of a style of music occurs, groups that have accepted the label previously begin to reject the label in an effort to rebel against mainstream constructions. This conscious rebellion can be easily witnessed within contemporary Garage Rock. Many bands that were thrown into a classification have begun to reject the terminology and grouping that now goes along with the label. The Dirtbombs are one of these groups that have gone against the notions of mainstream marketing. They refuse to call themselves or their music Garage, when in fact they do play a style of music and carry an image that was originally viewed as Garage Rock at their outset. What the Dirtbombs are rallying against is the assumption that all Garage bands are similar.

The musical styles within the label of contemporary Garage are not in any way consistent. There are bands that play completely different styles of music being linked together under the term Garage. For many, the label is failing when this becomes the case, and groups such as the Dirtbombs continue to display a desire to be removed from the label that has affected the surrounding members of the scene. This strong resistance to the label is often viewed in a positive light within Detroit and is constructed as the attitude that should be taken towards the label. While other groups attempt to make money on the label, the Dirtbombs and others remain fixated against it.

What becomes interesting about the labeling of a musical style is that within that label are such extreme variants that one cannot believe they are considered the same style. This can most readily be viewed when looking at what is considered Garage by the mainstream music press. The differences in many bands are so apparent that it makes one conceptualize the label as immediately false to the underground musical society. When we consider what has been dubbed Garage Rock by the mainstream, we can view the extreme differences in sound, appearance and outlook within.

A review in *Rolling Stone* of the Hives' album *Veni Vidi Viscious* states, "If the success of Sweden's Hives proves anything, it's that balls out garage rock is evergreen."[3] This reviewer makes a statement that at least suggests a difference in the sonic representation but continues to link the band to the Garage Rock moniker. This continues within *Rolling Stone* with a completely different sounding band in the White Stripes. From a review of their recent album *Elephant*: "Singer-guitarist Jack White and his ex-wife Meg—the undisputed king and queen of the new garage movement—finally romp and rattle like a fully armed band."[4] These two groups are very different in sound and their approach to style and music, but have consistently been linked through the same classification.

The differences within the label of Garage Rock stem from the many different appropriations of nostalgia that have been used to construct appearances and sound within the bands. Many of these groups do not outright deny the label of Garage Rock, but do not champion it either. The extreme difference between the hyper-stylized group the Hives and the band the Von Bondies can easily be witnessed, but both groups have been labeled Garage. From the outward appearance of each group to the style of music played, these bands differ in content and musical expression. The Hives nostalgically represent the Hard Mod concept of fashion, while the Von Bondies exemplify the rebellion of the Hollywood 50s. There are many other conceptual differences within these two groups, but the aspect of sound and appearance are obvious.

The question of why these bands are both considered to be Garage

Rock brings up the question of what is Garage Rock and who is the champion of the scene. When the term Garage Rock is discussed, who are the fans speaking of and what is their reaction to a band being labeled Garage without carrying the requisite sonic or representational similarities? When this issue is discussed, many performers align themselves with their inspirations, while the participants in the scene will cite specific contemporary bands. The responses are as varied as possible, with Punk and Mod Soul bands being cited as Garage. The majority of participants within the scene do not have a clear picture of what Garage Rock is, and the difficulty with classification continues to expand as more and more groups fall under the moniker of Garage.

An in-depth comparison between groups is necessary to view these extreme differences within the label of Garage Rock. To begin, let us again look at the Hives and the Strokes, two major label bands a majority of the press and mainstream fans have labeled as Garage Rock. These groups share similar qualities, but their differences are immense. Along with these variations comes the outlook towards music that both bands take. Both groups can be said to have started in an effort to achieve mainstream success, and with this, they differ from earlier contemporary Garage bands.

The Hives, a group from Sweden who took American charts by storm and disappeared soon after, had an outward appearance that led to the discussion of nostalgic representations of the Hard Mod culture in England, as has been noted. They have continued to rely on this presentation in performance and in public appearances, and have continually embraced the notion that they are a Garage band. With this aspect, they align themselves with the many groups that claim similar labels for themselves, but they also further the distinction of what it means to be a Garage band. Their musical output is in relation to a harder Punk feel, more so than the 60s Garage sound, and their music is produced thoroughly, which contradicts the notions of the original contemporary Garage bands from Detroit.

The Hives have assimilated the label of Garage for a multitude of reasons. The immediately obvious one is for marketing purposes. This reason alone is often cited for their removal from the Garage underground, but their inclusion allows the majority of people to construct the label of Garage Rock in a specific way. The Hives are considered by those in the underground scene to be one of the first and few bands that used the underground culture of Garage as a means to achieve monetary success and capitalist gain.

There is a sense of resistance to the Hives by the underground of contemporary Garage. Due to the use of the label and the manipulation of the mainstream, many people align this band with mainstream music and associate them with sellouts or other derogatory terminology that demands their removal from the underground scene. The Hives' consistent marketing of the term Garage has forced them out of the underground and separated them from the pioneering contemporary bands. Their attitude is different, and the desire and goal of the band are structured with an entirely different approach than that of the original contemporary Garage groups, and this has led to their removal from the Garage underground.

The Strokes are another instance where the incorporation of a label has led to mainstream success. The Strokes share many similarities with contemporary Garage bands, and their output of music is linked more directly to 60s Garage Rock; but through their immediate incorporation into the mainstream, they have been viewed as apart from the underground movement. The Strokes are oftentimes viewed as being representations of what the mainstream label of Garage can do to a band's sound and appearance. Their most recent release, *Room on Fire,* is an attempt to regain an underground acceptance, since their first album of what was called Garage Rock was a result of the mainstream conception of the label.

The immediacy of the Strokes' success was the reason behind many participants removing of the group from the underground. It appeared as if the Strokes were simply manufactured to latch onto the trend of Garage, and this led the underground to align the group with mainstream ideals and representations of what can happen to music in the hands of the mainstream. The Strokes represented to many the exact opposite of what it meant to play Garage music. This is gradually changing, with the acceptance of the Strokes growing, but the band's beginnings led them into this classification.

What happens when groups like the Hives and the Strokes acquire the label of Garage Rock is a split within the underground scene and the beginnings of a dissolution that could have been prevented by the limiting of the label to a certain form or style. Contemporary Garage Rock consists of a multitude of musical styles and appearances and has been harmed by the bands and the music industry's marketing that has extended this label. Many people claim the White Stripes as Garage, alongside the Hives and the Strokes. These bands are vastly different in musical approach, their dress and image, and their relationship to the subculture of Garage. Even though each group has achieved mainstream success, they represent completely different styles of music.

While many bands continue to remain a part of the underground, there still remains differences in sound and approach to musical performance. This difference can be witnessed throughout the underground culture by comparing contrasting bands such as Wide Right and the Come Ons, both of whom have been labeled Garage bands. These groups are linked within the underground through the shows and venues that both play and the participants that continually group them together within the scene. The associations that both share with recording studios and record labels allows the comparison to be extended even without the music being considered. These two bands differ in style and song format but have been placed alongside one another under the moniker of Garage Rock.

The makeup of the bands are similar, with both having lead singers that are women, but that does not automatically make them Garage Rock. Both bands also recorded at Ghetto Recorders in order to achieve the raw sound that has been the focus of many Garage bands, but this is where the similarity between the bands ends. Their approach to music is extremely different in nature, with Wide Right focusing on a harder approach and lyrical content derived from the New York area, from Buffalo to Brooklyn, and the Come Ons offering a strong dance sound with a different lyrical focus. It is difficult to understand how these bands can be considered within the same label of music.

The grouping together of these two extremely different sounding bands by the majority of mainstream music critics prompts a new listener to believe that both will hold up to their vision of Garage Rock. The sound of both of these bands alone should separate them into different categories, but they continue to be linked within the same genre of music. This linking has allowed both bands access to success and popularity that would have been denied them had they not been associated with the label. By being considered under the same label, they have drawn audiences from differing scenes together to witness a different sound and style of music. By focusing on the approach to music as the link, both of these bands have succeeded by remaining apart from the overgeneralized notion of Garage Rock.

It is often assumed that offering a different sound or original approach to music is necessary for success. This is true, but when a label is generalized to include any type of music that has a certain attitude or element, the label and the first incarnation of the music begin to lose their focus and power. To play Garage in this postmodern era can mean many things, and herein lies the difficulty of a label. If a band attempts to play in a style called Garage, they are not considered a Garage band; but they *will* be considered as such if that band plays with a certain attitude and approach. It is this confusion that will eventually lead to the dissolution of the scene, and the term will revert back to the underground, exactly as was used in the 60s.

The different approaches to music have arisen through the multitude of influences to which many of the musicians have been exposed. As has been discussed, what is considered contemporary Garage is a hybrid of the British Invasion, the original 60s Garage Rock and many other formats. However, these differences lead to an extreme reliance on setting oneself above the conception of the label of Garage Rock. Recently, a large number of bands have attempted to further rebel against the mainstream conceptions of music.

This rebellion has come about due to the insistence of marketing representatives on labeling this particular musical style. The Dirtbombs, the Sights, Detroit City Council and others have begun to seek outsider status regarding this label as a way to set them apart from what is considered Garage by mainstream society. This re-constructs the band as a fully underground entity even when monetary rewards are gained. Through this rebellion these groups challenge what it means to be a member of the underground and mainstream. Here they are rebelling within the underground scene. All of these bands share similar characteristics in musical output and appearance and have at some point considered themselves Garage bands. As the label grew to include copycats and those simply willing to accept the label for monetary reasons, these bands have removed themselves from the Garage label in rebellion against the mainstream.

The importance of this rebellion against the label of Garage Rock cannot be overlooked. With the majority of the bands being labeled Garage falling outside the original conception of the term, the founding bands have again separated themselves into a different category. The category that has been established is one that resides outside of the label of Garage but within the original underground of Detroit. The underground takes on the most important aspect of this rebellion against the term Garage and continues to shape the way that bands view themselves. This attempt to remain outside of mainstream categorization again allows these bands to break into a form of individuality that is opposed to postmodern late capitalism.

With this form of rebellion occurring within the scene, the issue of whether or not the label of Garage has been a benefit or a hindrance becomes clearer. With the beginning of the scene came a realization that allowed many people the opportunity to group differing bands together. It was not necessarily the music being played but the rebellion against suburban ideals that brought these bands into similar groupings. This has been transformed into a means of marketing by the mainstream, and suburban ideals have begun to creep back into the scene and the music being played. With the instance of labeling often overshadowing the effectiveness of a band's music and talent, the scene has begun to split in two different directions.

The newer groups that are being labeled as Garage and allowing the label to stand are viewed by the underground as antithetical and sometimes even as a threat to the development of the music being played. The attitude of these new bands is often one that is geared towards capitalist goals of monetary and celebrity gain, and the music played is often limited compared to the original groups that were playing before the label of Garage was in place. When this occurs, the newer groups begin to develop outside of the current underground and attempt to play shows that are separated from the original bands. These new groups are detrimental to the scene because their musical prowess does not accurately reflect the original groups' outlook and approach.

The label of Garage Rock is even being used in a negative way by clubs and bands within Detroit. Even the Garden Bowl is beginning to hold nights labeled as Punk, without Garage Rock as their advertising point. "100% Garage Rock Free Thursdays" has begun at this venue, one of the founding places of the Garage scene. The event is viewed as a way to escape the label of Garage and remain outside of the mainstream classification of music. Records played during this event can be linked to original contemporary Garage, but the label is now different.

The withdrawal away from the label is now being seen as the way to reclaim the individuality of the scene in Detroit. When a band removes itself from the mainstream label it is a different type of assertion and continues the challenge to dominant mainstream music. This reclamation is demonstrating that the label of Garage Rock has finally pushed the music and the scene into the mainstream of contemporary culture. The aspect of non-acceptance of the mainstream has caused a backlash against the label of Garage Rock, but has also allowed for the proliferation of the culture throughout America and the world.

Without the label of Garage Rock, many of the bands that have achieved mainstream success would be limited in their appeal to new music fans. This limitation would have hindered many bands a great deal. With the White Stripes paving the way for a "new" type of sound within the mainstream, the label of Garage Rock took significant hold throughout the world and Detroit became the focus of the music and fan-based press. Although this withdrawal from the label has occurred, many of the original bands would not have achieved success without being grouped into the culture and scene.

The groups that began contemporary Garage did so in an effort to bring a new sound to the underground that was nostalgically rooted in Rock and Roll. With the incorporation of a label, they achieved success and began to influence others around the world. The labeling therefore allowed these groups to gain success, and now they are continuing their success by rebelling against the label that made them. The confusion is immense, but contemporary Garage Rock continues to thrive based on the band's relationship to the label that has been forced upon them.

At the onset of the contemporary Garage scene, many bands were playing a style of music that could not be lumped into a category. This limited many of these bands in playing shows and gaining widespread recognition. With Sympathy for the Record Industry grouping bands together for their seminal compilation, a new label began to be associated with the groups on this disc. This compilation allowed the original bands to be considered together, and a large number of performances and accolades followed. Labeling alone did not lead to the success of Garage Rock, but in the beginning it allowed for fans, booking agents, record labels and others to compose a notion of what these types of bands were attempting to do.

With the marketing of a label within music, the scene began to build and a new conception of Garage was forced into the underground, as well as mainstream society. This conception led to the incorporation of many bands that did not fit within the original conception of contemporary Garage Rock, and bands became popular based on very minimal differences. Jean Baudrillard states, "...the more conformist the system as a whole becomes, the more millions of individuals there are who are set apart by some tiny peculiarity."[5] Contemporary Garage Rock has become based on these differences and has gained recognition based on the incorporation of new styles under the moniker of Garage Rock. Along with this fame and mainstream acceptance comes the bands that have begun to rebel, and this again leads to their eventual popularity due to a small difference and outside stance regarding the mainstream.

The labeling of Garage Rock by the mainstream has benefited the underground status of Garage as well. By labeling a form of music and combining different groups under one moniker, the underground has again separated from the original stance within the movement. By aligning Garage Rock with a mainstream ideal, bands that are going against this ideal remain a part of the underground. Much like the similar occurrence in Punk, Garage has begun to split into what is being considered in the underground as groups that sell-out and others that remain in the underground. By aligning a band with either of these concepts, the fans and the underground are allowing for underground progress alongside the mainstream popularity.

Without the label of Garage Rock being significantly in place, the underground culture that has surrounded it would be limited in its structure and power. In the beginning, Garage Rock was a statement against the suburban ideals, and now it continues to promote that statement with even more authority due to its label. By denying the label of Garage Rock, the original bands, including the Sights and the Dirtbombs, have again subverted themselves to an underground status while achieving monetary gain and popularity within the label of Garage. In this way, the labeling of a subculture and the defining of a musical structure has allowed the underground to remain a responsive and thriving entity.

While other bands within the scene continually shape the sound that has been called Garage, the bands that continue to challenge these notions are beginning to break into the underground and mainstream. These bands, including Electric 6, the Wildbunch and others, have gained popularity by inserting a different sound into the Garage moniker. The majority of these bands cannot be considered Garage for one reason or another, but have received attention by going against the labeled notions of Garage Rock.

What begins to play a role in the labeling of a band as Garage are the concepts that are brought to the label. These concepts are generally predetermined by the reviewer's or critic's background and standpoint. It has come to the point where Garage represents completely different aspects depending on what the term means to the individual. Therefore, many differing bands have fallen into and out of the Garage label rapidly within the last few years. The label of Garage Rock means very different things to many people, and while this label once carried a rebellious connotation, it has now become immersed in the mainstream and is being rebelled *against*.

Garage Rock is focused on injecting something different into the mainstream and into underground musical society. This stems from the desire to rebel against the contrived norms of late capitalist America and mainstream musical constructions. The original 60s Garage bands were focused on the attainment of capital based on the assimilation of British Invasion style, while the contemporary scene is braced against such notions. To be a contemporary Garage band, the musical style and performance must be based on concepts that move away from the mainstream and break into a constructed individualism outside of the cultural norm. Also, contemporary Garage Rock must contain multiple referents to a past form of music or style, such as Delta Blues or Mod. These referents allow the participants in the scene to bear witness to a constructed break into individuality away from the late capitalist, postmodern world.

The label of Garage Rock can then be expanded to include multiple styles of bands and performance. The style range within the mainstream label is easily witnessed through the differences in the White Stripes and the Hives. The music played, the image appropriated and the formation of the groups are completely different, but these bands have been grouped together due to their insistence on representing past ideals in music and style of performance. By taking on nostalgic roles of rebellion, and by insisting on a return to the "real" form of Rock music, these and many other bands construct themselves as Garage bands.

These concepts of rebellion and nostalgia were crucial at the beginning of the contemporary Detroit Garage scene and continue to play a role in the association of bands with the label of Garage. The extent of a band's inclusion within the scene completely relies on these notions of rebellion and control. The participants and band members remove and accept bands based on these thought processes and continue to perpetuate the notions of the original contemporary groups. In order to be classified as a Garage band within these guidelines, the conscious or subconscious drive remains against the mainstream constructions of music and aligns with nostalgic aspects of rebellion.

With this distinction made, the issue of other types of music falling into this classification comes to the forefront. What differentiates groups that have been labeled Garage from bands playing other types of music is the reflection of certain time periods. With other forms of (especially underground) music there is a desire to reclaim a past form of musical presence and style. What distinguishes bands that have been labeled Garage is their attempt to reclaim music from the British Invasion and later Garage bands of the 60s. This is not the only aspect that unites the bands that have been labeled Garage, but the majority of these groups reflect this type of music, as opposed to others who reflect different periods and locations.

The impetus for deriving a classification of Garage Rock is based on a multitude of desires. Whether it is to claim a label for success or to insert a different type of music into the underground, these bands have stood on the classification of Garage as a way to gain acceptance and approval from the underground. Now that this label has been co-opted by the mainstream music press and recording industry, a backlash against the label of Garage has begun. For the majority of bands within the early contemporary scene, the label began as a way to associate with other bands and participants. The label of Garage Rock has again gone from the underground to the mainstream and back into the underground in a revolt against such a contrived label.

With the entirety of music being forced into labels and classification, contemporary Garage Rock has again found a way to stand against the mainstream contrivances of music and late capitalist suburbia. It is the bands that are again seeking a removal from the label that remain as the first incarnations of postmodern Garage Rock and continue to uphold the original premise of the underground scene. Garage Rock is a form of music that allows for the established notions of suburban capitalism and mainstream musical demands to be challenged through nostalgic representations of the British Invasion, Garage Rock of the 60s and later Mod culture.

PART II
Implications

7
Mainstreaming
the Underground

With the label of contemporary Garage Rock in place and the many instances of mainstream success, many people began to form certain alliances within the Garage Rock movement regarding the definition of Garage Rock, leading to the discussion of what has become mainstream and what remains in the underground. Within contemporary Garage Rock is a strong crossover from the underground to the mainstream that is not as violently opposed as in earlier underground musical movements. This is due to the bands' reliance on notions of anti-conformity and withdrawal from suburban capitalism. The aspect of bands crossing over into the mainstream of society has been detrimental to many underground movements, but for contemporary Garage Rock the expected downfall seems to have been limited in its effect. There are still instances where it is believed that certain groups have "sold out," but these are much less common within this movement than in those preceding it. The concept of giving in to mainstream capitalism and seeking fame from the general populous does not engender the same disdain within contemporary Garage Rock as it did in past underground scenes.

The surprising issue within the Garage scene is that the music is not specifically championing any kind of rebellion. Almost every other previous style of underground movement has been an attempt to deliberately challenge a faction of society. In this case, the Garage scene has often been viewed in a limited light. The scenes of Punk, Hardcore, and Grunge all played heavily into this rebellion against society. What the contemporary Garage scene is doing is even more subversive because it is using the mainstream in a way that attempts to destroy it from the inside. By almost embracing the success of bands that maintain underground ideals,

121

the scene states that these ideals are in some way something to strive for. This is the major contradiction within the scene and will eventually lead to dissolution as underground participants begin to lose faith in the musical movement.

Through the use of nostalgic representations and musical constructions, the contemporary Garage scene asserts its rebellion in a far less shocking and "in your face" manner than preceding scenes. The rebellion of Garage stems from a reversion back to past forms of rebellion within society, and is therefore slightly limited in its approach. This is not the screaming aggression against those in control of society as witnessed in Punk, or even the ironic detachment of Grunge. This is the rejection of the mainstream through an incorporation of older technologies and styles that subvert the contemporary trends of music and fashion. Subcultures have gone through all of the formats of rebellion and have reached a point where there is no way to shock the society without reusing past forms.

A pervasive postmodern thought is that everything has already happened or occurred. While this notion seems negative, it is the champion of postmodern times because with this thought anything becomes possible. This is easily witnessed through any form of pop culture in which multiple genres are crossed with minimal backlash from critics. Contemporary Garage Rock is no different in its postmodern outlook. The combination of past referents is the only way that the underground can attempt its rebellion. Herein lies the importance of nostalgia for the scene. Contemporary Garage Rock achieves its underground success by combining elements of past rebellion into a postmodern construction against the mainstream.

This construction is extremely important within society because it allows the music and scene to challenge the many facets of our present society. The main issues of rebellion here are not the government, a feeling of separation from society or even a hatred of mainstream music; they are ways to construct success and the means to attempt individualization. By assuming nostalgic dress and using methods of recording that reflect older technologies, the Garage scene rebels against mainstream capitalist ideals. While doing so, the scene structures itself within the realm of our postmodern times. Garage Rock then becomes a way to posit a sense of individuality within the current society. Without the occurrence of Garage Rock in music, society would be lacking in a way to construct itself outside of the dominant cultural sphere.

Looking at the surrounding music that has attempted a rebellion in recent times this issue can easily be observed. To begin with, a similar musical underground that has attained worldwide recognition and success, with roots in Detroit, is the dance culture of Techno and all of its variations. This scene is the pure representation of postmodernism in its reuse of songs, sounds and musical constructions within a completely different format. The Techno, House, Jungle and other variations of this musical scene incorporate any sound that can be found and use it to construct various forms of dance music. The scene began in an effort to bring people together and form a culture that was underground and very effective in its influence on the culture. To date, Detroit is still the home of dance culture around the world, where it holds its annual festival of Dance music—"Fuse In," formally called Movement.

The main difference between this underground and contemporary Garage Rock is that the Dance culture does not rebel but instead champions mainstream capitalist ideals in its construction. While the scene began in Detroit underground and had a gritty start, it used technology as a main component. It has now become something that anyone can do with the proper equipment and some creativity. This is not to limit the extreme artistry that it takes to construct and perform live within this scene, it is simply to say that the artists that began this scene and continue to be its main proponents use technology in a way that supports mainstream goals. By relying on technology so heavily that some performers use computers on stage in an effort to incorporate sounds and formats, members of this scene continue to reinforce the notion that one must have a certain amount of monetary capital to participate within the scene.

Contemporary Garage Rock began as a reaction against this type of musical construction within Detroit and the rest of the world. At the time of its inception, the city was limited in its live music, and the underground was dominated by sounds of the Electronic and Dance culture. This was Garage's rebellion and what continues to link individuals within the scene to the music of contemporary Garage Rock. The return to live music and performance that everyone can create with limited monetary means is a key aspect of the contemporary scene. By reverting to older technologies of musical performance and even musical construction, Garage Rock asserts that society must escape the present reliance on technology.

This form of rebellion is not as harsh as the preceding musical scenes, but it is more important in our postmodern times because without a musical movement rebelling in this way, one would be forced into mainstream offerings filled with technology and their slick production and performance. The way that contemporary Garage Rock uses nostalgia to construct itself is extremely powerful in the rebellion against our technologically advanced society. In a culture that assumes every individual has access to a computer and e-mail, Garage Rock reminds listeners that nostalgic formats of expression were, and still are, extremely beneficial and important. Herein lies the rebellion of the scene and why it has been welcomed throughout the world.

While the Punk scene in England and America were set against different cultural realms, they both expressed a focus on the failures of government and society to support every individual. The extreme lyrical content and powerful music was often seen as a way to scream against the mainstream and a threat to the surrounding society. When it was incorporated into the mainstream, it began to fail in its effort of rebellion and became limited in its shock value. Again, the effort that mainstream capitalism makes to thwart rebellion is easily viewed. The incorporation of a form of expression into shopping malls and fashion magazines put Punk on notice and inspired the famous expression that Punk is dead. Although the Punk movement stemmed from the Beat writers and musicians of the 50s, another purely postmodern movement, it was limited in its continued effect to go against the capitalist mainstream.

The contemporary Garage Rock scene is not as animated in its rebellion, but continues to insert a different viewpoint into society through the use of nostalgia. By doing so, the scene is often viewed differently from Punk, but it is still making a strong statement about the way to seek individualization within society. Many performers within the scene are rooted in the Punk movement and have developed this sensibility into a musical style that reflects and incorporates the rebellion of Punk but with a different aesthetic. With this, the Garage scene continues to rebel against the same society as Punk but in a way that maintains connection to the mainstream.

Rebellion in postmodern times is limited and complicated by the multitude of definitions of rebellion. Contemporary Garage Rock states that the only way left to rebel is to manipulate past forms of rebellion into a constructed individualism against the capitalist mainstream. While this is not as obvious as the Punk movement's rebellion, it is effective in the postmodern construction of rebellion. Looking at how some of the most famous artists of the postmodern world rebelled can easily demonstrate this aspect of rebellion. From Andy Warhol to Jack Kerouac and countless others, the incorporation of past elements into a new form with the most basic of instruments was the key to rebellion.

These artists chose to combine multiple past influences into a constructed form that became their own. This has often been viewed in a manner that gives these artists credibility within society. Contemporary Garage Rock is reinstating these artistic theories of use and nostalgia, and continuing postmodern thought about constructed art. Whether it is Warhol's soup can or Kerouac's *On the Road*, the postmodern means of recombining past articles to form a new creation is present. The entirety of contemporary Garage rests on these notions of collective nostalgia and benefits from the postmodern use of the past.

All of these previous movements within the underground shared an extreme desire to break away from mainstream accumulations of wealth and success. The most readily accessible example is that of the Punk movement in its disdain for bands signing with mainstream record labels and achieving monetary success by following these companies' demands. This has always seemed a logical development in underground movements. With contemporary Garage Rock, these instances seem to be limited in their focus and scope within the underground participants of the scene.

There are many examples of bands that have achieved mainstream success and have not been considered sell-outs by the underground. It is these bands that challenge the preconceived notions of what is meant to be an underground band. While these bands allow this distinction to be made, they also challenge the underground's notions of what is meant by mainstream and what it is to be a sell-out. Contemporary Garage Rock is concerned with opposing suburban ideals of late capitalism. The bands that have gained mainstream success can be viewed as supporting these suburban ideals and notions, but are not removed as quickly within the current underground as Punk bands who played within the mainstream ideals.

The band that immediately springs to mind regarding this crossover is the White Stripes. Many people within the underground still consider this band to be a strong part of the culture. This band has achieved an immense amount of mainstream exposure and acclaim, even being considered as the world's dignitaries of contemporary Garage Rock by the mainstream press. They have achieved their success through notions that remain consistent within the underground movement of Garage and remain as ideals of the postmodern Garage movement. Their inherent crossover to the mainstream has led the White Stripes to late capitalist suburban accomplishment, but their musical presentation and performance style allows them to remain within the underground.

With the White Stripes' mainstream accomplishments also comes the discerning nature of the underground participants regarding their musical style and performance. When the White Stripes were beginning, they were seen within the underground as a band that was challenging the preexisting notions of Rock and Folk music. They became the emissaries of Garage Rock during their first European tour and gradually gained mainstream acceptance. What becomes extremely important is that they have never lost their ties to the underground and the respect of its participants. This has led to the White Stripes gaining even more popularity through the incorporation of the underground with the mainstream. When the underground ideals are put into realistic terms, the White Stripes conceptualize and encourage success through them.

While the White Stripes are emblematic, many more bands remain a part of the underground and have shaped the mainstream reactions to and about contemporary Garage Rock. There are countless numbers of bands that rely on their underground participation to achieve local and regional success. While accomplishing this through the use of the label of Garage Rock, these bands allow the incorporation of the notions of underground Garage Rock into the subculture of America. These ideas are strongly adhered to amongst the bands that remain a part of this dominating underground movement.

One of the main bands that have strongly stuck with the underground notions of rebellion and anti-suburbia is the Von Bondies. This band has remained a vital part of the underground culture while attaining limited mainstream success. Their style of performance and the aspects of their rebellious fashion allow them to remain a part of the underground and at the forefront of exposing mainstream music to underground developments. They remain on the threshold of mainstream success and regard this success with an air of rebellious indifference. Their underground status has not been questioned and they remain as proponents of the subcultural status of contemporary Garage Rock.

The Von Bondies do not let the distinction between mainstream and underground play an influential part in their musical development. They stand solidly behind their original intent to play music rooted in real Rock and Roll and to rebel against late capitalist suburbia. While doing so they have garnered the attentions of many mainstream record labels and have been exposed throughout the mainstream musical community. They have also continually upheld the underground aspects of contemporary Garage Rock and allowed for these aspects to break into mainstream musical society.

While the Von Bondies strengthen the underground's rebellion through these elements, they are also linked with other groups that remain solely enmeshed in the underground of contemporary Garage Rock. Bands such as Detroit City Council and the Dirtbombs still remain a part of the underground in which they began. They claim to be asserting their underground status by rebelling against the labeling of music and involving themselves in the debate against popular musical conceptions, but they are still aligned with mainstream goals of success. All of these groups seek acceptance through rebellion against the mainstream, and it is this aspect that has allowed for many groups to cross over into the mainstream without an attendant removal from the underground.

This occurs often in the postmodern late capitalist world. Many bands have played completely into underground notions of rebellion only to be easily accepted into the mainstream through it. Society has often viewed these issues of rebellion as concepts readily available for mass market assimilation, and, as Fredric Jameson states, "...even overtly political interventions like those of *The Clash* are all somehow secretly disarmed and reabsorbed by a system of which they themselves might well be considered a part, since they can achieve no distance from it."[1] The secrecy of capitalist manipulation of the underground is not a large factor in contemporary Garage Rock and creates an opening within society for the bands to belong to both the mainstream and underground networks. With the acceptance of rebellion and anti-suburban goals as mainstream concepts, the contemporary Garage bands that remain a part of the underground set a strong value on musical production.

When musical production becomes such a strong factor, it serves to solidify the participants' notions of what is truly to be considered Garage Rock. Through the confusion of the Garage label, the decision of what bands to include within the underground is left to members of the scene. This power of determination continues the insistence on the style of music played and the production quality of recordings. The question then becomes: which mainstream bands continue to represent the underground ideals and which ones are merely using the underground in an attempt to gain success? This difference is entirely dependant on how the construction of Garage Rock is viewed by each participant, again granting the power of determination to the individual.

With this granted power, the notions that have been discussed as representative of contemporary Garage Rock come to the forefront. The bands that continue the proliferation of ideals away from suburban capitalism through the use of nostalgic representations are the groups that remain within the underground of Garage Rock, whether or not they gain mainstream success. This plays an important role in the determination of continued acceptance by removal from the underground when mainstream success is gained. The musical production and recording strategies can vary, but the ideals must remain for the band to continue the association with both the mainstream and the underground.

Without certain bands remaining within the underground of Garage Rock, the groups that achieve mainstream success would exist completely outside of a movement or development in culture. The validity of these underground bands and their attempts at rebellion coincides with the success of the mainstream versions, and the reverse is also true. Without the existence of groups such as the Von Bondies alongside bands such as the White Stripes, each representation would be limited in its appeal to both underground and mainstream participants.

Instances such as these have occurred in the vast majority of musical developments. With contemporary Garage Rock there seems to be a difference. Contemporary Garage Rock does not incite similar responses from mainstream and underground participants as the Punk movement did. The Punk community takes an extremely strict stance on fitting in to the contrived notions of the underground, but this is not the case within Garage Rock. These assertions of the underground can determine the inherent differences when it comes to the removal of bands from what is considered Punk and how this differentiation occurs within contemporary Garage Rock.

The original assertions of Punk stem from anti-conformity and anti-establishment viewpoints and how the scene is constructed through musical form. While these rely on bands supporting common viewpoints, they created an environment that was based on individuality and denial of certain traits that did not coincide with specific underground beliefs. These characteristics led the Punk movement toward an isolationist outlook that was founded on these traits and focused attention on diverting societal aspects to Punk norms. While bands in the Punk movement champion these concepts, there are many that have been disassociated with the underground through the attainment of popular success. The differences between Garage and Punk stem from the origination of musical and fan direction, and this has allowed for the proliferation of these differences in both underground communities.

Those that began the Garage Rock scene were attempting to separate themselves from the suburban music and style that surrounded them, whereas Hardcore and Punk offered music attempting to thwart the system or state a working-class mentality. This difference occurred within the specific context of Detroit and the surrounding suburbs. The relationship between the city and the suburbs of Detroit is a difficult and often extremely harsh one that is continuously demonstrated within the Garage scene. While both lifestyles have their place within the scene, the city is often used in an effort to disassociate from the suburbs. This break point within the communities of Michigan is extremely easy to witness from the interior, but to those outside of the state it is much more difficult to discern.

The main distinction between this city-suburb relationship in Detroit and that of other metropolitan cities is that the city of Detroit is not fully supported by the surrounding suburbs. In comparison to its closest big-city neighbor, Chicago, Detroit's surrounding suburbs neglect it. This occurs due to the surrounding cities steadfast determination to remain autonomous on every level. The lack of financial and cultural support from local cities has caused Detroit to become a city isolated from the surrounding suburbs by more than just physical location. This has led to an extreme difference of mentality between those who actually live within the city and those that use the city to physically or emotionally flee from their surroundings. The contemporary Garage scene has taken this aspect of suburban withdrawal and incorporated it into its music and outlook on life.

The members of the beginning contemporary bands were often originally from the suburbs, and they used the music and the culture to distance themselves from the traditional values that the suburbs implied. Many were simply rebelling from the suburban lifestyle and attempting to insert a difference into the surrounding community. Suburban society

has failed many participants in the scene in their attempt at individualization, so they are forced to rebel against it in order to construct themselves. Daniel Traber, in his study of the Punk scene in L.A., suggests,
"The extreme conditions of the sub-urban life are not ones many of them
are forced into by their parents' financial problems, so by turning away
from suburbia they challenge America's cherished shibboleths of prosperity and progress."[2] The participants in contemporary Garage Rock are
not simply fighting against a system of control; they are rebelling against
America's perceived suburban norms—the norms that dictate how many
subjects relate to one another. These issues have been questioned before,
but in a different and more abrasive way. This challenge is the biggest
difference between the preceding movements and contemporary Garage,
but one that is also extremely important in its statement and use of nostalgia.

The origination of contemporary Garage Rock was similar to Punk,
with its anti-conformist viewpoint. It differed in the outlook on society
that the beginning Garage bands put forward. Contemporary Garage
Rock began in an effort to insert a difference into the current musical
environment, with a determination to gain success. Garage Rock differs
from Punk in the notion that through the attainment of success a band
does not necessarily lose credibility. Through this extreme difference
from Punk, contemporary Garage Rock has allowed bands that have
achieved mainstream success to continue as members of the underground
networks of fans and musicians.

The bands that have remained a part of these networks continue to
support the city of Detroit and the underground bands and participants.
Whether this support comes from sitting in with other bands that are on
the rise or from giving opening slots to such bands, the groups that have
achieved mainstream success continue to show loyalty to the original
scene. Whenever the White Stripes play a show in Detroit, they book
less recognized local bands to play in their opening slot. The support
shown by this band for the local scene is completely different from the
attitude taken by mainstream Punk bands.

Underground Garage bands desire mainstream success. The original bands, and the ones that followed, were not attempting to remain in
the underground for street credibility or any other reason. They were
driven, either subconsciously or consciously, towards the attainment of
mainstream success. While many kept this drive hidden, within the

Garage underground there is not the same disdain for mainstream success as that witnessed within the underground Punk movement. Like the original Garage bands of the 60s, the modern day rebirth is goal-oriented towards some form of success. With these concepts in place, the aspect of confronting mainstream capitalist desires within the underground movement becomes challenging.

When attitudes that revolve around late capitalist suburban constructions of success inundate an underground culture, the typical underground culture begins to dissolve. With this occurrence, many underground movements have failed and have lost recognition due to the confrontation of goals and desires. Through the incorporation of capitalist desires into the underground bands, participants begin to see the conflict between desires. Underground members begin to argue with one another over certain bands representing capitalist intent and others maintaining complete underground beliefs. This has been witnessed in many previous underground musical movements and remains a fear of underground fans and participants.

With contemporary Garage Rock, the installation of capitalist desires has weakened the scene, but not to the point of threatening the underground's development. The instances of bands attaining mainstream success are not viewed with as much distrust and hatred as has been witnessed in previous transitions, and this has allowed Garage Rock to remain as an underground movement. The aspect of capitalist desires incorporating into the underground has encouraged a new type of band to form alongside the development of Garage Rock. Many bands have been formed in an effort to recapture the original aspects of Garage Rock and, in doing so, continue the proliferation of underground desires alongside mainstream demands. The inclusion of these groups under the label of Garage has led to the continuation of the Garage scene within underground networks.

With this continuation is the assumption that many bands will continue their pursuit of mainstream goals. This allows many of the underground groups to remain antithetical to the bands that reach mainstream success. Bands that continue to display this reaction to mainstream groups reassert the original feelings of contemporary Garage Rock. These concepts have been used in the past by groups that remain challenging to the mainstream ideals and capitalist notions of success in order to advance into the underground.

The pursuit of such goals and achievements is not uncommon in society, and when bands begin to cross into the mainstream realm, it is imperative that they remain as fixed points of rebellion within the cultural sphere. In order for the underground to continue and remain relevant, it must keep this rebellion throughout the mainstream. The mainstream must then be used in a way that proclaims the notions of the underground and does not subvert them. John Seabrook discusses this aspect regarding the advent of MTV and the Web within our culture from the very beginning, stating that "the mainstream market, once the enemy of the artist, even began to acquire a kind of integrity, insofar as it represented a genuinely populist expression of the audience's preferences."[3] The concept of genuine representation is what contemporary Garage Rock is attempting to reinsert into the mainstream. The bands that have achieved mainstream acceptance must continue to demonstrate the original underground ideals. It is when bands begin to follow the mainstream demands from the record labels and producers that the original intent begins to fail and the audience's original preference for the group begins to change.

The notions of individuality that contemporary Garage Rock's underground encourages are based (as previously discussed) on rebelling against suburban capitalism and using nostalgic representations to break into an attempted individuality. With these in place, it is necessary for the underground to assert their place within the musical scene. Without these assertions being upheld by the majority of bands, including the groups that break into the mainstream, the underground would be limited in its effects. This importance cannot be understated in the effect on the growth and development of the underground scene both within and outside of mainstream conception.

Alongside this development are the concepts that allow both cultures of music, mainstream and underground, to coincide with each other (as opposed to previous musical movements). Many of the underground participants consider groups that have made the break into mainstream music as not antithetical to the other groups that remain in the underground. With this attitude, the participants are encouraging, or at least allowing, the continuation of the desire to gain mainstream success. Without the participation of the people within the underground and the acceptance of groups that have achieved this mainstream success, the underground scene would begin its dissolution.

This aspect has been thwarted within the Garage Rock scene by the consistent reliance on mainstream depictions of rebellion and with the inclusion of events and representations that are put forward through mainstream outlets. In a sense, the underground scene continues to use mainstream cultural outputs to self-determine their independence. Without these mainstream assertions within the underground, contemporary Garage Rock would be limited in its effect. Therefore many groups and participants within the scene mandate the use of the mainstream to control the development of the underground. This allows for the continuation of both mainstream and underground developments alongside one another.

This allows underground culture and ideals to reshape mainstream musical thought. This can easily be witnessed through the many bands that are now simply guitar and drums–based, following the White Stripes' success. Leslie Haynsworth discusses the differentiation within society and determines that "the underground has begun to affect the mainstream while coexisting with it. Scholars such as Raymond Williams and others also allow for the possibility that subcultures can, albeit in perhaps limited ways, reshape the dominant culture in their own image."[4] This reshaping is a result of the insistence on underground ideals remaining within the bands and participants of the scene. Without a strong relationship to nostalgic thought and a determination to remain as a representative of the underground, many bands would not remain successful in the eyes of the participants.

This occurrence has been perpetuated throughout many underground music scenes and immediately challenges the notions of what it means to be a part of the underground. Peter Wicke, in his article on Rock music and society, claims, "Commercially produced mass culture on the one hand and the sub-cultures with their class-specific organization on the other merely form differing cultural contexts and relationships around the same objects."[5] It is this similarity that also allows for the myriad of groups to coexist within both realms. The organization of underground bands alongside mainstream groups stems from the aspect of similar objects playing a role in determination and allowing underground ideals to remain alongside mainstream acceptance.

These objects of similarity between both the mainstream and underground reflect the close relationship between both types of events in contemporary Garage Rock. While incorporating Hollywood signs of rebellion, the underground appropriates mainstream notions into underground music. This is merely one example of the inclusion of mainstream output in the underground, but this example allows for many mainstream bands, such as Black Rebel Motorcycle Club, to remain alongside underground developments within music. Also, with this acceptance of mainstream objects and incorporation, contemporary Garage Rock inserts its differing notion of what it means to be involved with the underground into musical society. The importance of contemporary Garage Rock's stance on these mainstream objects holds great power and control over what is considered underground and mainstream, as both musical spheres play alongside each other.

The ideals that were originally expressed within Garage Rock must continue to be portrayed when groups have been granted mainstream success in order for their underground popularity to continue. If bands that break into the mainstream sphere of music do not continuously champion these ideals, they fail within the underground conception of Garage music. This can be seen with the Hives in contemporary Garage Rock.

The Hives, originally, came onto the scene with nostalgic representations of dress and performance but failed to continue their assertion of underground ideals of Garage. This has led to their failure to be accepted within the underground networks of contemporary Garage Rock. They achieved short-lived mainstream success, but are considered by the majority of underground participants to be the embodiment of what mainstream ideals do to Garage music. With their incorporation of mainstream Hollywood depictions of rebellion, the Hives displayed a break from the traditional notions of mainstream music; however, they have not continued to champion this, and consequently failed within the underground.

The underground of contemporary Garage Rock continually asserts notions of rebellion against capitalist constructions of conformity and success. By doing so alongside bands that have achieved what is considered mainstream capitalist success, they have championed the existence of mainstream ideals alongside underground notions of music. This seems contradictory, but in doing so, Garage Rock has continued its successful ascent into musical society, and allowed underground networks and bands to remain and play within conceptions of success. Many bands have championed both mainstream and underground spheres of Garage Rock, and these bands have become successful based on their determination to communicate underground ideals within the mainstream sphere.

It is these bands that lead the challenge of contemporary Garage

Rock against completely mainstream, late capitalist notions of suburban success. They also most importantly assert the challenge of Garage Rock against the control of our subjectivity through capitalist ideals. While many underground bands do so, it is the groups that have achieved mainstream success and still champion underground ideals that lead this challenge. When bands such as the White Stripes and the Von Bondies broke into the mainstream of musical society through playing music and performing in the same manner as that of the underground, they took a strong stance against capitalist control of subjectivity.

By asserting this challenge, these bands continue the strong desire of underground participants to remain outside of suburban capitalist demands. They are allowed to remain as constructions of the underground and are not considered as sell-outs. The insistence against popular mainstream recording techniques and performance expectations continues the strong battle over late capitalist control of subjectivity. Whether they succeed is still to be determined, but it allows the majority of participants to view a strong statement within the conception of society in America. It is this assertion that allows mainstream bands to remain part of the underground conception of Garage Rock. When groups fail to accomplish this, they become removed from the underground conception of Garage Rock and become immersed in thoughts of destroying the underground desires of contemporary Garage Rock.

To fully reside within or alongside both spheres, bands must maintain their desire to rebel against mainstream concepts of capitalist control and success. Even monetary success must remain secondary in an effort to assert this premise. The desire for monetary gain must be subverted through the presentation of the band to the continuation of underground desires. The groups that continually do this achieve it through the use of nostalgic representations and musical differences in production and performance. When all of these elements are not present, mainstream success will alienate the underground participants.

There is a constant subconscious desire of many Garage bands that achieve mainstream success to present themselves in the press and through performances as continually linked to the underground through their assertion against capitalist desire and control. One must only look at the White Stripes' insistence on playing smaller venues. Especially in Detroit, the White Stripes continue to play in smaller venues than their ticket sales would warrant. A band that has attained the kind of mainstream success that the White Stripes have garnered typically plays concerts at large arena stadiums in an attempt to generate as much monetary wealth as possible. The White Stripes, however, choose to play smaller theaters such as the Masonic Temple in an effort to express their continued link to the underground. The White Stripes go against the assumed constructions of mainstream performance and perpetuate the break away from capitalist control of the groups and the participants' subjectivity.

In doing so, the White Stripes assume a position of marketability by controlling their venue selection and ticket sales every time they play, but they are viewed by many participants as the champions of this style. They are also considered to be holding up the values of the underground within the mainstream sphere due to this insistence on small venues. Many groups have followed their lead, allowing for the challenge against capitalist control to remain alongside the determination of the underground. When this attempt begins to fail, or the facade crumbles, the White Stripes and other bands that participate in this manner will begin to lose underground acceptance.

The mainstreaming of the contemporary Garage underground encourages the bands and participants to challenge postmodern late capitalist constructions of success. To further this challenge is the goal of contemporary Garage, and many other underground musical movements. The methodology of Garage Rock revolves around its use of nostalgia, thereby injecting a strong statement into the mainstream cultural arena. By doing so, bands that achieve mainstream success and continue to proliferate underground ideals demonstrate a break away from capitalist control over subjectivity. Through constructing this break, bands that challenge late capitalist suburban notions of subjectivity maintain consistent ties to both mainstream and underground cultural spheres. These groups have been allowed to remain part of the underground conception of contemporary Garage Rock, and have allowed for the mainstreaming of the underground within the music of Garage Rock.

8

Nostalgic Benefits

In postmodern times, nostalgia has been constructed in a negative light that is often limiting to societal constructions of self. Consequently, the beneficial aspect of nostalgia on the discussion of constructed individuality is left behind. Contemporary Garage Rock benefits from the use of nostalgia when participants construct a form of their individuality through the incorporation of nostalgic dress and ideals. It is this use of nostalgia that has come to play an immense role in the movement of postmodern Garage Rock and its assertion of attempted control of self. Nostalgic benefits within the underground scene are determined from the formation of a band. Through incorporation within the mainstream, these benefits are witnessed by a large amount of participants, and this nostalgia is perpetuated within the cultural sphere. Although the concept of individuality is often considered as unreachable, the subjectivity of the participants of contemporary Garage Rock is based on nostalgic actions and thought. While many people in late capitalist America construct notions of individuality through the use of capitalist appearances and ideals, Garage Rock asserts a difference that has not been seen within previous underground movements and accounts for an aspect of popularity and appeal within the scene.

Late capitalist America harbors an extreme desire to remain independent and individualized. While some may argue that this is unattainable, it is the notions, concepts and ideals that are put forward in this attempt that allow for postmodern thought and action to occur. These concepts have generally been regarded in a negative light and seen as limiting in their potential to gain an aspect of self; but within postmodern times, society still clings to these in an often futile attempt at self-realization. Within American society, these concepts revolve around notions of late capitalism and its effect on societal structures. American society has become rooted in capitalist notions of success and has continuously used these notions in an effort to reclaim individuality. To many people in America, capitalist goals determine their subjectivity. The conflict arises when these goals are challenged in a similar attempt at self-actualization.

A general discussion of nostalgia usually revolves around the negative connotations and thoughts behind the terminology and occurrence. Nostalgia is generally viewed as a method of upholding old-fashioned thoughts about gender, race, class and familial structure by reclaiming certain aspects of the past for self-determined goals. The majority of critics and scholars that discuss nostalgia are attempting to rid postmodern society of nostalgic concepts, with some going so far as ascribing a death to nostalgia. Kirk Curnutt, in *GenXegesis: Essays on Alternative Youth (Sub)culture*, even suggests that nostalgia is used in marketing to create a split: "By breaking history into discrete units of pop-culture styles, nostalgia exaggerates the discontinuity between periods, rendering even relatively contiguous moments remote, distanced, and disconnected."[1] This line of reasoning is a limiting conceptual thought process when a country, such as America, is so rooted in nostalgic desires. To discuss the faults of nostalgia, the conceptual notion of nostalgia must be the focus.

The concept of nostalgia stems from the definition of homesickness that was used to discuss soldiers' reactions to being on the front lines of war, allowing for a series of disease-and-cure-related hypotheses to be instilled within the societal framework. Nostalgia is often discussed with this definition as a starting point, moving from the concept of a longing for home to a more abstract definition of longing for the past. In postmodern thought and terminology, nostalgia focuses on this longing for a specific past time period and continues on towards a past form of society. While this is still the case within the majority of nostalgic thought, it is the discussion of nostalgia in a negative way that needs to be challenged.

To view nostalgia as negative, one must begin by making different assumptions about nostalgia. To many, nostalgia fails to represent the past accurately due to the conceptions held and expressed by the subject. It depends on *who* is nostalgic as to what characterizes the time period discussed. Two subjects may become nostalgic for the same time period and come to completely different conclusions. This is where negative concepts surrounding nostalgia gain their support. To the man growing up in the 50s, to be nostalgic for that time period may mean that women are in the kitchen and the kids are perfectly behaved, when in reality this situation rarely occurred. The false representations of nostalgic thought allow for the constructions of negativity towards race, class structures, gender, etc., and allow for critical discussion on how nostalgic thought leads to limited societal constructions.

Throughout postmodern criticism, this insistence on a negative construction of nostalgia is prevalent. The use of nostalgia is generally constructed in a way that discusses limitations of the preceding society. With the focus on the 50s in America, the limitations of social class and gender are often clearly visible. These must be thought of as constructions that existed but were often construed in such a way that allowed people to benefit as well. Stephanie Coontz suggests, "Even people who found that moral order grossly unfair or repressive often say its presence provided them with something concrete to push against."[2] This desire for change was set up in relationship to social determination. With postmodern nostalgia, many people tend to reference the decade of the 50s in a way that shows it as limiting, when in reality this limitation was and is beneficial to cultural criticism.

This limitation plays a large role in the determination of self within postmodern times. By allowing a limited view of a time period that one is almost completely removed from, nostalgia gives the subject the opportunity to construct self in relationship to it. The nostalgic use of the past centers on memories and what is shown through the media. In order for nostalgia to become beneficial, society must continuously challenge the notions of what the media represents. Contemporary Garage Rock centers on portraying this nostalgia in a way that forces the question of the reliability of images from the past.

Within this construction of nostalgia is the criticism of nostalgia as failing the progression of society. Critics often reference nostalgic events in a way that shrouds them in negativity towards progress. While this can be easily witnessed in a discussion of race, class and gender, it is a constructed notion that is limiting in many ways. The argument stems from the notion that nostalgia allows the subject to forget the present and descend into a thought process that limits the impact of the present. An example of this criticism comes from John Frow when he states, "our world is characterized by an acceleration of history and thus by the slippage of the present into a past where it disappears from consciousness."[3]

It is this movement that has become the focus of the majority of the critics of nostalgia. What has been labeled as slippage has been reincorporated within postmodern times to reflect differing aspects of subjectivity.

While the concept of losing the present in favor of the past is often times valid, nostalgic thought places a distinction on differing time periods in an effort to comprehend the present, not to disallow it. In order to state that nostalgic thought forces a loss of the present, one must ascribe to a thought process that puts the present time period ahead of the past. Many people claim that nostalgia limits our ability to distinguish the present from the past. Nostalgia is being used significantly as a way towards the reincorporation of past ideals within the present cultural sphere. This does not limit the view of the present but perpetuates the discussion on the lack of the present in our search for subjectivity.

Through this occurrence, many subjects are drawn to nostalgia in an attempt to displace the present negativity of society. While this does limit the expression of the present, it also allows for the continuation of the past as a strong influence on the present. Through this notion, nostalgia gains a strong reinvention against the incorporation of present postmodern occurrences. While the claim of disappearance is relevant, it fails to consider the importance of nostalgic thought in the determination of self. Without a sense of the past and strong nostalgia, many subjects would fail in constructing their individualism. The movement of the present into the past is necessary in the continual search for the constructed individual in postmodern times.

While nostalgia is often seen in a negative light (as a slippage away from the present), this criticism of nostalgia has been viewed with disdain lately by those enamored of nostalgic thought. For the majority of Americans, nostalgia allows for a remembrance of a perceived better time in American society. This may be faulty, but through the use of nostalgia comes the desire to reclaim a certain aspect of past Americanism that is relevant to subjectivity. To limit the discussion of nostalgia only to negative constructions allows for the benefits of nostalgia to go unnoticed. It is relatively easy to continue a discussion about the negative concepts of nostalgia; however, through positive assertions of nostalgia, many people attempt to gain their subjectivity away from late capitalist desires.

Throughout society, multiple reconstructions have allowed access to a feeling of nostalgia. These reconstructions have mostly been limited to a type of nostalgia that has been perceived with negativity. Movies and television that construct the past, specifically the 50s, as a "perfect" lifestyle are deemed insufficient in their attempt to ascertain our current society. These types of constructions of society's past are often made in order to demonstrate how the present postmodern society is superior. Movies such as *Pleasantville, Back to the Future* and others have used such constructions as a way to show that the current time is more advanced.

This attempt to demonstrate separation from the past is greatly abused by Hollywood. Movies like this have made millions of dollars based on their flawed and underdeveloped representations of our past. These movies allow Americans to view their own society in this way and feel superior, much like how they feel about a third world civilization that is considered undeveloped. This leads to the majority of critics and audience members to view the past and these nostalgic representations as flawed and undeserving of comment.

What needs to be asserted is the premise that these nostalgic representations serve as much more than simple reminders of how far society has come. As these images of the past allow one to feel superior, they also serve as representations of a lifestyle to which many people are drawn. The image of the *Leave It to Beaver*–type family, though considered flawed by many people, has increasingly become more appealing to people in the postmodern world. In a time of increasing divorce and family restructuring, the "nuclear" family is seen as a depiction of falsehood that many people aspire to achieve. These nostalgic representations are becoming reshaped again into the desirable depiction of family life. Although most people are aware that this type of family structure could never occur again, there is a drive to reclaim this type of family setting in our late capitalist world.

This drive can be connected to society's suburban migration. With this migration came the desire to reclaim the family as a place where people spend the majority of their time outside of daily activities such as work and school. These movies, such as *Pleasantville* and *Back to the Future*, attempt to reclaim a view of family as consisting of members that are happy spending time together; in current society, this has again come to be something that is strived for but more often remains unrealized. According to Laura J. Miller in her article "Family Togetherness and the Suburban Ideal," "...the suburban ideal has, from its beginnings, been associated with a particular vision of family life. This vision regards the family not only as a domestic alliance that creates a household to take care of its members' basic needs for food and shelter, but also as a group of people who enjoy one another's company and share leisure pursuits."[4] This ideal, striven for but not often realized, is depicted through nostalgic representations within these movies.

This attempt to reclaim the ideal family arises from the extreme demand of capitalist conformity. At the present time society is completely focused on desires to conform to the capitalist constructed world. With this desire in place, subjects are forced to look to nostalgic representations to find a way out of these constructions. This leads to society looking towards such familial constructions as a way to break out of the current notion of both parents having to work in order to provide adequately for their children. These nostalgic representations also allow people to construct ways of life that have been found lacking. By viewing these nostalgic representations as good for the postmodern society, subjects strive to find their way outside of capitalist goals.

Postmodern goals and constructions of the family are not merely limited to capitalist desires. These goals are relative to individual experience but become constructions of our society in every way. These goals include raising children in a nurturing environment, making enough money to be happy, and keeping up with the Joneses. With these goals in place, society becomes mired in its desire to fulfill capitalist images of family. Movies that depict families from the 50s as flawed allow these postmodern goals to assert themselves. It becomes interesting when these movies are considered as a way to escape from capitalist constructions of conformity.

The movie *Pleasantville* depicts the 50s family as a construction that must be saved from itself. When David and his sister Jennifer are thrown into the past society from the postmodern world, Jennifer becomes determined to save this society by inserting the postmodern world into it. As the movie progresses, she attempts to fix a society that is considered flawed because of its lack of knowledge. Throughout the movie is the extreme desire to come back to present-day society. With her attempt to reconstruct that society as her own, one realizes that it is not always better to progress with knowledge.

When Jennifer asserts her viewpoint in the perfect community of Pleasantville, the community begins to change. With a small conversation about sex with her mother, the society of Pleasantville begins to shift. This change is seen from the beginning as a positive thing and continues through to the end to expose the audience to a way of thinking about the past as something that was sheltered from itself through lack of knowledge. In the postmodern world, one tends to view society as in decay, but through the nostalgic representations of *Pleasantville,* one begins to see that it is a better place due to the continuing progression of knowledge and thought.

This progression is viewed as the preferred society in the late capitalist world. Viewers begin to believe the main character's assertion that this is for the best, and then rely on her to change the entire town. When this occurs, the movie begins to be seen as a normal construction of capitalist desire. The family should be able to do what they desire, and both parents should be able to work to support their family. These desires change the community in the movie and allow the viewer to witness a change of society. When this occurs, the flaws of this change within society become visible. The characters in the movie begin to assert capitalist desires and to reflect the postmodern times, with all of its dilemmas.

Viewers of this movie can easily see the faulty construction of this past and the need for change. This movie, however, also demonstrates nostalgic representations of the past as a way to break away from complete capitalist reliance. Although *Pleasantville* is a Hollywood construction of this past, it constructs a view of the family that is desirable. This construction has become desirable due to society's immersion in the late capitalist world. The society depicted within this movie is seen as lacking but also as a desirable alternative to the current situation.

By viewing an alternative to the current familial structure, the opportunity to break away from postmodern capitalist desires is presented. Although this construction is still a part of the postmodern time, the 50s, it has come to represent an outside opinion of the current time. This current opinion restricts the family under the hegemonic will of late capitalism. With movies such as *Pleasantville,* an alternative to the current submission to this will, and an attempt to discern a way into a different construction, is placed into the surrounding culture.

Nostalgic representations of familial constructions are centered on many things that the postmodern world deems faulty. These include Hollywood stereotypes and visions that have been deemed sexist and flawed in our contemporary time. The notion of the wife being relegated to the kitchen and serving as the only homemaker has come to be considered undesirable and sexist within postmodern times, but these constructions of family structure also come to represent a somewhat desirable alternative to the current familial state within America.

Many people view these constructions as a way to get back to a more family centered time within society. By going against the capitalist desire that the more money one possesses the happier one will be, these familial constructions allow a view of a time when family came before money. By viewing these constructions through movies, a different type of family that finds a way out from under capitalist control is offered as an example.

As discussed, the concept of nostalgia relies on the faulty representation of the past, but it is through this specific representation, even though faulty, that many people gain a sense of belonging and self. American society is interlaced with notions of nostalgia, as demonstrated by whole television channels being based on nostalgic shows, and new programs consistently being produced to reflect a better time. Arthur Dudden argues that society has always related to nostalgia, and states, "Nostalgia was, and still remains, a continuous undercurrent of American life, as compelling perhaps for the masses of people as any visionary glimpses of progress."[5] With this undercurrent comes a desire to return to a constructed notion of the past and a reliance on nostalgia as beneficial to American life. Nostalgia is a consistent notion that has become a blatant focus of corporate marketing, the media and others to allude to a time of superiority within American society. The negative connotations of nostalgia focus on this type of construction but fail to discuss the beneficial aspects of nostalgic thought.

The way that nostalgia has been discussed and presented has greatly shaped these negative connotations. Nostalgia, in this manner, reflects a desire for a better time in the past. It is shaped to allow a feeling of disgust for the present and to focus on what is wrong with postmodern times. With this focus on nostalgia, many postmodern critics look upon the conception of nostalgia with disdain. What has continuously been discussed is the distinction of nostalgia as limiting to artistic pursuits and as an easy alternative for the majority of participants in the artistic realm. Nostalgia is oftentimes viewed and constructed in this way, and it has been claimed by critics such as Fredric Jameson and others, " ... the producers of culture have nowhere to turn but to the past: the imitation of dead styles, speech through all the masks and voices stored up in the imaginary museum of a now global culture."[6] It is this distinction and ability to view nostalgic acts with an abhorrence that has led to nostalgia being viewed in a negative light.

What makes these negative constructions of nostalgia limiting is the postmodern conception that nostalgia is a defining instance of the lack of control over subjectivity in postmodern times. Those who consider nostalgic thought limiting and non-empowering focus on the ability of nostalgia to draw the subject back to a time of complete removal of control. By assuming nostalgic thought, the postmodern subject falls back into the previously constructed forms of hegemony that have continuously remained dominant. It is often stated that subjects fall into this hegemony and limit their construction by viewing the world with little or no control. Jameson again confirms the argument: "Here in a nutshell is the full nostalgic narrative of a decline from use value to commodity, from immanence to instrumentality, from the observing traveler to the possessive tourist, and from the world as being to the world as simulacrum."[7] Making the world a simulacrum is a constant criticism of nostalgia and restates the premise that through nostalgic thought the present self is lost. Nostalgia again is said to allow the subject to relinquish control over their subjectivity to a past creation.

This thought process includes the dominant notion of the lack of control in postmodern times. If subjectivity is definite, to whatever order of hierarchy, then any thought process that allows for the construction of subjectivity within that control is still limiting with its influence. Subjects are continuously said to fail in their attempt at individuality due to the hegemonic positions in society that control subjectivity. Through the use of nostalgia subjects again attempt to construct themselves within these parameters and fall back onto these patterns of control. What must be stressed outside of this is that nostalgia within Garage Rock is used as a way to construct subjectivity away from capitalist notions of control.

As subjects continue an attempt to construct themselves in the postmodern world, they must relate back to the past in order to form ideas and attitudes about the future. Nostalgia then becomes a way to construct the self when subjects are forced into the realization of a future of conformity. To go against the trend of conformity and to work within the postmodern cultural sphere requires a thought process that is based within the past. Theodor Adorno contemplates this action against conformity and suggests, "In this search for history, the exploration of the no-places, the exclusions, the blind spots on the maps of the past is often invested with utopian energies very much oriented toward the future."[8] This orientation stems from the desire to attempt a construction of self, which is based within a time that everything has already been tried.

Although nostalgia has been used within the mainstream for advertising and often becomes a tool for marketing, the music and scene of Garage Rock reinstates nostalgia in a way that asserts a power over the capitalist driven notions of sales and marketing. In *Rock 'n' Roll Soundtracks and the Production of Nostalgia*, David Shumway claims, "There are many occurrences of nostalgia as marketing and the Twentieth century marks a new stage in the commodification of nostalgia because the eras to be revived had already been defined by representation in the mass media."[9] This representation is again being reconstructed into a musical format that takes a strong stance against the commodification of the individual within our society.

Contemporary Garage Rock uses nostalgic thought to attempt realization of subjectivity away from capitalist desires and control but within the hegemonic control of postmodern America. There is dominance over subjectivity and a continuous attempt at individualization that is arguably unreachable, but within this constraint nostalgic thought allows for Garage Rock to assert a subjectivity against the late capitalist notions of suburban control. The power of contemporary Garage Rock to assert this break in postmodern thought lies within the nostalgic conceptions that dominate the contemporary Garage Rock underground.

In order to establish a new determination for nostalgic thought and criticism, the effort to distinguish nostalgia in a positive manner has begun. How this is done varies between scholars. Jerry Herron regards the positive nature of nostalgia and states, "Fredric Jameson's nostalgia, which is both eloquent and influential, in addition to being indicative, is not so much for the present—as he claims it is—but for a particular form of nostalgia itself: one that would script the individual subject into a specific position historically."[10] To position the subject in this manner allows for the limiting notion of nostalgia to come forward and continue to dominate the thought process in society. What needs to be addressed is the aspect of how nostalgia can be beneficial in late capitalist times.

Beneficial aspects of nostalgia include intercessions within the postmodern condition of subjectivity to capitalist constructions of self. Along with such intercessions, nostalgic thought allows the subject to form constructions outside of the contemporary vein of determination and surround themselves with a notion of reflection on the past and how it can be manipulated into contemporary distinction. The postmodern construction of Garage Rock allows participants and outside viewers to form their subjectivity away from the suburban capitalist realm through the use of nostalgic representations and thought processes.

One of the main aspects of contemporary Garage Rock, as has been discussed, is the reliance on being linked to the urban city through music and lifestyle. This concept is linked with nostalgic thought in the desire to get back to a glorified remembrance of the city and what it claimed as significant in its prime. Within Detroit, this glorification revolves around notions of independence and survivability within a city known for being harsh and cold. This has allowed the participants of Garage Rock to construct a fixed identity away from the suburban realm. In *The Future of Nostalgia*, Svetlana Boym claims, "Urban identity appeals to common memory and a common past but is rooted in a man-made place, not in the soil: in urban coexistence at once alienating and exhilarating, not in the exclusivity of the blood."[11] Coexistence is allowed within a set context that is based in the concept of nostalgic thought within contemporary Garage Rock. The continued dominance of inner-city appeal allows for bands' and participants' desires to remain fixed in depictions and desires that have links to the city.

This inner-city reasoning and desire has been witnessed within many underground movements. The difference with Garage Rock is its dependence on such representation for credibility. While other beginning underground movements did not fixate on the location of the band's beginnings, Garage Rock participants continue to respond to inner-city bands, or ones they perceive as such. The allowance of participants to associate bands in this manner is a function of their nostalgic thought and what is considered the city.

Many participants within the underground and mainstream scene of contemporary Garage Rock have a specific picture of the city of Detroit in their head. This picture oftentimes, if not always, is dependant on a nostalgic representation of the city and its contents. Whether this picture is positive or negative, the participants are informed by their nostalgic images and thoughts that go along with experiences and discussions. It generally revolves around durability and conditions of non-dependence relating to inner city life and experience. What is not considered, however, is the faulty circumstances in which these nostalgic thought patterns are constructed.

The faultiness of images and memory based in nostalgia is often cited in a discussion of the negative connotations of nostalgic thought. Within Garage Rock, this faultiness allows for the continuation of an image of strength that is far removed from suburban life, goals and ideals. Within Garage Rock, the concepts of inner-city development and determination figure intensely in the construction of underground ideals. Svetlana Boym again states in *The Future of Nostalgia,* "The aesthetics of nostalgia might, therefore, be less a matter of simple memory than of complex projection; the invocation of a partial, idealized history merges with a dissatisfaction with the present."[12] Although the majority of this nostalgia is faulty, it allows for this empowerment and it distinguishes itself from previous underground musical movements.

Along with the construction based on the inner city comes a redefining of a time period in America that is considered by contemporary Garage Rock as positive and more closely related to postmodern times. Through the use of nostalgic thought, the period of music borrowed from discusses and creates a link to America in the 50s and 60s. Most of the contemporary Garage bands and participants structure themselves on nostalgic patterns that relate to these time periods in America and England. By doing so, they attempt to demonstrate a positive side of American and British culture that is set apart from late capitalist thought. This reflection stems from the use of nostalgic thought and representation, so that, again, contemporary Garage Rock inserts a difference into postmodern culture.

With 50s and 60s America and England a focus for the nostalgic representations within the music and the scene, the past is brought forward in a positive manner to create a distinction within the Garage scene. Many of the participants are seeking to get back to a time of no self-restraint that they falsely project onto the 50s and 60s. This time period is represented in a way that challenges what is traditionally advanced within postmodern times in relation to the 50s and 60s. Contemporary Garage Rock challenges these notions in an effort to portray an individualized stance within late capitalist times. What becomes important is the use of nostalgic thought in a positive manner.

The importance of this reflective stance cannot be overstressed within postmodern America and beyond. Society is in need, as shown by record sales and events, of a musical scene and environment that takes a different stance within late capitalist times. This musical stance is structured on the facet of rebellion against mainstream constructions of music through the use of nostalgic thought. America has become focused on the progression of music into technologically advanced realms, and contemporary Garage Rock seeks to distance itself from such advances in order to reinvent past forms of expressive thought. By doing so, a different thought on subjectivity is inserted into postmodern music and thought.

With the use of older recording strategies, Garage Rock again nostalgically represents the past. Going against mainstream conceptions of recording techniques allows contemporary Garage Rock to produce music that significantly differs from other musical constructions. The demand that musical production nostalgically linked to past forms of recording again solidifies the aspect of returning to a perceived better time period of music within American society. Again, the desire to reflect a style and presence that goes against the traditional conception of postmodern music is witnessed. By moving away from the over-stylized and over-produced mainstream popular music and toward a nostalgically represented form of production and sonic quality, a new form of subjectivity is constructed.

For many participants in contemporary Garage Rock, the notion of nostalgia is associated with a romantic feel. The desire to reconstruct the past stems from a longing for what is gained from faulty romantic representations of the past. In Linda Hutcheon's *Irony, Nostalgia, and the Postmodern* she states, "The object of romantic nostalgia must be beyond the present space of experience, somewhere in the twilight of the past or on the island of utopia where time has happily stopped, as on an antique clock."[13] It is this romantic ideal that proliferates and takes hold within contemporary Garage Rock. This ideal is based on the desire to remove oneself from contemporary notions of subjectivity and break into a constructed subjectivity based on these romantic notions. Contemporary Garage Rock is strictly based on these notions of romantic nostalgia, which continues to play a large role in postmodern America.

As discussed, contemporary Garage Rock uses nostalgic modes of appearance in order to assert itself in postmodern America. The method of dress allows for participants to readily witness the effects of nostalgic representation in response to late capitalist times. While doing so, the nostalgia represented through dress also allows the members of the scene to incorporate a status of attempted individuality and apparent nonconformity. This aspect of appearance again separates contemporary Garage Rock from the preceding underground musical scenes and distinguishes it from capitalist, mainstream driven music.

Many concepts within our society stem from the removal of the past in an attempt to move away from retired notions and conceptions. When this occurs, and it does so throughout postmodernism, subjects begin to see the failings of the past and use them for the progression towards the future. With this being the case, nostalgia bears the weight of negative criticism and has continuously been linked to the non-progression of our society. Throughout philosophy and postmodern thought is the continuous attempt at a removal from the past. This attempt, while promoting distance from, keeps nostalgia and the past as a common referent within postmodern society.

While discouraging certain viewpoints from the past that are considered overdone, trite, or boring, these past forms are given a rebirth and maintain a status of support through negation. When this process of negation and sublimation occurs, nostalgia and events in the past are allowed to remain and gain important status within underground and mainstream thought. With the inception of contemporary Garage Rock, those concepts that have continuously been rejected as inferior are embraced in an effort to regain a desired individuality.

The nostalgic concepts of music referenced within contemporary Garage Rock stem from the time periods that have been discussed. Concepts such as poor production quality and simplistic song formats that convey meaning and power through voice have continually been discounted as amateurish, crude or lacking in enough distinction to break into a new format of thought. These concepts have been embraced and championed in a way that allows postmodern Garage Rock to assert its independence away from preconceived notions of popular music. Within musical criticism is the desire to discuss classical and neo-classical music as breaking convention and going against preconceived notions of culture and music. The mainstream of popular music, regardless of time period, is generally left behind, or not even considered, due to notions of it being inferior to classical formats in music. The depiction of contemporary Garage Rock as a less challenging musical style has allowed it to remain within the underground of music and criticism.

What is significant and important to discuss is the movement away from these more traditional forms of music as a way for Garage Rock to distinguish itself from the majority of mainstream music. A determination that has allowed this musical development to remain critical to underground music is the conception of playing unforced music that is rooted in formats of the past. Musical constructions that revolve around notions of independence from, and rebellion against, the classical formats of music and thought allow performers to base their sound on vocal meaning and prowess. This also creates the distinguishing aspects of the underground and brings out the characteristics of nostalgia.

Garage Rock allows nostalgia to again play a role in the determination of subjectivity within late capitalist times. Contemporary Garage Rock determines its subjectivity based on nostalgic concepts and representations. While doing so, the participants construct themselves in opposition to traditional views of postmodern late capitalist thought. The reliance on nostalgia for this attempted break into individuality allows nostalgia to become beneficial within our society. Nostalgic benefits revolve around removing society's basis for subjectivity and transforming these conceptions in relation to the past. Nostalgia is defined as homesickness, or a desire for the past as a better time and place, and continues to allow for the discussion of the past in a positive light. The continued discussion of nostalgia in a negative light must be countered by including the beneficial aspects of nostalgia in the determination of subjectivity and attempted individuality.

9

Removing the Constraint: The Confines of Late Capitalism

In postmodern America people are continuously inundated by concepts derived from late capitalism. These concepts seek to wall in society as subject to strict desires and aspects of the self. Consistently driven by capitalist goal structures, the majority of the population structures their attempted individuality based on these goals. These goals and concepts are limiting in their structure and dependent on continued dominance. Many of these structures are enmeshed within society and self. Continuous claims seek to position subjectivity within these confines. Within postmodern times, many people are drawn to these demands as a way of defining and structuring self. People also continue to seek ways to construct a break in subjectivity that moves away from these concepts, and they do so by relying on movements that attempt to go against late capitalist desires. While these movements contain aspects of capitalist control and dominance, they allow society to bear witness to a differing view of hegemony as it is placed into culture. Contemporary Garage Rock, through its use of nostalgic representation, seeks to serve as an alternative to the dominant capitalist confines of postmodern times.

The desires continuously involved with the American citizen revolve around capitalist goals and demands that have been a part of society from the very beginning. These desires continue to play a large role in what is considered important within this society. The majority of people within mainstream America continue to base their subjectivity within the realm of late capitalism and go along with the concept that this is the desired way to incorporate oneself into the society. In *The Cheating Culture: Why*

More Americans Are Doing Wrong to Get Ahead, David Callahan explains, "Opinion surveys confirm an explosion of material desires over the past two decades, along with a growing focus on financial success and the increasing linkage in people's minds between meeting these goals and achieving happiness."[1] The material desires of postmodern America are becoming more important to this determination than most people realize. Many people cling to the belief that one cannot be a part of the postmodern society without a determination of self that is based within late capitalist desires.

The insistence on remaining fixated on these desires as a way to claim self-determination has become a major issue within the postmodern world. While assertions of rebellion are prevalent, the majority of people are continuously fixated on using capitalist determinations to find justification in life. Often, subjects attempt to gain success through corporate structures, through any means necessary, simply to find a way to express their self worth. To rise within the mainstream business world is often viewed as the only way to truly find one's place as an individual within American society and the surrounding capitalistic world.

To be a part of capitalist society is the goal for many people in America and the surrounding world. The desire to gain the most monetary benefits and have the best life is reflected in the hegemony of the postmodern world. What this leads to is an extreme focus on determining self worth through the relationship with others based on monetary and capitalist assertions. Subjects have become rooted in these desires and continue to make demands that perpetuate this dominant thought. By doing so, only one form of attempted individualism is expressed, and this is detrimental to the entire society.

Although alternative viewpoints have always existed, the majority has continued to assert this construction of self-determination. Consequently, people are limited in their viewpoints regarding different aspects of individualism, and the hegemony is reinforced. This must be redefined in order for individuals to have as much control as possible in determining their own definitions of worth.

Society has been constructed through capitalist goals that are set up to support the existing hegemony within America. These goals continue to dominate the majority of thought in America and have extended throughout the world. Said goals and constructions seek to keep the conceived order that is inherent within society by forcing subjects to conform to strict notions of capitalist control and dominance. When this occurs, the desired effect is the manipulation of the individual to conform to capitalist desires and demands. Many of these demands are met through the use of specific capitalist elements for the determination of the self.

Since the inception of capitalism, the notion of monetary gain leading to happiness has prevailed. While this may be the case in some instances, this theory has often been proved wrong within postmodern society. Despite this, the majority of society is bent with determination on the acquiring of wealth. Subjects constantly measure their happiness and life by the amount of money obtained.

Through consistent pressure, people are geared to take positions in business and are goal-driven to claim social status by achieving monetary success. To the majority of people in postmodern America, these positions are the only proper way to become a fully individualized subject. This leads to confusion within many people because in order to become individualized, people must gain access into a world that does not encourage such thought. It is this type of confusion that leads to depression and eventual questioning of value and self worth.

The confusion within our society is not simply based on place within but also on how one defines the self. Because many people view themselves in relation to their work positioning, they often fall into despair when these positions come to an end. When this occurs, the majority find that they have defined their lives based on job positioning and come to an emotional crisis, which leads to depression. The question then becomes how to define self and what leads to the depiction of self within our society.

Work that deals with money or business practice is given greater value within late capitalist America. Consequently, these jobs become structured on a concept of greed and power that, even as movies, television and others seek to go against this myth, continues to gain popularity and acceptance. As this occurs, the concept that money leads to happiness is continuously enforced throughout postmodern times. The insistence of this thought process plays into the residing notions of hegemony and continues to dominate America. What becomes important is the extreme determination of this thought process throughout the dominant forms of expression in postmodern times.

The dominant forms of artistic expression and thought have consistently played into capitalist notions of control. Popular music, film and mainstream fiction have all allowed money to dictate production output. As a result, any group that has gained mainstream pop success continues to support the notion of the attainment of wealth at any or all cost. With this in effect, popular mainstream constructions do not challenge the existing hegemony, and instead fall into its system of support. Throughout mainstream music, groups and individuals are bent on achieving success, with that being defined as album sales and chart ranking. This, again, continues the culture of late capitalist dominance within postmodern America, and it is up to groups that remain in the underground to go against such notions. Fixing one's place in society based on a musical underground is one alternative to mainstream culture, and an important distinction within it.

The groups within the underground that promote desires different from capitalist goals are the groups that continue to enjoy success with participants. These bands achieve their success through representing a challenge to the capitalist mainstream thought process. In order to continue this challenge, bands must remain focused away from capitalist goal structures. Many groups that attain mainstream success find themselves being associated with goals that are counterintuitive to the goals they first established. When any band chooses to give in to a mainstream record label's influence on thought and creativity, they lose the important underground in which they began.

Within our capitalist vision of society, artistic vision and forms of expression cannot compete with the means of production. Business allows for the accumulation of wealth, not art, which forces the artist into struggling with whether or not to remain true to their own artistic vision or to transform their art into a viable commodity. Even when going the viable commodity route, the corporate share of the profits generally dwarfs the amount of wealth accumulated by the artist. This leads to the subversion of the artistic vision by the capitalist-driven economy within this society. Musicians, artists, playwrights and others must take this drive into account when producing their art, which leads to a diminuation of the artistic vision of the author in favor of capitalist gains.

With this subversion taking place in society, the creator of such artistic visions must remain determined on their focus at the onset of their career. Once capitalist acceptance occurs, the artist is allowed to work within these two worlds and a much clearer representation of their art becomes apparent. This acceptance also grants the artist the power to express the state of the society in which they reside. Gyorgy Lukacs, in his article "Aesthetic Culture," discusses this power by saying, "If it is indeed true that there are primary forces in culture that move everything else and each movement is not just the unpredictable result of complicated interactions, then those who count on them and influence them through their life's work may also be granted the power to influence culture."[2] To be able to influence culture is an important part of the Garage Rock underground, and the goals of the underground are heavily aligned with this power of control. Contemporary Garage Rock uses this power to discuss the struggle between artistic vision and capitalist desire throughout musical society, but it would not have been able to do so without first being accepted within the capitalist realm.

Through the acceptance into the realm of capitalism, contemporary Garage Rock is allowed to remain fixated against certain goal structures that form the hegemony within postmodern America. The groups that have gained acceptance must remain situated against these notions in order to remain popular within the underground. By doing so, they insert the viewpoint of the underground and strengthen the challenge to capitalist goal structures. If groups that have achieved acceptance do not hold to their original goal structures they will be viewed as outside of the underground and placed completely within the mainstream of music.

Monetary happiness directly coincides with capitalist goals of production and market. This concept allows for the dominance of capitalism to continue by equating the notion of success and happiness with the accrual of wealth. While this concept plays a direct role in the formation of many businesses and even bands, there is a consistent stream of artists and individuals who continue to go against the notion of money leading to happiness. For most Americans, the value that is found in work is most often monetary. This has slowly begun to change, but is still rooted in the idea that work, and therefore subjectivity when defined by work, is based on monetary value. This often forces a person into a position of deciding on a job that is not the first choice and therefore is determined by the surrounding capitalist goal structures. In a study on definitions of work and placement within society, George England and Antonia Ruiz-Quintanilla found that "fewer members of the labor force retain the view that work is a way to contribute to society."[3] This lack of contribution through work becomes a key point in the society's view of work in the capitalistic framework.

The contribution to society is then based on what the subject does within the community and their family. If work is not considered an effective way to contribute to society, then what is the reason for work? This is the general confusion that has plagued America for decades. Work is now being defined as a way to survive within our society, not as a way to support it. When our production value is equated only with monetary gain, and the structures of what subjects do for a living is consistently founded on capitalist goals, there is a sense of loss. Without a feeling of support for society, work has become a place to contribute to the hegemony of postmodern America.

Another notion of late capitalism is the idea of obtaining a sense of subjectivity from one's position in the capitalist realm that is acquired through work and production. The majority of citizens have completely determined their sense of self through their position in the marketplace. While this is not entirely faulty, it is extremely limiting in the formation of a concept of self worth. The concept of self worth for many resides in the difficulty of their workplace position and how much control they have over their day-to-day work responsibilities. This is often improved through the attainment of a higher rate of autonomy in relation to a higher-class-based position. In many cases the amount of self worth is reliant on these positions of control over production, and, according to Monica A. Seff and Victor Gecas in their study on efficacy entitled, "Social Class, Occupational Conditions and Self-Esteem," "the distinction between self-efficacy and self worth as dimensions of self-evaluation upon which self esteem is largely based is a justifiable one...."[4] For the majority of subjects in American society, what they do designates who they are. By limiting subjectivity, capitalist notions of self are reinforced constantly and play a large role in the concept of determination.

The desire to claim aspects of self worth through capitalist positioning remains a strong impetus for many people and continues to gain support through the notions of production value that are aligned with each work position. The higher the capitalist positioning, the greater the sense of self-determination that goes along with monetary gain. Through the construction of subjectivity with the use of capitalist positioning, many people limit their self worth in a desire to maintain the dominance of late capitalist America.

These notions of constructed subjectivity within American society continue to wield influence through the continued stress on monetary gain through work. By allowing job positions that hold little relevance to artistic and creative avenues to hold the highest import based on monetary value, late capitalism continues to enforce its control over the self. When teacher and professor job positions receive little importance based on how much money is accrued through each, the desires of capitalism are continually strengthened. The importance of this is clear, but what is being discussed is the effect on subjectivity.

Positions of instruction and educational development provide a much greater impact on the construction of subjectivity than what is determined through the position of production within the society. Why then are such positions consistently regarded as inferior? It is due to the lack of monetary wealth associated with these job positions. Without teachers, professors, instructors, and coaches, society would not have the background of understanding and many would not even be able to define themselves through their job position. Georg Simmel, in "The Metropolis and Mental Life," suggests that "the deepest problems of modern life derive from the claim of the individual to preserve the autonomy and individuality of his existence in the face of overwhelming social forces...."[5] Positions of instruction allow the individual to develop a solution to this problem. The solution is not always a successful one, but these positions within our society inform the person of avenues towards individuality. Therefore, the misplacement of importance must be corrected in order for an alternative stance to be encouraged within late capitalism.

Since the inception of capitalism, these concepts have played an immense role in the determination of subjectivity and have plagued America with a hegemony that is limiting in its constructions of self. While the concepts of money leading to happiness and attaining determination through capitalist positioning still continue to dominate postmodern America, there are people and expressions that go against these conceptions of subjectivity and allow for a difference to be placed within society. These expressions and outputs play an immense role in subverting the dominance of capitalism and strive to offer an alternative outlook on self-determination and subjectivity.

While alternatives exist, late capitalist desires still dominate. This dominance is responsible for the demoralizing aspects that have become inherent in American society. When subjects begin to base their self worth on late capitalist constructions, they fall prey to the limiting aspects of these constructions and fall into a circle of dependence that leads to demoralization within our society. By allowing the attainment of subjectivity to be based on notions of money leading to happiness, people allow themselves to be contained in a sphere of production that does not account for outside requirements involved with subjectivity.

The majority of people that believe these conceptions express a desire for something outside of what is merely acquired through work. There are those who are extremely satisfied with their determination through work, but the majority feel slighted or limited by this approach. This demoralizes subjectivity in order to gain capitalist goals and capability. It also plays a strong role in the depression and negative constructions of self that have plagued American society for so long. It is an important conceptualization that is based outside of these notions of determination that allows for a strong statement against late capitalism's dominance.

The demoralization of the subject within postmodern America is rapidly approaching levels that are harmful within any society. When subjects are completely reliant on their social positions obtained through work, they begin to devalue themselves. This then leads to depression and a lack of self-control over value. Through the insistence on remaining part of the goal structures that are set up in postmodern capitalism, individuals continue a spiral of depression over the attainment of goals. The way out of this cycle is through witnessing alternative individualities and examples of people that reside outside of these goal structures that have led to the depression.

Contemporary Garage Rock seeks to insert this type of determination into the late capitalist realm. The musicians allow the participants and other subjects outside of the scene to obtain a sense of self-determination that is different from the standard conceptions of capitalist dominance. Through the use of nostalgic representations in dress, the participants make a statement against the hegemony that is prevalent within postmodern America. They continue many of the underground notions that have previously been placed within society, but are allowed to remain within capitalist spheres because they maintain a sense of capitalist determination. By this positioning, contemporary Garage Rock displays this constructed break into an alternative subjectivity.

This break is witnessed within the mainstream because of contemporary Garage Rock's less harsh rebellion. While Punk, Hardcore and other musical formats shared similar ideals and expressions, the way that they rebelled was too harsh to garner any acceptance within the mainstream. This is where Garage Rock is extremely important within postmodern society. Through proclaiming a rebellion against capitalist dominance from within the mainstream and underground of society, these bands and performers provide a reconstruction of subjectivity.

While many people subconsciously realize that contemporary Garage Rock inserts this view into mainstream popular culture, it is due to the insistence of the participants that a difference is placed within the culture. This difference stems from the musical style of production and performance and consistently asserts a strong impetus for self-determination away from the continued capitalist desires. While the mainstream press has championed this musical scene, they have continued to allow this important concept to remain at the forefront of thought. As contemporary Garage Rock continues to play a role within popular and underground culture, it will continue to portray this alternative thought process towards subjectivity.

Through the use of nostalgia to reflect back and take concepts of rebellion from a time period that was ripe with change in America, contemporary Garage Rock makes headway against capitalist forms of thought and conceptions of self. Without Garage Rock providing this alternative conception of self, the demoralization of subjectivity that is inherent within America would continue unopposed. It is the goal of many people within postmodern America to react to late capitalist dominance, but it is through underground musical uprisings that these reactions can grow towards a determination within the capitalist sphere. The construction of many bands around nostalgic aspects of rebellion allows these concepts to take center stage and hold power within postmodern America.

Within postmodern times are many attempts to break away from capitalist determinations of self. Many of the underground musical movements offer a concept of alternative self. The extremity of each musical movement is based on how forcefully they portray this break. With Punk as an easy referent to this harsh determination, one can see how musical movements seek to obtain subjectivity away from mainstream capitalist desires. While doing so, they often alienate participants in mainstream society due to specific influences on dress and music. Punk arose in reaction to a society that was contained completely within capitalism, and contemporary Garage Rock continues this stance, although in a much simpler way.

There are many other forms that play into this determination within postmodern society. Any art format that challenges contemporary definitions of art offers an alternative. Formats that promote the importance of art moving away from strict notions of control and definition contain referents to other distinctions of subjectivity that do not conform with late capitalist notions of self. Many artists, with differing techniques, express their disdain for postmodern capitalism throughout their work and determine a way outside of contemporary mainstream thought. The main difference between Garage Rock and other artistic formats of attempted rebellion is the latter's lack of acceptance within the capitalist sphere. Contemporary Garage Rock is a movement that remains within the capitalist sphere while challenging the existing notions of capitalist thought.

While all of these attempts have been successful to varying degrees, they are not defined by their success rate. The importance of success is not relevant within the discussion of contemporary Garage Rock because of the removal of value that is placed on this break from late capitalist subjectivity. The majority of Garage Rock participants are not consciously attempting this break into subjectivity and therefore have been allowed to remain part of mainstream popular culture. With other formats of expression, the success of an alternative approach to subjectivity was limited because of a major clash with the mainstream, resulting in a reaction against underground music and the participants due to the severity of rebellion.

Contemporary Garage Rock and other formats of rebellion allows the attempted removal of mainstream late capitalism to be encouraged within mainstream and underground thought. Throughout history rebellion has allowed subjectivity to be based on outside occurrences, and with Garage Rock comes the latest method of forming subjectivity away from the mainstream through the use of nostalgic representations.

With this use of nostalgia, the success rate of this break has little importance within underground and mainstream society. The fact that this nostalgia is being used in a positive manner to construct a break into subjectivity carries the importance in the discussion of Garage Rock. By allowing this break to be viewed, the amount of success and failure carries little importance. The desired effect of rebellion is generally viewed as having little or no worth—merely a marketing tool—but while this is occurring, the move away from capitalist desires is being championed as an alternative to the contemporary notions of self-determination.

There is a consistent desire within America to be drawn to alternative formats of thought. With the use of music and performance techniques, contemporary Garage Rock reflects the desire to remain outside of the hegemonic norm within society. The participants have claimed an underground musical format as a way to portray a desire to break away from the demoralizing aspects of late capitalist postmodern time, and by doing so, place Garage Rock into a category that continues to promote viewpoints that champion this break. Many of the bands do not consciously strive for this, but remain adamant in their stance against mainstream musical ideas of construction and performance. It is these bands that allow the progression of thought outside of the capitalist sphere to remain a part of postmodern society.

As the members of bands initiate these statements throughout the underground and mainstream scenes, the participants gain access to this form of subjectivity. The participants are drawn into the surrounding musical development through the witnessing of rebellion and performance traits. These items are used with nostalgic reflection in a way that garners the attention of the surrounding fans and participants. When this fixation on subjectivity has occurred, the music and the importance of the message take hold within the participant's mindset. This is the point where contemporary Garage Rock asserts its claim on the outside stance within society. The participants are drawn into a culture of nostalgic rebellion and allowed to redefine their subjectivity and mindset.

Many issues arise when this is occurs; however, the majority of participants in the scene continue to construct themselves based on the nostalgic rebellion that is expressed. The problem with this is the way that the mainstream continues to dominate the thought of many people, even within the Garage scene. Contemporary Garage Rock continues to strongly assert a difference, but it is beginning to become reincorporated into mainstream thought. With groups being pre-packaged to reproduce the Garage look and sound, the deep dependence on underground groups continuing to express underground demands increases. Jude Davies continues this thought, stating, "The problem lies in the monopoly over the construction of identity held by the bourgeois hegemony. As soon as a sub-culture attempts to establish a communal identity, it becomes recuperated, since the only tools for doing so are already hegemonic."[6] These tools have consistently been challenged, and the contemporary Garage scene continues to attempt to insert a difference into the postmodern world.

Throughout the development of Garage Rock, the goal has always been to inject a difference into the music of the time. While this difference has become something that can be marketed and given monetary value, this fact has not severely changed the outlook of the original bands. These original bands, as discussed previously, began with this desire and continue today with the same desire to affect a difference away from the mainstream. This allows the Garage Rock scene to remain separate from mainstream capitalist thought, even when some bands are attaining mainstream success. The importance of asserting this difference cannot be overstressed regarding the popularity of contemporary Garage Rock and its continuation into the present thought processes.

This occurrence in postmodern times has been empowered through the participation of members that follow the prescribed attitudes that go along with the contemporary Garage Rock scene. Without adherence to the principles of nostalgic dress and performance, the contemporary Garage scene would not have achieved as much as it has. The underground would have been limited if Garage Rock was not capable of appealing to a large portion of the community through the assertion of a different musical format and different stance on subjectivity. To form subjectivity based on nostalgic instances and thought patterns was a key to the beginning of Garage Rock and also to its continuation into the present. These desires have permeated the entirety of the underground and have come to be used as a guarding point for musical production and incorporation.

The growth of contemporary Garage Rock into the mainstream has led to a backlash against groups that have falsely claimed the label. This backlash stems from the inability of these bands to insert a difference into mainstream society. The White Stripes and the Von Bondies have acquired mainstream success but have remained part of the underground due to their insistence on expressing an outlook on subjectivity through nostalgia. When groups performed a tour under the moniker "the All Garage Tour," it deflated the assertions of the original participants and caused a backlash against the label. These groups consistently rely on the depiction and use of the underground for strictly capitalist gains and fail in their stance within the underground.

By using the underground to achieve this type of success, bands remove themselves from the original thoughts and constructions of contemporary Garage. In doing so they promote capitalist notions of success. These bands limit the success of the underground within the mainstream and challenge the existing underground's removal of capitalist goals. In doing so, these groups diffuse the rebellion put forward by the original bands and continue to allow the mainstream to control subjectivity.

With the instances of selling out and ascription of the label to improper bands for capitalist gains, the hegemony of late capitalism begins to strengthen within contemporary Garage Rock. These groups have allowed the capitalist goals of production value to infringe on a mindset that was set against these ideals in the first place. This in turn causes the beginning of demoralization within the underground and continues into the mainstream of the scene. When groups are allowed to represent a form of music and an underground scene that do not adhere to the concepts originally espoused by that scene, then the breakdown of the underground begins. For many people, contemporary Garage Rock has begun to fold due to the influx of bands that have been formed for strictly capitalist gains. These groups fail in their approach to the underground and split the movement, thus demoralizing and leading to a collapse.

This is not to say that contemporary Garage Rock will collapse, but the moniker has already begun to shift focus and meaning. Many participants now shy away from describing the underground scene as Garage. This has occurred due to capitalist notions of subjectivity again being forced upon a musical underground that was set up to go against capitalist formations. When capitalist desires and formations of subjectivity begin to infringe on underground ideals, even if they are faulty, the scene begins to suffer and eventually folds.

To differentiate again from late capitalist ideals and control warrants a shift away from the existing moniker and determines another break into a constructed subjectivity. Within contemporary Garage Rock is a desire to break into a subjectivity away from capitalist desires, and when this, and the focus of the bands, begins to change, the scene begins to break down. Participants that were originally drawn to this break begin to view it as simply a way to make money and begin searching for another outlet that stands firmly against capitalist desires and controls. The main reason for Garage Rock's success was this determination of self through nostalgic thought, and without this stance the underground, and eventually the mainstream, will begin to dissolve into something else. When this aspect of demoralization occurs, it sets up a representation of the capitalist control over our subjectivity.

Society uses underground modes of performance in an effort to view alternative stances on subjectivity. Once these have been co-opted by capitalist desires and demands, people begin to see the limiting aspect of basing their subjectivity on postmodern capitalism. The unsettling aspects of American society are again brought forward through the use of the underground and its fall within the capitalist sphere. Society must begin to realize that determining subjectivity through the use of late capitalist demands is extremely limiting. With the incorporation of capitalist demands and desires, modes of production that once allowed for this break come into conflict with their original intent and begin to fail in the eyes of the participants.

With the effects of late capitalism fully in place within postmodern society, it is up to participants who insert a different form of subjectivity into the mainstream to allow for an alternative self-description. Contemporary Garage Rock offers a break into a constructed form of subjectivity that resides outside of capitalist demands. By placing this viewpoint alongside mainstream demands, Garage Rock champions a desire to remain apart from the hegemony in place. Without art forms such as Garage Rock, society would be mired in a sense of disillusionment based on capitalist desires. Because of this, the importance of underground music cannot be overstated. With contemporary Garage Rock, we see this extreme impetus towards change.

Postmodern demoralization stems from the reliance on capitalist goals for constructed subjectivity and has been continuously reinforced by what is considered success. By allowing these goals and desires to remain in place, American society will continue to decline. Basing subjectivity on monetary attainment and production value leads to a sense of loss of what has been considered self. The structure of support for capitalist desires remains strong and coercive. The strength of the hegemony that is ingrained in American society continues to support a culture of otherness and debasement of self. This perpetuates the cycle of demoralization and leads to the dissolution of a strong society.

As the postmodern era continues and American society determines self through capitalist desires, underground formats of expression gain strength by rebelling against the mainstream thought processes. By doing so, they risk failure, but still construct an alternative viewpoint that is easily witnessed by participants. As the progression of these viewpoints continues, these underground scenes gradually face challenges from the capitalist sphere and either continue or fold in resistance to them. Even at the event of failure, underground and alternative viewpoints allow for the mainstream hegemony to be challenged and a culture to begin to form and grow away from traditional goals and desires.

Through the use of nostalgic representations in performance and appearance, contemporary Garage Rock asserts its stance against main-stream capitalist desires and promotes the importance of self-determination away from mainstream desires. By gaining mainstream acceptance, bands that continue to champion the original goals of the underground scene are allowed to remain part of the underground and its effort to assert this difference. The continuance of an alternative construction of subjectivity relies on these bands remaining aligned with this original intent in some way. As soon as bands and participants begin to conform to capitalist intent and desires, the scene begins to lose power and influence in underground society. This is beginning to occur in contemporary Garage Rock and may lead to its decline and failure. Even so, Garage Rock will still have left its strong statement against postmodern late capitalism through its use of nostalgic representations.

10

The Break Into Individualism

Contemporary Garage Rock expresses the desire to break into an individualism that is constructed through nostalgic traits. This break is imperative for success within the underground and mainstream music scenes. It has continued to allow the proliferation of nostalgic thought, encouraged by participants and performers alike. To remain a relevant and influential part of the Garage Rock scene, one must be successful in this attempted break and display a removal from capitalism that is directly based on nostalgia. Many participants rely on this break to establish a consistency within the scene and a determination away from capitalist control. There are many types of underground movements that have attempted this break but have failed in the eyes of the populous due to their inability to remain free from capitalist desires. Through nostalgic facets within music production and performance, and a reliance on structured forms of nostalgic dress, contemporary Garage Rock has continued to succeed in its constructed individualism.

The discussion of individualism is problematic because of the limitations of the term and the arguments surrounding its meaning. With the differing semantics of the word, individualism has been seen throughout history in both a positive and negative light in relationship to the surrounding society. Often, the definitions are rooted in social and political reactions. Steven Lukes states in *The Journal of the History of Ideas*, "For some, individualism resides in dangerous ideas, for others it is social or economic anarchy, a lack of the requisite institutions and norms, for yet others it is the prevalence of self-interested attitudes of individuals."[1] In postmodern times, individualism is often considered impossible because of the subjectivity of all humankind. For this discussion, this last thought is being used in a way to construct the framework for an attempted individualism that is based on a differing subjectivity.

Another instance of individualism within contemporary Garage Rock is the Puritan ideal of the individual. This ideal was the antithesis of the surrounding society that preceded it and served to represent an attitude of rebellion. V.F. Calverton states, "Individualism thus represents struggle against social organization and regimentation, and to the extent to which it advances and social organization recedes, its influence is able to deepen and intensify."[2] Although this thought process is extremely old and representative of the modern period, it closely resembles the ideas behind contemporary Garage Rock's attempted break. By struggling against the hegemony from within, the music and participants construct their individualism based on subverting the social organization of late capitalist thought.

The use of individualism within our society is often misconstrued and has been consistently debated since the word's inception. What is specifically relevant to this discussion is the way that self is constructed and defined through the use of Garage Rock. The ability to use a form of music and the surrounding culture to create a form of self is necessary within today's society. The use of the term individual is always flawed, because people are consistently relating to others and subjectively influenced. Where contemporary Garage Rock gains its strength is in its display of an alternative construction of self within the hegemony of postmodern society.

The argument and debate over the definition of individuality allows a look into how contemporary Garage Rock uses a definition to expound upon the subjectivity of every person. By creating an avenue by which one becomes distinct within society, Garage has allowed people to become individuals. The only way to become an individual within our postmodern times, and arguably all times, is to find a method of differentiation within the society. For many, contemporary Garage Rock is this difference. E. Jordan, in "The Definition of Individuality," claims, "Distinctness is not the logical differentia of individuality, but the practical formula by which individuals find their station and function within the complex of inter-individual relations which constitutes an individuality of higher degree."[3] Through contemporary Garage Rock, performers and fans break into their own individuality within postmodern time.

This break constitutes the ideas of the contemporary Garage scene. The effort to reclaim a place within the music world of Detroit through the reassertion of the past led to the development of Garage Rock and continues to define its relevance. The way that fans and members of the scene base their individuality on specific traits within the culture places the surrounding musicians and what is displayed through them at the forefront. By creating an image, sound and performance attitude, these musicians allow participants to form their individuality based on differentiation within society.

The differentiation has come about due to the limitation of postmodern America and the capitalist control of culture. To stand within and against this control is the goal of contemporary Garage Rock, and by offering this differentiation, the subculture allows members to take an alternative stance within a culture that is often viewed as limiting and controlling. To regain this control over self and to attempt to individualize is the goal of every person, and in the venue of contemporary Garage Rock this can begin with the use of nostalgia.

By using traits of the past to differentiate and define individuality, the participants of contemporary Garage Rock structure their individual thought along similar lines of interest. While this is often conforming, it allows the subject to assert a difference within the realm of mainstream capitalism. Lawerence Grossberg claims in "Another Boring Day in Paradise: Rock and Roll and the Empowerment of Everyday Life," "Rock and Roll removes signs, objects, sounds, styles, etc. from their apparently meaningful existence within the dominant culture and relocates them with an affective alliance of differentiation and resistance."[4] The relocation within emotional control and organization is crucial to the development and consistent appeal of contemporary Garage Rock, and determines the assertion of individualism into our society through musical relationships.

By using musical developments and the preceding underground as a way to gain a foothold, Garage Rock inserted itself and the thought process carried with it into the underground and mainstream society. By building a following that is based on a rejection of older underground processes that were thought to be detrimental to the development of a scene, contemporary Garage Rock picked and chose from the entirety of the underground culture. This allowed the groups and participants to develop a strong relationship to the past. Through this relationship the process of becoming an individual was again demonstrated throughout the music community.

The culture of Garage Rock systematizes the process of breaking into individualism by demonstrating ways to achieve subjectivity based on an entirely different hegemony within postmodern America. Since Garage Rock remains within mainstream musical society, the use of nostalgic traits becomes the focal point for the assertion of individual thought. The nostalgia of music, fashion, sound, and styles challenges the dominant cultural construction of the time. This challenge incorporates the same feeling of disdain and apathy for the generation that is used as the referent. The nostalgia therefore incorporates the removal of capitalist constructions from the past as well as the present.

Unlike previous musical movements that have been based on finding a family or club to belong to, Garage Rock is determined by the aspect of remaining an individual. There are not any clubs to belong to or gangs to join; simply following a specific band or sound will include you in the contemporary movement. This is extremely different from the preceding Punk and Hardcore movements. In the preceding cases, belonging to a group of people that provided an aspect of family that was not found elsewhere was extremely important. Garage Rock does not discount this, but there is not a significant demand to belong to a specific group.

The concept of individuation was founded on a removal from such groups and a restructuring of the definition of how a subject belonged to a certain group. When the definitions began to change, so did the aspect of the individual. Contemporary Garage Rock is again attempting to reconstruct the framework in which subjects attempt to individualize. In his study on Puritanism and individuality, Adam Seligman suggests that "the development of the morally conscious individual was predicated on a fundamental transformation of the terms collective identity and social solidarity."[5] The shift in terms that took place previously is again challenged through the use of music and the reformation of the definitions of the group within underground society. Unlike preceding musical undergrounds, Garage Rock does not require specific solidarity to a group and, while demonstrating a collective identity, does not force the participant into any particular concept of individualism.

What these instances led to in the preceding scenes was a feeling of belonging and dependency that eventually resulted in dissolution, stemming from the participants' reliance on the surrounding scene for their defining qualities. Garage Rock does not place such strict requirements on the surrounding members of the scene and allows participants to decide on their own qualities of individualism. Although these qualities are generally shared within the scene, the scene does not remove participants as readily as previous underground movements.

Contemporary Garage Rock does not promote an attitude of exclusion. Participants are not completely removed from the scene because they choose to listen to a different type of music or band. This has allowed for the expansion of the music community and strengthens the contemporary Garage Rock underground. The scene originally developed out of a myriad of other musical developments; therefore, to restrict access to other bands that seemingly do not fit the Garage sound or attitude would be detrimental to the scene. While this is often confusing in aligning members and participants, it also allows for the continued expansion of the underground and mainstream.

Through the confusion of where certain groups are placed, Garage Rock has greatly increased its influence within the music world. Although many of the groups linked with its expansion are viewed as latching onto a trend, there are still others that remain tied to underground ideals and continue to perpetuate the notions that the original groups placed into the surrounding society. Bands like Brendan Benson, the Waxwings, Electric 6 and many others continue to benefit because of contemporary Garage Rock's growth in mainstream music and society.

The insistence on remaining an individual within the scene is extremely relevant even to the band members. Many members state that there is a lack of family in the scene but a specific desire to be an individual within a community. This seems contradictory but reflects the desire of the Garage Rock community to break into an individualism that remains within the community. The challenge is still relevant and the goals remain fixed on this break within a capitalist sphere, but the route is extremely different from preceding scenes.

Within preceding musical undergrounds was the desire to force individualistic thought on a society that was not really willing. The case of Punk is a prime example in the way members would attempt rebellion through hair color or style of clothes, and attitude towards the mainstream. This harsh approach was not very effective and led to the incorporation of fashion and style into the underground. While the rebellion was important and relevant, the outcome was not, which let the hegemony of postmodern late capitalism advance. The construction of Punk within mainstream society allowed many people to view the scene and music as dead on arrival when mass markets began using Punk as a means for capitalist gain. The incorporation of this musical underground and rebellion led to a split and eventual dissolution of the underground.

There are other musical formats that posit similar notions of individualistic construction. The importance of Garage Rock lies in its nostalgia for the specific forms of rebellion. It is also imperative that the mainstream be able to relate to this assertion even though it is against it. Unlike Punk or Hardcore before it, Garage Rock is attempting to assert its individuality from within. The scene continues to do so by using specific formats of nostalgic reproductions. To be within the community of the mainstream is extremely relevant and important to contemporary Garage Rock and leads to the rebellion through nostalgic traits that many bands and participants express.

The way that musical movements of the past have rebelled from within the mainstream is very different from contemporary Garage Rock. It has often been assumed that rebellion cannot be co-opted by the mainstream and still be effective. This assumption is interlaced with a great deal of past exposure and support; however, Garage Rock is attempting to rebel and challenge the mainstream from within and to create a space for a constructed individuality outside of the dominant view. This has allowed many participants to construct their position in society away from the dominant view but maintain similar desires.

By continuously demonstrating a viewpoint outside of the dominant ideology, Garage Rock champions a position of rebellion and maintains an outsider status that continues to relate to a large portion of society. The preceding youth movements have now gained control of the means of production, and it is up to the underground movements of today to challenge this control. To assert this challenge through music is to break into individualism, and Holly Kruse, in "Subcultural Identity in Alternative Music Culture," suggests, "...there is a lot at stake for all who cling, through their social and cultural practices, in some small way to the possible identities offered to them by a baby boom generation which is coming to control most of the material resources, and will therefore hold most of the power within our society."[6] Through the use of images and sounds from the past, this has been accomplished thoroughly.

With the use of nostalgic recording techniques, performers base one aspect of this break on recorded potentialities and realities. Participants are drawn to this sound through the recordings and become immersed in the techniques and strategies that have been used to represent the music. With the limited recording techniques used within contemporary Garage Rock, the members of the scene can easily witness a break away from the capitalist methods of recording that dominate mainstream music. The ability of a band to express thought and sonic capability through limited recording techniques is an essential element of the success granted by the participants of the scene to them. If a group cannot express what is intended through these types of recording methods, participants will question their success.

Many subjects within the scene are bound by the types of musical construction that employ recording techniques originally established by the first group of bands to be labeled as Garage Rock. It is this sonic quality that has become enmeshed within the underground scene and continues to influence a large part of the groups and participants that have followed. Subjects allow their musical desires to become dominated by sonic representations that are recorded through nostalgic methods and sound as if they were recorded in a previous decade. This allows participants to construct their break into individualism through the use of recording strategies and sonic qualities expressed by the performers.

The sound quality of these early recordings is often limited in its professionalism and quality. This allows the performers and subjects within the scene to distance themselves from the streamlined, slick production of mainstream music. While many outsiders view this type of recording in a negative light, the performers champion this style in their effort to construct their individuality within the myriad musical scenes. The first recordings, many on Italy Records, demonstrate the thought that anyone can make this type of music. Much like the first incarnations of Hardcore music, where the do-it-yourself ethic came to fruition, these first recordings allowed anyone to believe they could be in a band. While many of the groups admit that the sound and song structure on these early recordings was limited, they do not outright dismiss them as bad or unimportant to their development. In fact, many claim that these first recorded songs are better because fans or record producers have not yet influenced them.

While the influence of producers and record labels is not always negative, to many fans of Garage it is considered unwanted mainstream manipulation of music that is supposed to be as simplistic as possible. The use of specific producers then becomes increasingly linked to the band's reputation within the scene. Many of the original groups choose to use Jim Diamond as a producer because of his relationship to the studio and the scene. The groups that choose to work with outside producers often risk removal from the underground because their sound will become too "slick" and over-produced. This has occurred many times within preceding scenes, but with contemporary Garage Rock it plays a larger, specific role in the determination of whether or not a group will continue to be aligned with the underground.

The effort to sonically represent older styles of recording is a big factor in the continuation of Garage Rock today. Many groups consistently use recording strategies that do not allow multiple takes or overdubs in their music. This challenges them to continue the dominant style of music within their recordings. Instead of overdubbing vocals or guitars, the bands that make single- or double-take recordings continue to represent the original ideals and thought processes of the Garage Rock bands.

While postmodern mainstream music continues to stress the importance of overdubbing and the use of multiple tracks for every instrument or voice, the older style of recording has resurfaced in an effort to regain originality and an individual sound. Through the use of these techniques, Garage has expounded on the importance of the past within music and allowed many new fans and participants to hear an older sound within a newer context. This is where the groups that remain fixated on recording in this manner succeed in continuing the notions put in place by the original Garage movement.

This method of recording also allows for the construction of individualism through the primitive. By supporting the older technologies, the performers are effectively challenging the new modes of recording and championing the primitive use of tape in order to assert their individuality. Many groups even refuse to work with producers that use newer techniques and strategies. The link to the primitive has always been a nostalgic trait, but with contemporary Garage Rock there is a demand to recreate the sounds of the past in a similar way that at least sounds primitive and is removed from the technologies of the day.

These qualities are also expressed through the stage performance of the many groups that have successfully remained part of the underground. The performances of groups such as the Hard Lessons and the Dirtbombs continue to rely on nostalgic elements to make their statement within musical society. These bands continue to offer limited stage shows from the standpoint of effects and choreographed movements, and, by doing so, draw audiences to a show in an attempt to get back to "real" Rock and Roll. This sustained dominance of stage performance as a representation of music only allows the participants to become drawn in, witnessing another way to break into a constructed individualism. The requirements placed on bands that continue to express these distinctions rely heavily on the participants' preconceived notions of what Garage Rock should look and sound like.

Many participants continuously place ever increasing demands on what contemporary Garage Rock should be and become. These demands are rooted in the aspects of nostalgia and how the subject, breaking into individualism, uses them. With the instance of Garage Rock, the members of the underground scene have placed strong requirements on the bands and their musical output. Many people continue to rely on notions of what was originally considered Garage Rock, while others make demands that are linked to the first occurrence of the contemporary scene. These two differing outlooks on contemporary Garage Rock are easily seen as conflicting viewpoints, and it is the bands that continue to satisfy both that have achieved the most success.

The demands of underground participants are often very structured and fixed in their depiction of a band or group. Demands on performance and recording strategies are just the beginning, and, in order to claim an increasing number of members within the underground, bands will go to great lengths to meet these demands. Performers, oftentimes unconsciously, continue to use what is successful with the participants, and the relationship of meeting demands continues. With contemporary Garage Rock, the exchange of demands is based on the accrual of nostalgic aspects in performance and sound. Without these aspects, the band and the participants would not agree on a commonality within the scene in their attempt to break into individualism.

With the limited use of special effects and choreography in performance, bands that have been labeled as Garage Rock meet the demands of the participants. Even in the event of a group attaining mainstream success and popularity, their shows must continue to remain stripped down, displaying only the music, in order for them to remain a viable part of the underground. When the use of an elaborate stage show occurs, bands appear to be succumbing to capitalist desires and begin to fail to meet the extreme demands of underground participants. To counteract this, many groups, upon achieving mainstream success, play smaller venues without much fanfare or stage displays. This maintains their underground status and creates the space necessary for participants to achieve an attempted break.

While continuing to conform to underground demands regarding stage performance, Garage bands are also forced to embrace the desire for nostalgic dress. Without a reliance on dress that displays a removal from capitalist mainstream musical goals, bands that have recently gained success through the underground would lose the participants' support. This can be witnessed by attending any show performed by mainstream Garage bands. They may have a uniform, such as red and white or all-jean jackets, but this dress is set up to reflect a nostalgic link to the original 60's Garage scene or Mod culture. When this style of dress is changed, the band risks losing the favor of the underground as well.

Members of the underground use this nostalgic dress as another factor in their attempt to break into individualism, and without the bands' portrayals, they would determine another form of break through other outlets. Many participants begin to conform to the style of dress witnessed through performance and use this style to display an alliance to the underground scene. They begin to base their removal from late capitalist society on the dress displayed by performers. Without such a display, many of the participants would not have access into this constructed stance. The distinction placed on dress throughout the Garage Rock scene cannot be overestimated. The participants and performers continuously enforce a code of dress that is critical to their removal from the mainstream.

Within the participants of the scene is a strong impetus to structure their individualism around the demands of the performers. The performers, within Garage Rock, continue to influence participants throughout underground society, continuing into other aspects of their lives. Many participants remain set in their notions of attempted individuality and allow these notions to dominate their lifestyle for a period of time. What occurs is a reliance on self-determination away from capitalist constructions through the use of performers as focal points. Many subjects assert a strong notion of not conforming to the performers' demands, but rely on them for determination and approval of a lifestyle that is not fixed in traditional late capitalist modes.

This often occurs within musical developments and is not limited to contemporary Garage Rock. One only need look at any other music genre to see instances of fans dressing in similar ways to performers, with some performers even creating clothing lines. What becomes important is the way that Garage Rock structures its dress. The nostalgic look that is used reflects a time when rebellion was possible within any class level. There is no attempt to gain street credibility through dress or to shock the surrounding society; this dress is used to assert a rebellion within a class-structured society.

Garage Rock promotes a break into individualism that continues to influence a great many people. Through the performers' use of nostalgic sounds and dress, subjects witness an important determination away from traditional goals. The scene began in an attempt to insert a difference into the musical community and get back to the roots of Rock, and has succeeded in this respect. There is a great underscored desire within the scene to remain outside of traditional concepts, and this has been a driving force in the continuation of Garage Rock, from both the performers' and the participants' viewpoints.

Even when bands that have achieved mainstream success play in venues in Detroit, there is a desire to perform with different sounding bands. A growing number of participants within the scene consider bands playing with similar sounding bands on the same bill detrimental to the scene. This continues to play a large role in the apparent dissolution of the scene because many groups gained their popularity by playing with different sounding bands from the onset. When bands play a show that has three or four Garage Rock groups on the bill, the fans view this as limiting and the venue management is beginning to notice. It is not uncommon in Detroit to have a show with the Dirtbombs, the Von Bondies, and the Go on the same bill. This becomes another way that participants begin to place demands on the performers.

Although outside observers may see such demands as unappealing, the success of contemporary Garage Rock is reliant on assertions of individuality being based on demands from both sides. Through underground networks of participants, and with the performers support, this assertion of attempted individuality is shared and remains within the contemporary scene. Even with mainstream acceptance, these demands remain intact, allowing the dominant thought to continue moving away from late capitalist desires. Without these distinctions from the participants' standpoint, contemporary Garage Rock risks the decline faced by Punk and other musical movements.

The inherent nature of an underground musical scene is demonstrated by its concern for the usage of these forms of individuality. Participants affect each other through their constant insistence on moving away from capitalist desires. Through the use of techniques that lead to acceptance, the participants determine who is able to remain as part of the constructed scene. There is a strong reliance on communication of these desires at shows. Through the witnessing of the surrounding participants and performers on the stage, underground members express these demands to one another.

The use of this power over participants comes to fruition with the constructions that the band members portray as effective in asserting an attempted individuality. Through these performers, participants are given a consistent viewpoint that is upheld by the underground. It is this viewpoint that members hold onto so strongly in their attempt at constructed individuality. Contemporary Garage Rock strives to keep this aspect aligned with performance in order to easily gain acceptance within the underground sphere. In wielding this type of power, the performers are faced with the issue of determination away from capitalist desires. This leads to the extreme importance that is placed on the bands' portrayal of nostalgia, along with their determination away from capitalism.

Many of the original groups attain their success through these concepts of performance-based individualism. Although many that followed were based on similar aspects but were viewed negatively, the original groups offered something different to the surrounding participants. This difference is what has become dominant within the underground scene and has allowed for the distinction to be placed on Garage Rock. This difference is based on nostalgic individuality and continues to be expressed through the current bands that remain at the forefront of the contemporary movement. The groups that have removed these differences have become at least partially removed from the underground scene.

With the removal of specific nostalgic traits, the underground participants are not specifically distanced from mainstream society. The bands then no longer distance themselves from capitalist desires, and their decline in popularity begins. Many of these groups begin with the ideals that contemporary Garage Rock shares, attain mainstream success and then change their representation to follow mainstream requests. This construction forces the group's removal from the original importance that was placed on their statement of individuality. The most obvious example of this is in the one hit nature of groups like the Hives, whose significant challenge to the mainstream is removed with their acceptance.

This has led to the Hives being severely criticized for their apparent conformation, while other groups that have achieved mainstream success did not lose underground support.

The most popular group that has successfully withstood criticism and remains part of the underground is the White Stripes. From the beginning, this group has challenged the notions of mainstream music by performing as a two-piece band. With their extreme success as performers, they have inserted their version of individuality throughout the mainstream and underground spheres. Participants continue to respond to the White Stripes due to their stance against the mainstream. They remain a part of the underground through the expression of notions that reside away from capitalism and conformity. This allows for an extreme distinction to be placed within the participants of the underground scene in regards to what is considered selling out.

When it comes to underground musical scenes, participants rapidly change their minds about the determination of characteristics of the scene. When a group attains mainstream success, they are generally removed from the underground, with the thought that they have sold out and have failed to maintain the elements of the underground. With the White Stripes and others attaining mainstream success while keeping underground notions of individuality, the participants are left with a challenge to the normally constructed definitions. The distinction then falls into the performance of individuality and how these groups allow for a determination away from mainstream capitalist demands.

Throughout the contemporary Garage Rock underground the control wielded by the performers over the participants is evident. When performers begin to fail the notions of acceptance that are put forward by the participants, this control shifts to the members of the underground scene. With this shift in control, the participants are allowed to influence the performers' appearance and musical output. In order to gain acceptance, now bands must play into the thoughts of the surrounding scene. These ideas are based heavily on the use of nostalgic representations and continue to influence the newer groups claiming to be part of the underground network of contemporary Garage Rock.

In order to continue the removal of capitalist desires and promote the attempted break into individuality, participants rely on these demands to communicate their interpretation of Garage Rock. The continuous shift of what is considered important to the underground creates a short period in which power and control are wielded by the participants.

Throughout this period, bands must conform to ideals that have been displayed previously by bands and members of the underground. The risk becomes the issue of conforming and how the participants in the development of a new group will view it.

Within underground musical movements is a constant desire to go against the mainstream musical world. With Garage Rock this statement is translated into specific requirements bands must meet in order to remain within the underground network. The importance of Garage Rock lies in its allowance for mainstream success, something that previous underground movements did not accept. Garage Rock participants are not as likely to immediately write off a band simply because they succeed in the mainstream realm, differentiating Garage Rock from Punk and other types of underground musical developments. The importance placed on mainstream success, however, falls second to the need for a constructed individuality away from capitalist desires.

Through the use of these traits, the participants are allowed to form their own construction of what it means to be a Garage band and what it entails to be a part of the underground scene. Without an allowance for mainstream acceptance, Garage Rock would have been limited in its effect and scope and probably would have experienced the downfall that affected the Punk movement. This allowance has remained a consistent trait of contemporary Garage Rock, and is a defining part of the continued success of the scene. Through the underground's extended notions of acceptance, Garage Rock has remained an affective part of postmodern society. The extremity of demands that have occurred with previous musical movements resulted in the eventual downfall of the underground scene, whereas with Garage Rock these extreme demands are more malleable—as long as the performers continue the insistence on nostalgic individuality.

There is an overwhelming amount of support for bands that begin in the city of Detroit and gain acceptance and success beyond local venues. These groups have occasionally garnered mainstream support while continuing to allow the local scene to follow their progress and effect on the surrounding musical landscape. With this support, bands remain loyal to the underground participants that gave them their start. With contemporary Garage Rock, this relationship between performers and participants is crucial to the survival of the scene. If the bands that attain mainstream success begin to alienate the underground, their survival rate and longevity will be affected. It is through the underground's support and the band's removal from mainstream desires that the most popular Garage bands continue their dominance of the charts.

This insistence is critical to the continued success of many contemporary Garage bands. When these bands begin to disassociate from their original goals and intent, they suffer (from the underground's standpoint). When this occurs, many begin to drop from the charts and lose their dominance within both spheres. The participants within the scene hold dominance over mainstream acts from this standpoint, and if bands begin to falter in regard to these demands, the bands will lose their appeal. For many groups, this is the turning point in their career and the start of their decline. For others, it may be considered a highpoint of success. It is those groups that gain mainstream acceptance while remaining true to the underground that will experience continued success.

The participants continually base their demands on what has previously been constructed and accepted within the underground scene. They view clothing and sonic representation as paramount. The impetus for removal from the scene can be varied, but falls back to a lack of nostalgic display. These demands generally take hold within the participants as well. Towards the beginning of the scene, the requirements for participation were not strict, but they have begun to dominate as the popularity of Garage Rock grows. Through the use of fixed notions of acceptance, many participants control their surroundings, and as the success of contemporary Garage Rock continues to dominate the underground, these attitudes continue to gain strength.

Nostalgic dress and knowledge of previous bands play a large role in the determination of acceptance within the underground network. While these factors are significant, the largest determining factor is the movement away from capitalist desires. Without this anti-capitalist sentiment, members of the surrounding underground fail to accept a participant. Throughout contemporary Garage Rock the importance of nostalgia is displayed, and when it comes to determining who is a member of the constructed scene, this nostalgia and the ability to stand against late capitalist desires plays the largest role. Although many participants cite goals that seem contradictory, they refer back to these notions of nostalgia and anti-capitalism for a starting point of conformity.

Contemporary Garage Rock has continually promoted an attempt to break into a form of individuality that resides away from mainstream American society. By doing so, the importance of the music and the scene is defined. This allows contemporary Garage Rock to maintain an influence within other countries, particularly Europe, where American values and norms are questioned. Success within Europe has often influenced the amount of success in America. With Garage Rock this is also the case. The important difference with Garage Rock is the reason behind its success. Garage Rock uses its American and British nostalgia to impart desires that go along with European constructions of America, and by doing so, Garage Rock continues to gain acceptance and exposure throughout both continents.

Many bands believe that through success in Europe comes success in America. There is a large discrepancy between success in both areas, however, and Garage Rock began challenging this difference. With the success of the White Stripes in Europe and America, many Garage bands believed they would also find mainstream success in both arenas. The White Stripes' success stems from their nostalgic sonic representation in recordings and performance, and their use of this nostalgia to demonstrate a constructed break into individualism. While other artists attempt to gain success in Europe and America, they seem to fall into capitalist desires and do not have the same impact upon their return to the States. Without a strong anti-capitalist stance and an attempted break into individualism, the bands do not hold the same power and control over the underground and mainstream scene.

Throughout contemporary Garage Rock is the drive to proclaim an alliance to music that has been rooted in Americana and past forms of music. This alliance is focused on a belief in nostalgic betterment and allows the distinction to be made on what Garage Rock is attempting to claim as its defining voice. This stance is shared by the majority of participants and allows the underground, as well as the mainstream, to draw comparisons and distinctions between contemporary Garage Rock and other formats. The importance placed on nostalgic traits allows the distinguishing characteristics of the music and the movement of contemporary Garage Rock to be placed within society. Without nostalgia as the basis for this movement, Garage Rock would fail to affect postmodern society and would go the way of the preceding musical movements.

With nostalgia as a base for the construction of an attempted break away from capitalist desires and demands, contemporary Garage Rock solidifies its effect on participants as well as performers. There is a solid distribution of power within the scene regarding the controlling aspects of this break and how it is allowed to remain a significant part of the music. Participants and performers often do not realize the importance of this constructed individualism and continue to enforce restrictions and codes within the scene that play into these shared, inherent desires. Through success in Europe as well as America, Garage Rock has asserted its claim on this break and gained popularity along with it. The insistent use of nostalgic representations to effect this break binds the performers and participants in their construction of the scene and the demands of incorporation.

The reliance on these demands to assert this break is an essential part of the success of contemporary Garage Rock throughout the mainstream and underground musical spheres. Without a set construction of goals and a defined outlook, the scene would not be affected. This has given contemporary Garage Rock a continued dominance throughout the underground musical community while simultaneously attaining mainstream success. Without constructions in place that proclaim a break away from late capitalism in America, contemporary Garage Rock would not have held the same power and would not have attained the same amount of success.

Individualism within Garage Rock stems from these notions of nostalgia, with the means of attainment coming through the performers. When the participants begin to assert dominance over the scene, they must be aligned with the ideals that have previously been championed. By doing so, they continue to enforce those thoughts and allow the recurring theme of nostalgia to be brought forward. For the participants, there is a strong desire to remain away from the mainstream and to insert these differences into the underground musical world. They allow these assertions to champion the music of the scene and continue to promote the original intent of the surrounding culture.

To construct a break into individualism, contemporary Garage Rock uses nostalgic representations throughout the underground, continuing on to the mainstream musical community. This use of nostalgia radiates out from the performers and is embraced and continued by the participants. Both function in a way that allows nostalgia to influence an attempted individualism away from postmodern late capitalist mainstream thought and towards a stronger sense of individuality. Whether or not this is an actuality is not important, and the contemporary scene does not place relative value in factual representations. Members continue to use nostalgic artifacts and cultural representations in order to define themselves within the late capitalist sphere. When this begins to erode, contemporary Garage Rock will face the fate of previous musical developments.

11

This Will Wake
the Neighbors!

In postmodern society there is a constant desire to break away from capitalist notions of constructed individuality. Many people are drawn to forms of music that allow for the expression and continuation of ideals that help construct an alternative form of subjectivity. Through contemporary Garage Rock's use of nostalgia, society is given a new way to look at constructions of individualism and self. Garage Rock uses these forms of nostalgia, which include dress and sonic representation, in an effort to express the inherent nature of rebellion. Many participants within the Garage scene have consciously chosen to follow particular groups in order to self-determine their stance within society. Through the use of 60s Garage Rock, Hard Mod culture and the British Invasion, bands demonstrate their desire to return to a time when rebellion was the main drive behind music. Many groups also demand a particular sound that represents these movements and become bound to recording practices and songwriting styles that reflect these nostalgic ideals. Getting back to the roots of Rock and Roll is the beginning determination within contemporary Garage Rock, and with this expression, participants construct themselves outside of mainstream capitalist desires.

There is a strong relationship between the extreme demands of capitalism within postmodern America and the downward spiral that society has taken in these times. The strain of meeting capitalistic goals causes many people to enter fields they don't like and continues the propagation of capitalist dogma. The resulting, often unrealized, depression causes individuals to react in ways that are deemed uncivilized within the mainstream, including an outpouring of aggression and/or violence. In order to keep meeting capitalistic demands, many people give up their original desires to pursue these constructed notions. They become fixated in a subjectivity that is based on how they support the capitalist quota and how they continue promoting the desires of mainstream America. This majority is allowed to continue through their insistence on following the mainstream ideals of capitalism and conformity. It is through underground musical developments that an alternative is placed into postmodern America.

Other underground artistic outlets also allow people to view alternative notions of self. With these other formats, there is a tendency to either go to the extreme limit of rebellion in order to demonstrate their removal, or remain fixated in late capitalist desires. The goal of other undergrounds then becomes to separate fully from the mainstream, whereas with contemporary Garage Rock the goal is to rebel from within. Gaining acceptance from the capitalist sphere of production is necessary and warranted in postmodern times, and Garage Rock serves as the vehicle for the attainment of this break.

By achieving a place within the mainstream sphere, contemporary Garage Rock determines its power through the assertion of a different subjectivity. This is disturbing to the multitude of people who remained focused on keeping mainstream capitalist demands in place. By rebelling from the interior and challenging this thought process, Garage Rock continues the fight where Punk and other movements left off. The main difference here is the harshness of previous movements and the way that the mainstream has taken to contemporary Garage Rock so rapidly. In some ways, this could be detrimental, but as of now the scene has not failed in its attempt and has propagated a new thought process within postmodern society.

By looking at previous musical movements, including Punk and Hardcore, one can easily see their different positions within the mainstream. Their stances were often viewed as overly harsh and critical of the surroundings, and therefore the movements suffered in their attempts to sustain success. This led to a removal from the mainstream, which eventually led to the dissolution of the original underground. Punk and Hardcore were both thought of as non-commercial, but as the music became mainstream, the rebellion became saturated in capitalist desires and failed. While many people still champion Punk and Hardcore music and claim it as their defining style or sound, its effect has been limited in a society that has been witness to everything prior.

When society has been exposed to every form of rebellion from both extremes, it is difficult to effectively change the system with overly harsh sentiments. What Punk and Hardcore music did was to force the notion of angst and rebellion onto underground society and place strict demands on the participants of both scenes. Contemporary Garage Rock, however, seeks to simply provide an alternative to the capitalist mindset and to allow the subject to witness a difference within society. The aspect of forcing attitudes or trends is limited within Garage Rock, and this lends strength to the movement.

Postmodern constructions within art and music have always needed to be removed from the mainstream to gain a large following, but that removal has been viewed with complacency in the majority of groups. This complacency has allowed mainstream capitalist desires to remain intact and continues to demoralize the majority of individuals within postmodern America. Music and art that challenge these referents through the use of nostalgia create the opportunity for people to witness a differentiation of individualism and a way out of the imposed dominant ideology.

This way out can consist of simply listening to a certain song in a specific place, or by going to a performance and witnessing other subjects that share similar outlooks. What's important is that the music is founded on nostalgic thought in an effort to demonstrate an alternative path to this individualism. Without this nostalgia, the path would be singular and driven towards the standard hegemonic viewpoint of late capitalism. This is detrimental to society, since the more ways into individualism that are offered, the more prominent our society will become.

The importance of nostalgic thought and construction cannot be overlooked within postmodern times. Society is constantly striving to provide its members with what is considered a place in life and a way to individualize. Since every alternative "new" way has been attempted, individuals must begin the process of looking back and reconfiguring the past for their own uses and benefit. Through nostalgia, contemporary Garage Rock constructs its focus and frames rebellion based on the past. This continual usage and reliance on the past forms the basis of the rebellion and allows Garage Rock to retain relevancy throughout postmodern times.

The relevancy of underground music is often challenged and leads to a discussion on access potentialities for differing races and genders.

With Garage Rock, these access points are not limited in any way, and every individual is given the means to display a similar type of rebellion through contemporary Garage. For many in the scene, this is the goal and foundation of the music, and the ability of every person to have access to this form of nostalgic rebellion keeps the movement from becoming linked to other underground musical developments that have suffered from the constricting viewpoints of its participants.

The beginnings of contemporary Garage Rock drew from the surrounding musical scenes in Detroit. A city that is considered by many in the press to be one of the worst cities to live in America spawned an underground movement that has traversed multiple language and cultural barriers. Garage Rock began with the insistence on the reclamation of Rock and Roll and the spirit of rebellion that was issued in the 50s, 60s and 70s. By constructing music and performance based on these eras, Garage Rock began with a nostalgic outlook. Garage Rock developed and grew due to its relationship with the surrounding underground musical structure, and was allowed to remain because of these nostalgic issues.

With the use of the 50s as a nostalgic point of rebellion, the contemporary scene aligns itself with the foundations of Rock and Roll and the development of the rebel within postmodern society. The cultural shift within culture from radio to television and the market shift from Big Bands to Rock and Roll performers was especially relevant to the growth of contemporary Garage. While this could be said of many genres of music, the beginnings of Rock and Roll are readily and consistently referenced throughout postmodern Garage. The beginning of the Rock era demonstrated that music could be used as a form of rebellion even within mainstream cultural arenas. Jazz had done so previously, but on a limited scale due to its outsider associations, and now Rock could allow anyone in the mainstream a chance to rebel.

The previous musical movement of Jazz was structured around a harsh outlook of rebellion that demanded the removal of participants from the scene that did not conform to underground ideals. With original Swing and Big Band music, society was inundated with certain traits of conformity. Then Jazz again broke these barriers, thereby creating one of the first underground scenes. The importance here is in the harshness of this break and the strength of the musicians within the underground. With Rock's arrival the majority of people were accepted into the rebellion through mainstream avenues.

The 60s are often referenced in nostalgic rebellion for a multitude of reasons, mostly due to the age of the baby boomers, but that is a different discussion. In the case of postmodern Garage, it is the decade that gave the world the original Garage sound and the British Invasion. The era consisted of many other formats of rebellion and created the first subcultures that were easily viewed by the majority of American society. The rebellion championed by these groups was slightly different from the 50s style and the Beats, but still held the connotations of going against mainstream society by challenging it from within.

The specific usage of the three decades discussed is extremely relevant due to the way these eras in society shaped postmodern culture today in the form of music and art. By referencing the late 50s through the early 70s, the contemporary movement encourages a similar thought process to be brought to the forefront of society. Each decade plays a large role in determining what a band will sound like, and the influences taken from each era frame the sound and style of every band in the scene. Determining what era to nostalgically represent is usually based on influences, but is always consciously attempted.

The insistence on nostalgic thought within the Garage scene is very different from preceding musical movements. The fact that Garage readily admits to the use of the past is completely unique in a movement that believes itself to be completely original. By referencing song patterns and creating stage performances that are linked with the past, contemporary Garage depends on nostalgic notions to exist. Garage Rock depends on the past and differentiates itself from other movements because of this dependence. Bonnie Jo Lundblad, in her article "The Rebel Victim: Past and Present," states that there is a "...feeling that today's youth regard themselves and their culture as unique—quite unlike anyone and anything that has gone on before."[1] With the realization that the past is an influential and important resource, contemporary Garage has succeeded where other youth movements have failed.

Through the support of the pre-existing underground, Garage Rock was encouraged as a musical format. The members of the beginning scene played a pivotal role in the development of the music that is today known as Garage. Without Ko Shih, Dave Buick and Long Gone John supporting the original scene, Garage Rock would not have achieved the level of success that it has today. These people were members of a wide variety of scenes before finding Garage Rock. Without their support and the support of participants that encouraged the growth of this new form of music, Garage Rock would have been destined to fail.

The majority of the beginning participants were members of the Punk and Hardcore scenes of Detroit before forming the newer sounds of Garage. Because of this relationship, contemporary Garage took on a harsh sound and a do-it-yourself ethic. The members of the first bands to come out of the scene held the same beliefs and goals as the Hardcore and Punk scenes, but accomplished them in a different and arguably more effective way. Through the usage of these hard techniques, the groups were often left on their own and developed a fan base based on the preceding movements and surrounding underground scenes.

The bands that began to form in relation to the scene were influential as well, and the Sights mimic the rise of the contemporary Garage scene. Many align this band with the beginning of the movement and view them as successful because of their relationship to the past and the rest of the scene. By being involved at the beginning and being accepted into the music world by their surrounding musicians, the Sights were allowed to become fixed in the movement. This fixation represents the shared desires of the scene and allows the Sights to stand as representatives of the underground of Detroit and contemporary Garage.

Although the Sights are often mentioned in relationship to the Garage scene, they do not champion the term nor the label, again allowing for a rebellion from within mainstream society. This also continues their alliance to the underground and strengthens their relationship with the city of Detroit. Many other bands have retained this focus, but the Sights have achieved a level of mainstream success that the others have not. Therefore, the focus on the Sights as representative of the movement's positive assertions into the mainstream remains effective and demonstrative of the surrounding scene's goals.

Without the aspect of nostalgia, contemporary Garage Rock would have been extremely limited in its appeal from its onset and often challenged for its credibility and musical style. Through the use of the preceding underground and nostalgic representations, Garage Rock was allowed to continue and grow. This continued dominance is beginning to be undermined by the various bands that latch onto the surrounding label and attempt to claim success through capitalist means. These groups consciously attempt to draw from the original Garage bands in their effort to claim acceptance within the underground. However, by doing so they alienate the majority of the underground, and it begins to fail.

This occurred with the preceding Punk movement and will continue to play a role in the end or continuation of contemporary Garage Rock.

The underground's reaction to the bands that are latching onto the trend is extremely negative. These bands are easily recognized and generally removed from the discussion of what is considered underground by many participants. These bands may play shows within what they consider the underground, but their goals remain capitalistic and therefore are removed from the conception of what it means to be a Garage band. Whether or not these bands will lead to the destruction of the scene is yet to be determined, but they have already begun the process of splitting the underground into two different thought processes and attitudes.

The differing attitudes and agendas have led to multiple groups again rebelling against the label of Garage and continuing to challenge the preconceptions of the underground. By doing so, these groups are reasserting their place in the underground and standing against the newer groups that are latching onto a trend. This allows Garage Rock to continue in two different ways and for participants to take conflicting sides in the debate about contemporary music. Nostalgia is again reinforced, as this harks back to the original split that occurred with 60s Garage. The continuation of the underground is based on participants' choices and the continuation of nostalgic ideals in mainstream music.

Groups that do not assert the same demands as they did within the underground scene when they gain acceptance within the mainstream realm begin to fail in their relationship with the original scene. These groups are mostly determined to remain within both spheres in an effort to continue their dominance of the underground. Without an extreme amount of success within the underground, many groups would not reach the mainstream arena; and when this is achieved, bands must remain attached, in some way, to the scene from which they originated. With the crossing between underground and mainstream genres of music comes the extreme demand of fixing groups with a label.

Garage Rock has continuously attempted to remove itself from the labeling that results when a musical genre is accepted by the mainstream. Many bands have resisted the label of Garage Rock after accepting it as a way to gain success. This has occurred often within underground musical developments, but with contemporary Garage Rock there is a complete reversal of opinion when it comes to this issue. The labeling of a musical style is oftentimes faulty and riddled with inconsistencies, and the mainstream press has shown a strong determination to label anything closely resembling the original groups as Garage. The label has gone back to the original connotation, nostalgically, to now represent a group that is defined by the original 60s definition of not being good enough to get out of the garage. In order to avoid falling into this classification, bands that attain the label of Garage must insert a difference into the classification.

The bands that have been purposefully given this label harbor an extreme desire to re-assert the original intents of contemporary Garage Rock. The groups that found success within the label of Garage were the ones that did not allow success to constrict their musical output, and who continue to challenge the mainstream capitalist notions of control within postmodern America. With this challenge comes the responsibility that accompanies contemporary Garage Rock. The bands that remain in the underground must continue to let the participants view this break, even when they reach mainstream society. The White Stripes and the Von Bondies continue to assert their stance in Garage Rock with mainstream success, and do so with the strong desire to remain part of the underground, especially in Detroit.

These two bands are often viewed as extremely different in musical approach and sound, but they both reflect the underground throughout their music. The White Stripes and the Von Bondies continuously assert that they desire to remain important elements within the underground in Detroit and elsewhere, even with mainstream success and monetary gain. The importance here is that they maintain the same goal structure that they first perpetuated within the music underground. The importance of contemporary Garage Rock remains with groups such as these and their relationship to both realms of popular music.

The aspect of coming from the city of Detroit greatly comes into play with all of the groups that are represented in Garage Rock. It has become another way to insert a strong difference into mainstream America by claiming association with a city that is viewed in extremely negative connotations. Band members and participants consistently rely on images of the city to enhance their popularity and sound. Without alignment with the inner city as a starting point, bands that have become known as Garage would not be as effective in their musical approach. This has gone on for years with various musical developments, but with contemporary Garage Rock this desire is extremely forceful. A group must come, or appear to come, from the inner city of Detroit to gain acceptance within the underground and even the mainstream of contemporary Garage Rock.

The retreat from suburban goals and desires is an important part of contemporary Garage Rock's success. Through the images and displays of the city, the members of the scene must continue to escape from the confines of suburban capitalist desires. The determination of being from the city comes from the participants' desire to flee from these suburban goal structures. The city continues to play an immense role in the way that Garage bands display this removal to participants and society. The importance of having urban beginnings has allowed Garage Rock to again assert its dominance in relation to nostalgic ideals.

The continued success of contemporary Garage Rock relies on the issue of nostalgic ideals being made accessible to mainstream postmodern America. These ideals reside far away from the capitalist demands that are continuously enforced throughout society, and are strengthened through Garage Rock's use of nostalgia. The crossover between mainstream and underground spheres allows an extreme amount of difference to be inserted into everyday surroundings. This is the importance of contemporary Garage Rock and its participants' continued demand on musical output and participation. Without these nostalgic representations of a break into constructed individualism, contemporary Garage Rock would be limited in its appeal across musical and cultural boundaries.

The use of these nostalgic constructions is extremely influential within our society and leads to a specific distinction within America that is highly controversial. This distinction is the ability of groups to rebel effectively from within a position of commodity. Contemporary Garage Rock champions the ability to attain this position and still insert a difference into the surrounding culture. Simon Frith, in "Rock and the Politics of Memory," approaches the issue similarly and suggests, "The problem is not culture *versus* commodity but the contradictions of the culture of the commodity."[2] These contradictions play out continuously within the underground and mainstream of Garage Rock and frame the discussion of the rebellion that is accomplished through the use of nostalgia.

By using nostalgia as one solution to the overbearing contradictions of late capitalist America, the contemporary movement strengthens its hold on the aspect of subjectivity throughout society. Nostalgic traits are not viewed as threatening and lead into the contradictions that are formed when art and music become commodities. Through the use of nostalgia in construction and displays of image, contemporary Garage bands mark a strong statement about forming subjectivity away from capitalist intent.

Nostalgia in America is continuously referenced as lacking in its ability to lend support for individualism. Throughout postmodern criticism is a strong disdain for what nostalgia is and what it does to subjectivity that has only recently come to be challenged. In a country that is surrounded by nostalgic media and thought, people are constantly looking for a way to escape from the now, the reality of our present day. Individuals search for this escape by using nostalgia as a starting point for the future. The past gains significant power when constructed in relation to the present, and in David Lowenthal's study *The Past Is a Foreign Country*, he states "However faithfully we preserve, however authentically we restore, however deeply we immerse ourselves in bygone times, life back then was based on ways of being and believing incommensurable with our own."[3] This is where individuals claim the largest amount of success in relation to the past. Challenging the notions of existence in relation to the appearance of the past that we witness in the media and throughout our culture conditions the subject to rebel through nostalgia. At a time when America is constantly in turmoil about sociological and political implications, we feel the strong desire to relate to the past in an attempt to find ourselves. Through contemporary Garage Rock, this past breaks strongly into the populous thought.

The exposure to the past that is offered through media outlets is falsified and completely based on nostalgia. Construction of subjectivity based on this past is then often seen as flawed. However, it is this reconstruction of subjectivity based on the past that allows for the assertion of individuality within the postmodern world. Television stations, music movements, and movies that fixate on the past center perceptions on a time that was thought to be better, even if such thoughts are faulty. This perception challenges what is going on in our society and strengthens the process of attempted individuality.

Garage Rock offers its participants, and those that witness it from the outside, an opportunity to reclaim their subjectivity based on nostalgic traits. This contradicts the conforming notions of late capitalism and allows the subject to determine himself or herself away from mainstream society. Though Garage Rock does produce a structure of conformation, it is far removed from the contemporary notions of capitalist success. It is this allowance that defines Garage Rock in its focus and scope and determines the way that participants and outside observers construct themselves in relation to it.

The demands placed on participants within contemporary Garage are not nearly as strict as those made by previous music undergrounds. While forcing certain aspects of dress, and occasionally styles of drink, Garage is fairly limited in its demands. Consequently, the scene continues to grow and maintains its hold on the underground and mainstream society. The way that the scene progresses will eventually determine its success or downfall, but for now the demands have been relatively few and the participants still remain fixated on the underground groups.

With the consistent intent of reclamation of the past through music and dress, Garage Rock inserts a difference into our postmodern world. This difference challenges the pre-existing notions of control and continues to ask questions about subjectivity in late capitalist America. If society must continue to follow the goals that have allowed this country to become trapped in a downward spiral, then the demoralization will continue. If subjects continue to base their happiness on monetary success, then the detrimental aspects of capitalism will continue. If there is another determining factor in subjectivity that society has somehow been conditioned to repress, then the dominant hegemony will come through. These statements and many others are brought out in an effort to expand the current musical domain.

The importance of these statements is reflected in the relationship of contemporary Garage Rock to mainstream society. With multiple groups achieving success, these statements are allowed to permeate the populous instead of simply affecting the underground of a small locale. The force of contemporary Garage Rock is expanded into postmodern society through mainstream avenues and groups that reside in both underground and mainstream spheres. By incorporating both realms of society, the statements of late capitalist control become forced into the consciousness of the populace. This constructs a new avenue towards individualism and maintains the underground sentiment of contemporary Garage Rock.

The mainstream record companies and the fans of the groups promoted by them are forced to create labels and categories for Garage Rock that did not previously exist. This is done in an attempt to make Garage Rock more homogeneous to the mainstream, and again to enforce capitalist goals throughout the music. If homogeneity of music becomes instituted through contemporary Garage Rock it will begin to fail and the mainstream conceptions of the music will be achieved. What becomes an important factor is that the groups that have enforced this acceptance have continued to base their music and appearance on nostalgic traits in an effort to challenge the previous notions of popular music.

With this challenge comes the opportunity for the mainstream, and therefore other countries, to witness a culture and musical style that is set in direct opposition to the current mainstream musical output. This extreme resistance to corporate ideals and control of the musical output allows bands such as the White Stripes and the Von Bondies to continue their popularity throughout both realms. This is an extremely important aspect to the members of both groups in their effort to maintain underground credibility.

Whether or not this break from capitalist desires is successful is not relevant to the discussion and allows another constraint to be placed on contemporary Garage Rock's intent. The importance lies with the break being established within America and the world through the impact that Garage Rock has had. Without contemporary Garage Rock's insistence on nostalgia and conformity away from the mainstream, this break would not be as accessible within the surrounding culture. Garage Rock has allowed a constructed break into nostalgic subjectivity to be continuously witnessed and commented on, and without this musical development our society would be limited in its ability to construct itself away from capitalist goals.

There may be an argument against granting too much credit to contemporary Garage Rock and its musical output; however, without this attempt at reclamation of "real" Rock and Roll, people would still be forced to acquiesce to pop music and capitalist dominance. Does Garage Rock fall into capitalist demands and desires? Yes, but it does so with the continued association with nostalgia and a strong determination away from popular constructions of music and band format. Dick Hebdige, in his seminal book *Subculture: The Meaning of Style*, states, "The cycle leading from opposition to defusion, from resistance to incorporation encloses each successive subculture."[4] The use of different appropriations of nostalgic worth, plays heavily into acceptance within the mainstream. With acceptance comes the responsibility of Garage Rock to remain faithful to its surrounding core.

To accomplish this, while still holding capitalist desires within the mainstream, is the challenge for many bands. The importance lies within the reconstruction of the musical output and the rebellion against notions that have dominated the mainstream for too long. Notions of pre-written music and heavily produced albums represent the antithesis of the underground scene. Contemporary Garage Rock asserts this structure of rebellion, even with the attainment of monetary and capitalist success.

The rise of contemporary Garage Rock's popularity is in direct relation to this break being expressed within the mainstream. Through past years Garage Rock has claimed a fairly strong foothold around the world, with the White Stripes being nominated for a 2004 Grammy. This extreme growth would not have been possible without something that strongly reverberates throughout society. While many people would say it is just the music, it is the music and the nostalgia and how they are drawn together within Garage Rock that has garnered its success. The mainstream is complicated and rarely allows a genre to stay popular for very long, but when contemporary Garage Rock declines there will still be a strong desire to return to an original period in music as a means of subjectivity. This is the effect of contemporary Garage Rock and what has led to its popularity and rapid rise to success. Its ability to grab people's attention through the assertions of simplistic nostalgia is the strength of the movement and the culture surrounding it.

Our postmodern arena has typically cast nostalgia in a negative light, which is just now beginning to be questioned. This negativity must continue to be challenged in order for a distinction to be made between the positive and negative aspects of nostalgia. Through contemporary Garage Rock's use of nostalgia for a positive outcome, people witness the importance of nostalgia to America. For too long nostalgia and nostalgic traits have been held in extreme disdain in regards to subjectivity, and now we are able to witness the positivistic notions that go along with a desire to return to the past. Nostalgia is a means for people to construct their subjectivity with a difference that has not been alluded to previously. The opportunity for this determination outside of the constructed norm is provided by Garage Rock and its consistent use of nostalgia.

The demands that are either implied or outright enforced are based on the premises that Garage Rock began with. The assertion of a difference within underground music, the alignment with the past as a beneficial element, and the focus on appearance as reflective of the past all play extremely important roles in the creation and continuation of Garage Rock today. These demands are structured around the concepts of nostalgia and force the participants to construct their outlook and subjectivity based on them. For Garage Rock to continue to progress, these demands must remain fixed on nostalgic notions of subjectivity, even with mainstream recognition and acceptance.

The importance of contemporary Garage Rock within postmodern society is reliant on the aspects of nostalgia that are incorporated throughout. When these aspects begin to fail in the eyes of the surrounding members, Garage Rock will begin its downward descent. Although this has not happened yet, it will cause the scene to crumble from within. The members and participants of the Garage Rock scene structure their musical output and appearance on nostalgic traits and base their subjectivity on these elements. Many preceding underground musical movements have attempted to accomplish this, with limited success; none have done so as thoroughly as the contemporary Garage scene, and this is what has garnered support and success within the underground and mainstream.

The idea of disturbing those surrounding the individual is extremely important for contemporary Garage and becomes the goal of the entire musical movement. By nostalgically performing song formats that were once rebellious, the bands champion a way into a subjectivity that is different and threatening to mainstream postmodern thought. This defines what it means to be a Garage band, and to wield this threat is the importance of the development in our time. Society has fallen into a demoralized realm and thought process, and through contemporary Garage it can again be woken up. Rebellion from within is much more challenging than simply alienating the mainstream, and Garage Rock accomplishes this rebellion through nostalgic representations.

This will wake the neighbors and begin the process of individualization away from late capitalist desires. Contemporary Garage Rock strives to offer this break, and by doing so continues to perpetuate aspects of subjectivity that contradict suburban goal structures. Waking the neighbors takes on an entirely different meaning than the original Garage Rock concept of simple loud noises. Contemporary Garage Rock can wake the subjectivity of its participants up to a new form of self.

To wake the neighbors is what contemporary Garage Rock is for. In order to do this a group must perform loud music that is challenging to the mainstream conceptions of subjectivity. Through challenging capitalist notions of success with the use of nostalgic traits, Garage Rock has successfully awakened the neighbors in its attempt to assert this difference within postmodern society. Whether they will succeed in defining a new subjectivity is yet to be determined, but through their insistence on a break into nostalgic subjectivity they have woken up the surrounding members of society and thoroughly disturbed the neighbors. The success is based on this disturbance and will continue as long as the neighbors (mainstream society) are challenged in their notions of subjectivity. Contemporary Garage Rock has played an immense role within postmodern society, and its influence has dominated the underground of Detroit and elsewhere. Without the appearance of Garage Rock in postmodern times our society would be left without such an extreme challenge to mainstream capitalist desires, and a nostalgic sentimentality of subjectivity would not be available as a basis for constructed individualism.

Chapter Notes

Chapter 1

1. In reference to Made in Detroit clothing company.

2. For more information on Detroit Hardcore music please see the compact disc entitled *Detroit Is Distraught*.

3. *Time Out New York*: Issue 391, March 27–April 3, 2003, "Black and White and Red All Over," by Jay Ruttenberg.

4. The definition of what real Rock and Roll happens to be is heavily and consistently debated throughout musical scenes and underground developments.

5. from interview question 5, dated 8/6/04.

6. from interview question 12, dated 2/2/04.

Chapter 2

1. "The Move History," Rob Caiger, *Face the Music* http://www.themoveonline.com/history.html.

2. Interview question 14, 4/8/05.

3. Interview question 6, 4/8/05.

4. *Metro Times*, April 13–19, 2005, "Got What You Want," by Brian Smith.

5. Interview question 12, 4/8/05.

6. Interview question 20, 4/8/05.

7. "The Sights: Got What We Want," by James Oldham. *New Musical Express* http://www.nme.com/reviews/11040.htm.

Chapter 3

1. From *Living on a Thin Line: Crossing Aesthetic Borders with the Kinks*, ed. Thomas Kitts and Michael J. Kraus.

2. From Jon Savage, *The Kinks: The Official Biography*. London: Faber 1984, 32.

3. Taken from *The Kink Kronikles*. 1971. Written by Ray Davies.

4. The Jam, "A Town Called Malice." *The Jam Greatest Hits*. Polydor, 1982.

5. Charlie Gillett, *The Sound of the City: The Rise of Rock and Roll*. rev ed. New York: Pantheon, 1983.

6. Groups such as Sham 69, the Angelic Upstarts, the U.K. Subs, etc.

7. www.thatsightsband.com, www.thevines.com, www.hives.nu

Chapter 4

1. Charlie Gillett, *The Sound of the City: The Rise of Rock and Roll*, rev ed. New York: Pantheon, 1983.

2. Peter Wicke, *Rock Music: Culture, Aesthetics and Sociology*, New York: Cambridge University Press, 1990.

3. Michael Hicks, *Sixties Rock: Garage, Psychedelic & Other Satisfactions*. Urbana and Chicago: University of Illinois Press, 1999.

Chapter 5

1. Kuper, Hilda. "Costume and Identity." *Comparative Studies in Society and History*, Vol. 15, No 3. (June 1973), 348–367.

2. From interview question 2, dated 2/2/04.

3. Lenny Kaye, *Rolling Stone*, 12/20/73.

4. Benjamin, Walter. "The Work of Art."

Literary Theory: An Analogy. Eds. Julie Rivkin and Michael Ryan. Malden, Mass: Blackwell Publishers, 1998.

5. Briley, Ron. "Reel History." *The History Teacher*, Vol. 23, No. 3 (May 1990), 215–236.

Chapter 6

1. Grossberg, Lawerence. "The Politics of Youth Culture: Some Observations on Rock and Roll in American Culture." *Social Text*. No. 8 (Winter 1983–84), 104–126.
2. Frith, Simon. "'The Magic That Can Set You Free': The Ideology of Folk and the Myth of the Rock Community." *Popular Music Vol. 1 Folk or Popular? Distinctions, Influences, Continuities* (1981), 159–168.
3. Jenny Eliscu. *Rolling Stone*. 6/20/2002. 898.
4. David Fricke. *Rolling Stone*. 4/17/2003. 920.
5. Baudrillard, Jean. *America*. Trans. Chris Turner. New York, Verso. 1988, 58–59.

Chapter 7

1. Jameson, Fredric. *Postmodernism or the Cultural Logic of Late Capitalism*. Durham: Duke University Press. 1991. 49.
2. Traber, Daniel S. "L.A.'s 'White Minority': Punk and the Contradictions of Self-Marginalization." *Cultural Critique*, No. 48 (Spring 2001), 30–64.
3. Seabrook, John. *Nobrow: The Culture of Marketing, the Marketing of Culture*. New York, NY: Vintage Books. 2001. 71.
4. Haynsworth, Leslie. "Alternative Music." *GenXegesis: Essays on Alternative Youth (Sub)Culture*. Eds. John M. Ulrich and Andrea L. Harris. University of Wisconsin, Madison. 2003. 41–58.
5. Peter Wicke, *Rock Music: Culture, Aesthetics and Sociology*, New York: Cambridge University Press, 1990.

Chapter 8

1. Curnutt, Kirk. "Generating Xs: Identity Politics, Consumer Culture, and the Making of a Generation." *GenXegesis: Essays*

on *Alternative Youth (Sub)Culture*. Eds. John M. Ulrich and Andrea L. Harris. Popular Press, 2003. 162–183.

2. Coontz, Stephanie. *The Way We Really Are: Coming to Terms with America's Changing Families*. New York, NY. Basic Books. 1997.
3. Frow, John. *Time and Commodity Culture, Essays in Cultural Theory and Postmodernity*. New York, NY. Oxford University Press. 1997.
4. Miller, Laura J. "Family Togetherness and the Suburban Ideal." *Sociological Forum*, Vol. 10, 3 Sep 1995, 393–418.
5. Dudden, Arthur P. "Nostalgia and the American." *Journal of the History of Ideas*. V. 22, 4, Oct.-Dec. 1961. 515–530.
6. Jameson, Fredric. *Postmodernism or the Cultural Logic of Late Capitalism*. Durham: Duke University Press. 1991.
7. *Ibid.*
8. Adorno, Theodor W. "Memories of Utopia: Longing in Artworks, Which Aims at the Reality of the Non-existent, Takes the Form of Remembrance." *Twilight Memories: Marking Time in the Culture of Amnesia*. Ed. Andreas Huyssen. Routledge, NY. 1995, 85–101.
9. Shumway, David R. "Rock 'n' Roll Soundtracks and the Production of Nostalgia." *Cinema Journal*. Vol. 38, No. 2 (Winter, 1999), 36–51.
10. Herron, Jerry. "Homer's Simpson's Eyes and the Culture of Late Nostalgia." *Representations*. V. 0, 43, Summer 1993, 1–26.
11 . Boym, Svetlana. *The Future of Nostalgia*. New York , NY. Basic Books. 2001.
12. *Ibid.*
13. Hutcheon, Linda. *Irony, Nostalgia and the Postmodern*. University of Toronto Library.

Chapter 9

1. Callahan, David. *The Cheating Culture: Why More Americans Are Doing Wrong to Get Ahead*. Harcourt; Orlando, FL, 2004. 114.
2. Lukac, Gyorgy. "Aesthetic Culture." *The Yale Journal of Criticism*. 11.2. 1998. 365–379.

3. Ruiz-Quintanilla, S. Antonio, George W. England. "How Working Is Defined: Structure and Stability." *Journal of Organizational Behavior*, Vol. 17 Special Issue: Work Values Worldwide. (1996) 515–540.

4. Gecas, Victor, Monica A. Seff. "Social Class, Occupational Conditions and Self-Esteem." *Sociological Perspectives*. Vol. 32, No. 3. (Autumn, 1989), 353–364.

5. Simmel, Georg. "The Metropolis and Mental Life." *Classic Essay on the Culture of Cities*. Ed. Richard Sennett. Appleton-Century-Crofts. NY. 1969, 47–60.

6. Davies, Jude. "The Future of 'No Future': Punk Rock and Postmodern Theory." *Journal of Popular Culture*. v29, n4 (Spring 1996): 3–25.

Chapter 10

1. Lukes, Steven. "The Meanings of 'Individualism.'" *Journal of the History of Ideas*. Vol. 32, No. 1 (Jan–Mar 1971), 45–66.

2. Calverton, V.F. "A New Approach to the Problem of Individualism." *Social Forces*, Vol. 9, No. 3 (Mar. 1931), 343–350.

3. Jordan, E. "The Definition of Individuality." *The Philosophical Review*, Vol. 30, No. 6 (Nov. 1921), pp. 566–584.

4. Grossberg, Lawerence. "Another Boring Day in Paradise: Rock and Roll and the Empowerment of Everyday Life." *Popular Music*, Vol. 4 Performers and Audiences. 1984, 225–258.

5. Seligman, Adam. "Inner-Worldly Individualism and the Institutionalization of Puritanism in Late Seventeenth Century New England." *The British Journal of Sociology*. Vol. 41, No. 4 (Dec. 1990), 537–557.

6. Kruse, Holly. "Subcultural Identity in Alternative Music Culture." *Popular Music*. Vol. 12, No. 1 (Jan. 1993), 33–41.

Chapter 11

1. Lundblad, Bonnie Jo. "The Rebel-Victim: Past and Present." *The English Journal*. Vol. 60, No. 6 (Sept. 1971), 763–766.

2. Frith, Simon. "Rock and the Politics of Memory." *Social Text No. 9/10 The 60s Without Apology* (Spring–Summer 1984), 59–69.

3. Lowenthal, David. *The Past Is a Foreign Country*. New York, NY: Cambridge University Press. 1985.

4. Hebdige, Dick. *Subculture: The Meaning of Style*. London: Methuen & Co. LTD. 1979. 100.

Bibliography

Adorno, Theodor. "Memories of Utopia: Longing in Artworks, Which Aims at the Reality of the Non-Existent, Takes the Form of Remembrance." *Twilight Memories: Marking Time in the Culture of Amnesi*a. Ed. Andreas Huyssen. New York: Routledge, 1995. 85–101.

Baudrillard, Jean. *America*. New York: Verso, 1988.

Benjamin, Walter. "The Work of Art." *Literary Theory: An Anthology*. Eds. Julie Rivkin and Michael Ryan. Blackwell Publishers, 1998.

Boym, Svetlana. *The Future of Nostalgia*. New York: Basic Books, 2001.

Briley, Ron. "Reel History." *The History Teacher* 23.3 (1990): 215–236.

Callahan, David. *The Cheating Culture: Why More Americans Are Doing Wrong to Get Ahead*. Orlando: Harcourt, 2004.

Calverton, V.F. "A New Approach to the Problem of Individualism." *Social Forces* Mar. 1931: 343–350.

Coontz, Stephanie. *The Way We Really Are: Coming to Terms with America's Changing Families*. New York: Basic Books, 1997.

Craiger, Rob. "The Move History." *The Move Online*. 25 Aug. 2005 <http://www.themoveonline.com/history.html>.

Curnutt, Kurt. "Generating Xs: Identity Politics, Consumer Culture, and the Making of a Generation." *GenXegesis: Essays on Alternative Youth (Sub)Culture*. Eds. John M. Ulrich and Andrea L. Harris. Madison: University of Wisconsin Press, 2003. 162–183.

Davies, Jude. "The Future of 'No Future': Punk Rock and Postmodern Theory." *Journal of Popular Culture* Spring 1996: 3–25.

Dudden, Arthur. "Nostalgia and the American." *Journal of the History of Ideas* Oct 1961: 515–530.

Eliscu, Jenny. "Review of 'The Hives'." *Rolling Stone* June 20, 2002: 898.

Fricke, David. "Review of 'The White Stripes'." *Rolling Stone* April 17, 2003: 920.

Frith, Simon. "'The Magic That Can Set You Free': The Ideology of Folk and the Myth of the Rock Community." *Popular Music: Folk or Popular? Distinctions, Influences, Continuities* 1 (1981): 159–168.

_____. "Rock and the Politics of Memory." *Social Text No. 9/10 The 60s Without Apology* Spring 1984: 59–69.

Frow, John. *Time and Commodity Culture, Essays in Cultural Theory and Postmodernity*. New York: Oxford University Press, 1997.

Gecas, Victor, and Monica A. Seff. "Social Class, Occupational Conditions and Self-Esteem." *Sociological Perspectives* Autumn 1989: 353–364.

Gillett, Charlie. *The Sound of the City: The Rise of Rock and Roll*, rev ed. New York: Pantheon, 1983.

Grossberg, Lawerence. "Another Boring Day in Paradise: Rock and Roll and the Empowerment of Everyday Life." *Popular Music* 1984: 225–258.
_____. "The Politics of Youth Culture: Some Observations on Rock and Roll in American Culture." *Social Text* 8 (1983): 104–126.
Haynsworth, Leslie. "Alternative Music." *GenXegesis: Essays on Alternative Youth (Sub)Culture.* Eds. John M. Ulrich and Andrea L. Harris. Madison: University of Wisconsin Press, 2003. 41–58.
Hebdige, Dick. *Subculture: The Meaning of Style.* London: Methuen, 1979.
Herron, Jerry. "Homer Simpson's Eyes and the Culture of Late Nostalgia." *Representations* Summer 1993: 1–26.
Hicks, Michael. *Sixties Rock: Garage, Psychedelic and Other Satisfactions.* Urbana and Chicago: University of Illinois Press, 1999.
Hutcheon, Linda. "Irony, Nostalgia, and the Postmodern." *UTEL.* 19 Jan. 1998. University of Toronto Library. 26 Aug. 2004 <http://www.library.utoronto.ca/utel/criticism/hutchinp.html>.
The Jam. "A Town Called Malice." *The Jam Greatest Hits.* Polydor 1982.
Jameson, Fredric. *Postmodernism or the Cultural Logic of Late Capitalism.* Durham: Duke University Press, 1991.
Jordan, E. "The Definition of Individuality." *The Philosophical Review* Nov. 1921: 566–584.
Kaye, Lenny. "Review of 'Quadrophenia'." *Rolling Stone* Dec. 20, 1973.
Kitts, Thomas M., and Michael J. Kraus. *Living on a Thin Line: Crossing Aesthetic Borders with the Kinks.* Rumford: Rock 'n' Roll Research Press, 2002.
Kruse, Holly. "Subcultural Identity in Alternative Music Culture." *Popular Music* Jan 1993: 33–41.
Kuper, Hilda. "Costume and Identity." *Comparative Studies in Society and History* 15.3 (1973): 348–367.
Lowenthal, David. *The Past Is a Foreign Country.* New York: Cambridge University Press, 1985.
Lukac, Gyorgy. "Aesthetic Culture." *Yale Journal of Criticism* 1998: 365–379.
Lukes, Steven. "The Meanings of Individualism." *Journal of the History of Ideas* Jan 1971: 45–66.
Lundblad, Bonnie Jo. "The Rebel-Victim: Past and Present." *The English Journal* Sept. 1971: 763–766.
Miller, Laura J. "Family Togetherness and the Suburban Ideal." *Sociological Forum* Sep 1995: 393–418.
Oldham, James . "The Sights: Got What We Want Review." *New Musical Express.* 25 Aug., 2005 <http://www.nme.com/reviews/11040.htm>.
Ruiz-Quintanilla, Antonio S., and George W. England. "How Working Is Defined: Structure and Stability." *Journal of Organizational Behavior Special Issue: Work Values Worldwide* 1996: 515–540.
Ruttenberg, Jay. "Black and White and Red All Over." *Time Out New York* March 27, 2003.
Savage, Jon. *The Kinks: The Official Biography.* London: Faber, 1984.
Seabrook, John. *Nobrow: The Culture of Marketing, the Marketing of Culture.* New York: Vintage Books, 2001.
Seligman, Adam. "Inner-Worldly Individualism and the Institutionalization of Puritanism in Late Seventeenth Century New England." *The British Journal of Sociology* Dec. 1990: 537–557.
Shumway, David R. "Rock 'n' Roll Soundtracks and the Production of Nostalgia." *Cinema Journal* Winter 1999: 36–51.
Simmell, Georg. "The Metropolis and Mental Life." *Classic Essay on the Culture of Cities.* Ed. Richard Sennett. New York: Appleton-Century-Crofts, 1969. 47–60.

Smith, Brian. "Got What You Want." *Metro Times* April 13, 2005.
Traber, Daniel S. "L.A.'s 'White Minority': Punk and the Contradictions of Self-Marginalization." *Cultural Critique* Spring 2001: 30–64.
Wicke, Peter. *Rock Music: Culture, Aesthetics and Sociology.* New York: Cambridge University Press, 1990.

Index